The Legacy of State
Socialism and the
Future of Transformation

The Legacy of State Socialism and the Future of Transformation

Edited by David Lane

ROWMAN & LITTLEFIELD PUBLISHERS, INC.
Lanham • Boulder • New York • Oxford

ROWMAN & LITTLEFIELD PUBLISHERS, INC.

Published in the United States of America
by Rowman & Littlefield Publishers, Inc.
An Imprint of the Rowman & Littlefield Publishing Group
4720 Boston Way, Lanham, Maryland 20706
www.rowmanlittlefield.com

12 Hid's Copse Road
Cumnor Hill, Oxford OX2 9JJ, England

Copyright © 2002 by Rowman & Littlefield Publishers, Inc.

British Library Cataloguing in Publication Information Available

Library of Congress Cataloging-in-Publication Data

The legacy of state socialism and the future of transformation / edited by David S. Lane.
   p. cm.
  Includes bibliographical references and index.
  ISBN 0-7425-1792-6 (alk. paper)—ISBN 0-7425-1793-4 (pbk. : alk. paper)
   1. Europe, Eastern—Social conditions—1989—Congresses. 2. Former Soviet
republics—Social conditions—Congresses. 3. Europe, Eastern—Politics and
government—1989—Congresses. 4. Former Soviet republics—Politics and
government—Congresses. 5. Post-communism—Europe, Eastern—Congresses. 6.
Post-communism—Former Soviet republics—Congresses. I. Lane, David Stuart.

HN380.7.A8 L46 2002
306'.0947—dc21

2001048483

Printed in the United States of America

♾™ The paper used in this publication meets the minimum requirements of
American National Standard for Information Sciences—Permanence of Paper
for Printed Library Materials, ANSI/NISO Z39.48-1992.

Contents

Foreword

The end of the Cold War has provided many benefits to the nations of the world, but it has also presented them with new challenges for which they were not prepared. Perhaps the most difficult has been for the newly emerging democracies to reinvent themselves, and to do so in a way that satisfies their populations, makes them economically competitive, and brings them into the global arena. We are still a long way from understanding the complexities of this adjustment or from adequately explaining the different paths these nations have taken. The contributors to this book have moved us closer to such an understanding, however, and in the process have made a valuable contribution to the social science of transition.

This book is part of a series of projects conducted by The Gorbachev Foundation of North America (GFNA). Created as a nonpartisan organization, and with Mikhail Gorbachev as its president, GFNA has as its mission the support of research and debate on important issues of the post–Cold War era. Among these are many that are closely related to Gorbachev's contributions to the twentieth century, such as opening up societies to the outside world, integrating them into the emerging global community, and moving them towards a democratic form of government. Our projects on global economics, on international relations, and on technology and democracy bring together people from politics, academia, business, and public policy to find ways to improve the lives of people in societies at all levels of economic and political development.

This volume is designed to focus attention on the extent to which the legacy of communism has influenced the ways in which transition is taking place. The variety of patterns of postcommunist transition has still not been adequately described, and the factors responsible for different paths remain to be properly defined and evaluated. There are of course some obvious reasons for the differences.

Thus, the length of time during which a society was a one-party state, the intensity of ideological and organizational penetration of life by the ruling elite, the level of economic development, levels of education, whether or not the system was imposed from outside, the experience of a nation prior to its communist period, and even the geographic position, may all be expected to create differences in the patterns of transition. In addition, there are a number of important influences coming from the global environment, including the activities of other nations and of international agencies, and the state of the world economy. The size and complexity of the task at hand is clearly beyond the scope of a single project, and the contributors are able only to address some major issues, identify more carefully the factors at work, and work in a fairly restricted geographic region. The chapters of this book, therefore, are to be seen as part of a long-term, collective enterprise on the part of a large number of scholars.

On behalf of the Gorbachev Foundation of North America I would like to thank the contributors to this book for their work and for their support during this rather lengthy project. I would also wish to thank the acting provost of King's College, John Barber, and the College Fellows who provided a congenial setting for our discussions.

In addition to the contributors to this volume, the following also contributed to its success: George Kolankiewicz, Soyoung Kwon, Alistair McAuley, Nick Manning, Mario Nuti, and Jim Riordan. My special thanks go to David Lane for his tireless efforts in bringing this volume to fruition. Without his leadership and hard work there would be no book.

Anthony Jones
Executive Director
The Gorbachev Foundation of
North America

I

THE LEGACY AND TRAJECTORIES OF CHANGE

1

Trajectories of Transformation: Theories, Legacies, and Outcomes

David Lane

By the year 2001, the transformation of the former Communist societies of central and eastern Europe have been in progress for some ten years, and this experience allows scholars to reflect on the significance of the societal changes that have taken place. The chapters collected in this book take stock of the developments in these societies and also address the legacies of state socialism and the ways such traditions interact with other factors to influence the course of social, political and economic change. The political cultures of the previous state socialist societies are analyzed in the context of the wills of actors, both domestic and foreign, who wish to create a different type of society and to introduce these changes from above.

Most of the chapters in this book highlight the transformation of the Soviet Union with comparisons to the countries of central and eastern Europe, though two focus on the latter. All of these chapters attempt to consider the extent that the footprint, or legacy, of state socialism has shaped, or is shaping, the course of development. The chapters cover a wide range of social and political institutions and forms of change. There is a focus on the institutions in transition: Linda Cook on the welfare state and Stefanie Harter on the defense and space industries; Stephen White, Paul Lewis, Cameron Ross, Lynn Nelson and Irina Kuzes on the political system; Ray Taras, Louise Shelley and Walter Connor on social groups; Greg Andrusz on the legacy and potential of cooperatives; Michael Cox on the global perspective, particularly the role of the United States.

The term *transformation* is the process by which the former state socialist societies, which rejected Communist Party hegemony and a planned centrally directed economy, embarked on major changes of their political, economic, social and legal institutions. It is problematic whether they were inspired by any revolutionary theory or led by a revolutionary class. Essentially, these movements had one thing in common: they "rejected" communism, but the degree of renunciation varied both between countries and between different aspects of "communism." The early postcommunist governing elites had a vision of a transition to a Western type of society characterized by wealth, markets, private ownership, democracy and civil society. What was meant by the more abstract of these terms was vague and the means to achieve transformation were ambiguous. The successful capitalist societies of Western Europe and particularly the United States became reference points of what the postcommunist states aspired to become; the "West" also defined the conditions under which the new states entered the global market and received financial and political support.

The perspective from which most writers view these changes is that of a shift from planning to markets, from communist autocracy to democracy, and from a totalitarian society to a pluralist one. But these changes, if carried out, present not a series of radical reforms, but in sum a revolution.[1] Scholars, however, have been reluctant to consider these changes in terms of revolution for several reasons: there has been very little or no internal violence, there has been no explicit ascendant and dominant social class, and there has been no revolutionary ideology of change.[2] This was to be expected, for the "totalitarian" interpretation of these societies entailed an absence of internal dissent, let alone a mass revolutionary movement, and leading commentators earlier concluded that such societies were even "revolution proof."[3] Following Tanter and Midlarsky's typology, the happenings in Eastern Europe between 1989 and 1991 would appear to have been "revolutionary coups."[4]

The essential point, which has been lost, however, is not that the "intentions of the insurgents" did not entail a mass revolution, but whether "fundamental changes in the structure of political authority and the social system" followed the replacement of the former political elites.[5] Western political scientists and economists, who have dominated the field, are ideologically well versed in democratic theory and market economics but relatively uninformed on revolutionary theory. Historians and theorists of revolution have been blinkered by the traditional Marxist trajectory of change from capitalism to socialism and classical Marxist class theory.

In this chapter, I detail these positions and the developments in Eastern Europe and the former Soviet Union from two perspectives. First, I analyze the literature that conceptualizes the changes taking place and devise theoretical paradigms of change. Second, the outcomes of transition are discussed in terms of these models. The objective is not only to determine the extent and success or failure of transformation but also to unravel the factors that have promoted or retarded social and political change and to evaluate embedded and imposed elements in the transformation process. To succeed, a transformation of state socialism to capitalism and polyarchy must occur concurrently in major sectors of society such as values, law, governance, the economy, and in exchanges with the external global economy. If these conditions are not met there is a failed or only partial transition.[6]

MODELS OF CHANGE

Understanding transformation is predicated on social science theories of social change.[7] Two aspects are usually distinguished: the collapse (or self-transformation) of the declining regime and the subsequent formation of another.[8] The extent to which transformations can be considered as revolutions will depend on the extent of the subsequent changes. A new elite intending to carry out "reform" may be impelled into more significant changes of a revolutionary quality.[9] Much of the literature, moreover, distinguishes between the preconditions of collapse, renewal (the process of the formation of a new regime) and the consolidation of postcommunism. These distinctions are useful for analyzing the different phases of change, but they need to be combined to understand the trajectory of transformation.

The major building blocks in the explanation of the transformation process are values and norms, structures, societal preconditions, interests and class relations. Different theorists combine these variables in various ways to define six major approaches to transition: political culture and modernization, elites and institutions, class and productive forces. These paradigms are illustrated on chart 1.1.[10]

These explanatory variables in turn are shaped by other independent factors such as societal preconditions, interests, class relations, values and norms and structures. Preconditions of transformation may be analyzed in terms of the norms and values of the population (box 1—the type of political culture: subject, participatory) on the one hand, and the level of modernization (box 4—the extent of urbanization, the levels of education) on the other. Interests include the types of elites that emerge and the values they embody (box 2—those within the political system, for example, political parties advocating certain types of change). Elites, either within the state or outside it, lead transformations. Institutions, which are embedded in the social structure, also act as constraints on action (box 5); examples here are legal systems—forms of, and rights to, property, the organization of science and technology and other institutional clusters. Class structure I define in the sense of aggregates of people sharing the same life chances and market situation. Classes can be defined in terms of values and norms they share (box 3)—beliefs about how a market and capitalist society or economic hierarchy should be organized and achieved (in a Marxist sense, "consciousness") and the structural constraints (box 6)—the type of market relationships, whether it be the

Chart 1.1.   Paradigms of Transformations

	Societal Preconditions	*Interests*	*Class Structure*
Values and Norms	1. Political culture	2. Elites	3. Classes
Structures	4. Modernization	5. Institutions	6. Productive forces

sale of labor or the ownership of property. Social scientists of the 1960s explained "transition" in terms of boxes 1 and 4; those of the 1990s dwelled on transformation in terms of categories in boxes 2 and 5, and theorists of revolution (conspicuously underrepresented in the transformation debate) would use the framework of boxes 3 and 6.[11]

Political culture, modernization and production relations approaches (boxes 1, 4 and 6) may be considered as necessary preconditions of change. Theorists adopting these positions point to the level of education, the class structure of the population, the type of political culture and the institutions of the external environment. Writers here assume that a successful transition of a society is dependent on an educated and urban population and/or the psychological orientations of citizens.[12] These factors are considered important preconditions for the type of regimes that may arise, but they cannot "determine" social change because they are not actors. Rather they are requisites for regime change that create the conditions in which actors may arise.

Much of the discussion on the process of transformation and the preconditions for the rise of democracy focuses on the nature of elites and whether elites have made (or are able to make) an elite pact or settlement (box 2). The strength or weakness of elites and the extent to which they are politically unitary determine whether or not there will be a successful "transition from above." The work of Higley and Burton is particularly important here. They hypothesize that elites lead economic and political change, and that democratic stability (in turn a condition for successful economic development) is only possible if there is an elite pact, or compromise, creating a consensually unified elite.[13] They postulate an important causal link: only after the settlement takes place can the conditions for stable democracy occur. Also of importance is that predominantly unmobilized nonelites facilitate settlements by allowing elites sufficient autonomy for negotiated compromises to take place. In this theory, elites are determinant, while classes are fragmented, whereas in the class structure approach (box 3), class consciousness is a prime determinant.

O'Donnell and Schmitter[14] shift the emphasis away from the structural "preconditions," which they consider to be "overdetermined." Leadership, even in uncompromising circumstances, they contend, can facilitate a shift to democracy, which is at the heart of transition. The stress is put on forms of consensus building, institutionalization, and the role of committed political actors who have secured democratic solutions. Box 5 illustrates the combination of correct "interests" and appropriate institutions. The foreign policy of hegemonic foreign states can also influence development by supporting the political procedures of liberal democracy, the division of powers, rule of law, electoral provision, political party choice. Hence the preconditions for collapse, and the way it was brought about, play a relatively unimportant role compared to the institutional and policy changes that new elites can formulate. The emphasis is on "crafting democracy."[15]

Box 5, however, may be used in quite a different way to emphasize the conditions that limit change. The neoinstitutionalists, such as North, Bruzst and Stark,[16] would contend that surviving institutions are constraints that limit and channel the activities of elites and those "transitologists" who seek to orchestrate macro changes. In the following chapters, Cameron Ross, Lynn Nelson and Irina Kuzes, Greg Andrusz, Ray Taras, Walter Connor, Stefanie Harter, Paul Lewis and Stephen White all stress the "institutional legacy" as defined in chart 1.1. Interests are wedded to the structures left from the Soviet period and act as constraints in the period of transition. A transition from above will not work if the social and institutional preconditions are not in place. This "path-dependent" approach either sees a top-down transition as being impossible or, optimistically, considers that capitalism and democracy may be built only with the materials (institutions, values and norms) left over from state socialism.

Traditional class-driven approaches (boxes 3 and 6) look to the level of productive forces as providing institutional constraints and possibilities for change and to the role of classes as agents of progression. Vocabulary moves from "transition" and "transformation" to revolution. It is class interest that is the motivating psychological factor defining the revolutionary interest of the ascendant class. Revolution favors one class at the expense of others.[17] For Moore,[18] the bourgeoisie was the driving force of the development of capitalism. From this viewpoint, democracy is the political shell in which a capitalist class is legitimately able to maintain property rights and the proceeds from labor. Following the line of reasoning of Rueschemeyer, Stephens and Stephens, democracy is a social mechanism derived from the contradictions of capitalism.[19] It originated as a means to ameliorate class inequality created by the ownership of the means of production and gave the subordinate class (the working class) the possibility of a greater stake in society without a change of regime. In terms of elite theory, discussed above, counterelites of labor and socialist parties become incorporated into the dominant ruling class.

Class theorists might claim that a class settlement, or the exhaustion of a potential ascendant class, may be a condition for a pact between elites to arise in the first place. Thus the transformation of communist-type parties into social democratic ones (in practice, if not in name) is an essential class compromise underpinning an elite pact. In this sense, democracy becomes part of a hegemonic ideology. What is clear is that the historical antecedents of capitalism must be derived from the rise of a bourgeoisie and this is a necessary (though not a sufficient) condition for the development of a democratic society. This discussion is in terms of developments that have preceded the collapse of state socialism. One of the few books to consider transformation from a Marxist standpoint considers the "upheavals" as "revolutions" but they are political (rather than social and economic) ones. The transformation is considered to be a shift between two types of capitalism[20] (state to multinational) and therefore is not an example of a true revolution. Lane and Ross outline a theory of class interest in terms of an "acquisition class"[21] essentially made up of people who may benefit by valorizing and privatizing their cultural, economic and political capitals through a market. The traditional class actors, bourgeoisie and working class, as defined by writers such as Moore and Rueschemeyer, have no explanatory role in this theory.

These approaches provide the major building blocks in the social sciences for the understanding of revolution and transformation. The assumptions made about the role of institutions, culture and human agency play an important part not only in the explanation of what happened but also in the formation of policy options and choices. Such paradigms have given rise to two methodological positions that inform the literature on policy-making: these are system transfer and path-dependency (or social and institutional embeddedness).

SYSTEM TRANSFER OR INSTITUTIONAL EMBEDDEDNESS?

The system transfer approach assumes that the legacy of the previous regime can be neutralized relatively quickly and that a move to markets and democracy can be ensured through the introduction of the appropriate institutional forms copied from Western practice coupled to positive political leadership.[22] There is a mild "End of History" triumphalism in the thinking of these theorists. It is often supposed that, when totalitarian controls had been lifted, the previous regime was subject to a spontaneous and complete collapse and its institutions and the psychological orientations of the population could be relatively easily replaced. Zbigniew Brzezinski, for example, has described its "state of general crisis, both ideologically and systemically."[23]

Economic reformers have assumed that the major social institutions in the old system were completely flawed and that reform was impossible. The economy was defective because a system of planning and state ownership could not and did not work. For Kornai, "the socialist system was a brief interlude, a temporary aberration in the course of historical events. [T]here is no alternative to the capitalist system."[24] State socialism had "major systemic incompatibilities caused by the absence of both a market and a mechanism of conflict resolution. . . . Because institutional arrangements deprive state socialism of the capacity to channel self-interested behavior into socially beneficial performance and condition its survival on the base of direct coercion, the whole concept of a politico-economic order is fundamentally flawed."[25] The logic of this position is that if the coercive powers of the totalitarian state are removed, a political and economic *tabula rasa* is revealed on which Western institutions (usually defined in neoliberal rather than social-democratic terms) may be freely constructed. These views derive sustenance from works such as those of von Mises and other neoliberal economists that under socialism "economic calculation is impossible . . . in the absence of criteria of rationality, production could not be consciously economical."[26]

A system change was necessary to correct the pathological shortcomings of state socialism. Such critics contended that systemic planning failures, poor economic performance and political stagnation of the communist system and the obvious superiority of the capitalist led the overwhelming mass of the population to have a natural desire for markets and capitalism. Analogous to the political, ideological and economic collapse of Germany in 1945, the state socialist system was discredited and people now identified with its ideological opposite, capitalism. System transfer, however, rather than revolution, characterizes this approach.[27]

The introduction of new institutions—markets, private ownership—would create a window of opportunity and incentives that would motivate people to change their behavior. People would become "future" oriented and would act like rational "economic persons" to maximize their own preferences and interests. Crucial to this policy choice is the implantation of the correct institutions (box 5) and their subsequent performance. People would choose the new institutions of democracy and the market only if they lead to prosperity and social satisfaction; they would reject them if they failed. The values of the people (box 1) in the transitional societies, it was contended, were congruent with a strategy of radical economic and political reform. The carriers of these policies would be the elites (box 2) implementing correct policies to move to Western-type capitalism.

The "system transfer" position assumes that state socialism was a fundamentally defective system and that a neoliberal policy of markets, private property and competition in economy and competitive polyarchy in the polity would be a strategy that would transform the ailing societies into prosperous democratic states. A system collapse approach would identify pathologies in all segments of the social system as summarized in chart 1.2. This scenario is explicitly reformist, but implicitly revolutionary. Gorbachev may have anticipated a change in social system when he defined *perestroika* as a "revolution from above."[28] What is lacking is a revolutionary theory and revolutionary actors. As state socialism experienced spontaneous collapse, transitologists needed merely to provide the appropriate Western institutions and processes.

Not one of the chapters in this book, all written by experts in their field, finds the above approach realistic.

The path-dependent approach, on the other hand, places considerable weight on the ways that people and institutions are socially embedded in society. Values and norms are socially based, and these may continue independently of changes of elites or of the introduction of new institutions. A principal difference between these two approaches is that the path-dependent theorists do not consider postcommunist societies to have emerged from a unitary "totalitarian" or "socialist" mold. Rather, each state socialist society had unique characteristics. They were mixtures of traditional, oligarchic societies with "socialistic" elements. Whereas the system transfer theorists viewed state socialism through the

Chart 1.2.   System Collapse of State Socialism

Values	Marxism-Leninism had failed and was repudiated by Communist leaders. History renounced, communist future abandoned.
Integration	Communist Party had legitimacy crisis.
Collective	Social identity was lost.
Governance	Planning failed. Instrumental bureaucratized rationality of means prevailed.
Adaptation	Decline in effective utilization of resources, underemployment of labor and capital.
External Exchanges	Hegemony of the West was incompatible with internal structural forms and processes.

prism of an organic systemic type of totalitarianism,[29] this school distinguishes more complicated sets of exchanges. The Soviet Union did not just collapse: as Ray Taras in his chapter reminds us in the Soviet case, transition was carried out through imposition from above.

Stephen White, in his chapter, reminds us that the dissolution of the USSR, "did not reflect the wishes of ordinary people . . . nor did it reflect the original intentions of the republican leaders who took part in the final negotiations."

Boxes 1 and 2 of chart 1.1 (the societal preconditions) apply both to system-transfer and path-embedded theories, but they entail different conclusions. For the path-dependent approach, values, beliefs and institutions from the old regime may be regarded as assets. The fall of the old regime, therefore, involves changes in only a limited number of institutional sectors of society; others continue more or less unchanged or are adapted and legitimated under new circumstances. Such writers take a more conservative view of the possible effects of "radical" political change: while the formal institutions may be replaced, the expectations of people and the processes inherited from the past may either continue or be reconstituted.[30] This is particularly the case with respect to the welfare state provision provided under state socialism, as brought out in the chapter by Linda Cook.

There are two major implications for policy: some argue that the previous structures are liabilities for the transition to markets and democracy and have to be quickly destroyed. Others envisage them as "assets" that could and should be utilized in the transformation process. What these writers want is a "bonding" between regimes.

In his chapter, Walter Connor defines seven legacies of the Soviet period that have constrained and determined the position of the working class. He points out that the legacy of state-fixed and controlled prices could be overcome quickly. Other aspects of the Soviet system could not so easily be changed. The legacy of not working hard, of "workers' control" in the factory, has been preserved in the context of privatization and marketization. Louise Shelley shows that abuse of women has a long history in Russia that predates the USSR. However, the flawed design of privatization and the collapse of state institutions concurrent with organized crime and corruption limited women's economic alternatives and has led to prostitution and trafficking on a large scale.

A crucial development here is the destruction of Soviet institutions that supported women and the absence of effective institutions in their place. As she points out, a major objective of economic policies of transformation was to ensure that a reversion to Communism would not happen. Women lost out with respect both to property rights and to the previous levels of support enjoyed. Even well-educated professional women sought employment in prostitution. Lynn D. Nelson and Irina Y. Kuzes also show how institutional practices of state socialism are reconstituted: the Soviet form of "executive-centered hierarchy remains the accepted approach to internal organization." Ray Taras points out that the previous traditional (prestate socialism) mindset of Russia as an imperial power was a liability to a movement to a less-expansive identity, but the West's foreign policy—Russia's humiliating treatment—has led to the strengthening of ideas of imperial identity. He argues that the institutional framework would be better adapted to social-democratic, rather than neoliberal, structures. The contradictions in the welfare state are clearly defined in the chapter by Linda Cook. The benefits system of state socialism was structured in such a way that it could not be easily adapted (if it could be accommodated at all) to the market-oriented reforms. The transfer to an American-type housing system based on private ownership and full cost-recovery rents did not work. However, the legacy was hardly an asset to reform because there was insufficient economic wealth to deliver to the population. New needs created by the introduction of a market system also have gone unheeded. "Inherited institutional deficits have limited reform possibilities and outcomes. . . ." Hence, the partial transformation not only does not meet old needs, but the ones it creates are not met.

On the basis of the previous discussion, we might clarify a number of theoretical possibilities about the trajectory of change under different combinations of circumstances. A fairly rapid transition to capitalism and polyarchy is effective when collapse is spontaneous, the extent of rejection of the old regime is complete, the new institutions are strong and elite values and norms are unitary. Transformation becomes path dependent when the collapse is imposed (by a political coup), rejection of the previous regime is partial, elite values and norms are divided, and when the new institutions are weak. Reform of state socialism is a more appropriate strategy. These hypotheses are discussed empirically in the following chapters. Paul Lewis shows the differences in the ways that state socialism was "rejected" in central and eastern Europe, where the renunciation of the old regime of state socialism was more complete than in the former USSR (with the exception of the Baltic states). Stephen White, in his chapter, uses the analogy of the "revenge of the superstructure" to illustrate that after the early postcommunist dedication to liberal ideas, there was a shift back to Russia's own traditions of collectivism, patriotism and social justice.

The conditions for reform and transformation are illustrated in chart 1.3; assets and liabilities for a move to capitalism/democracy are disaggregated by social, political, and economic sectors. *Assets* and *liabilities* are defined in terms of their relevance for a transformation to capitalism and polyarchy: features inherited from state socialism are "assets" for a move to capitalism when they are conducive to it; they are "liabilities" when they provide structural or psychological opposition to such a move. These factors are asymmetrically related to support and opposition to the previous state socialist regime. Hence, for example, a buoyant economy with rising standards of living under state socialism would be a liability for a move to capitalism; a social asset for a capitalist transformation would be an intelligentsia resentful of low differentials with the skilled manual workers and little opportunity for emigration; a political asset for transformation would be a unified elite strongly opposed to the Marxist-Leninist system (and/or Russian hegemony), but a ruling elite either divided or favorable to the virtues of state socialism would be a liability.

On the basis of these conditions one may define two types of change: reform and transformation and four different paths of transition: reform failure, reform of state socialism, gradual transformation, revolution. By failure (box 1), the conditions are such that no significant reform is possible. Jowitt has come closest to this position with his idea of the "Leninist legacy" in Eastern Europe (excluding Poland). He argues that the cultural, political and economic "inheritance" of forty years of Leninist rule will be so great that a transition to democracy and a market system are likely to be thwarted.[31] The "Leninist legacy," moreover, has to be considered in the context of traditional values. As we shall consider later in this chapter, countries such as the Baltic states, Slovenia, the Czech Republic, and Hungary have made relatively successful transformations. (These points find substance also in the chapter by Paul Lewis.) If we increase the number of years to seventy as in the case of Russia, then Jowett's reasoning seems intuitively more likely and is supported by much of the writing in this book.

The other extreme case is that of conditions suitable for a rapid transition (such as shock therapy policy), the conditions for success of such a policy are illustrated in box 4. Here state socialism had only economic, political or social liabilities—it was bankrupt. Such a revolutionary transformation is favored not

Chart 1.3.   Conditions for Successful Reform and Transformation (liabilities and assets for a move to capitalism)

	Reform	*Transformation*	
Economic Liability	1. Reform	2. Gradual Transformation	*Social Liability*
Economic Asset	3. Reformed socialism	4. Revolution	*Social Asset*
	Political Liability	*Political Asset*	

only by elites but has resonance among the population. The negative short-term effects of shock therapy will not be opposed, as the alternative might well be worse. Two other cases are exemplified in boxes 2 and 3. A reform of state socialism is possible when the economy and the social spheres are ineffective but when the political leadership is vigorously opposed to systemic change. Effectively the political elites can block any major shift to capitalism and polyarchy. (China and Cuba are cases here, though they are outside the scope of this book.) Gradual transformation can take place when the political elites are unitary and in favor of change, and where the economic and social elements of state socialist society remain effective and have considerable support. (The position under Dubcek in Czechoslovakia in 1968 is an example of this scenario.)

OUTCOMES OF TRANSFORMATION: LIVING STANDARDS AND DIFFERENTIALS

We now turn to consider countries experiencing "actually existing transformation." Transformation involves changes in economy, polity, external relations and lifestyles. Aspects of these developments will be discussed in detail in following chapters. In this one we discuss three aspects of the transformation process against which changes may be viewed. First, we examine comparatively the social and economic outputs of the new system—to measure the variations in standard of living and prosperity and the distribution of income. Second, we explore the degree to which the polity of state socialism, predicated on a hegemonic Communist Party, has been replaced by a competitive electoral process with polyarchic elites. And third, we appraise the extent to which the economy has moved from state ownership and central control to one with private ownership and market relations.

Following the collapse of the communist regimes and the move to markets, the first five years of transformation was characterized in all the postcommunist countries by a considerable fall in GDP and concurrently by increasing levels of inequality and poverty. The period is often characterized as a transformation recession. The downward trajectory for selected countries is shown in table 1.1. The first row shows the decline 1990–93 over 1989, then between 1992 and 1999, by year-on-year growth/decline in percentage terms. GDP declined in all countries and declined very considerably in Lithuania, Ukraine, Russia and Tajikistan.

From 1993, for some countries, an economic recovery took place though the levels of 1989 had not been achieved. Chart 1.4 illustrates the level of economic recovery measured by comparing GDP/NMP in 1998 with the level in 1989 (= 100).[32] The bars on the chart bring out the great variation in levels of recovery between the different countries. By 1999, only three countries (Poland, Slovenia and Slovakia) had achieved the level of GDP that they experienced in 1989.

Table 1.1.   Growth and Decline in Real GDP 1992–1999 (percent year to year)

	Poland	Czechoslovakia	Hungary	Lithuania	Ukraine	Russia	Tajikistan
1990–93	–3.1	–4.3	–4.8	–18	–10.	–10.1	–12.2
1992	2.6	–3.3	–3.1	–21	–13.7	–14.5	–29
1993	3.8	.6	–.6	–16	–14.2	–8.7	–11
1994	5.2	3.2	2.9	–9.8	–23	–12.7	–18.9
1995	7	6.4	1.5	3.3	–12.2	–4.1	–12.5
1996	6.1	3.9	1.3	4.7	–10	–3.5	–4.4
1997	6.9	1	4.4	6.1	–3.2	0.8	1.7
1998	4.8	–2.7	5	4	–1.7	–4.6	4
1999	3	0	4.2	2.5	–3.5	–5	3

Source: *Transition Report Update 1999*. London: (EBRD) 1999, p. 6. World Bank, *Transition*, Vol. 9, no. 3 (June 1998) p. 6.

At the bottom of the chart, eight former republics of the USSR reached less than 60 percent of the 1989 level.

Not only has income declined, but also the inequality of income distribution has increased markedly and there has been a significant rise in levels of poverty. The gini coefficient is a measure of income inequality: the higher the coefficient, the greater the inequality. A coefficient of 0 would show a completely equal distribution of income. Chart 1.5 shows changes in income distribution in two periods: before transformation (1987–1988) and after it (1993–1995). Before transformation, income inequality was fairly modest and relatively constant between all the countries. After the collapse of state socialism, however, inequality became more regressive in all countries (except Slovakia) and the differential between countries increased significantly. The bars on the chart in 1987–88 show the range from 19 to 28, whereas in 1993–95, the range was from 19 (Slovakia) to 55 (Krygyzstan).

Three countries of the former USSR top the group for income inequality: Kyrgyzstan, Russia and Ukraine. For this cluster, income differentials are much greater than the OECD average, whereas at the bottom of the table (Slovakia, Hungary, Slovenia), the Eastern European countries (at least in 1995) had levels of inequality lower than the OECD average.[33] In the first group of very unequal societies, real income decreased between the two time periods by between one-third and one-half, and the bottom quintile was severely affected; in Russia the top quintile increased its share from 19.45 percent of total income in 1988 to 39.52 percent in 1993.[34] The rich became very much richer. It is interesting to note that inequality of income is also high in China and Vietnam, suggesting that inequality is linked to the market.

There has been a steep increase in poverty. According to data collected by Milanovic, in eighteen central and east European countries, before the transition, there were 14 million people in poverty (4 percent of the population); this figure rose to 168 million or 45 percent of the population in 1993–95.[35] Table 1.2

Chart 1.4.   GDP Recovery 1998 (1989 = 100)

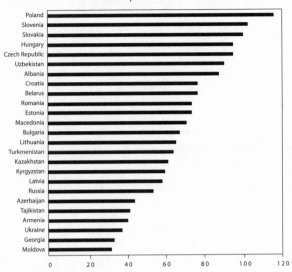

Source: Transition Report 1999. (London: [EBRD] 1999), 73.

Chart 1.5.   Gini Coefficients for 1987–1988 and 1993–1995

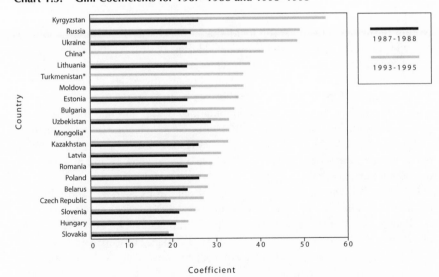

Source: Branko Milanovic, *Income, Inequality and Poverty during the Transition from Planned to Market Economy.* (Washington, D.C.: World Bank 1998), 41.
*World Development Report 1999/2000. (New York: Oxford University Press, 2000), 238–39.

Table 1.2. Levels of Poverty 1987–1988 and 1993–1995 and GDP per Capita 1998

	GDP per Capita 1998[a]	Poverty 1987–1998[b]	Percent of Population 1993–1995[c]
Slovenia	9760	0	1
Czech Republic	5040	0	1
Hungary	4510	1	2
Poland	3900	6	14
Slovakia	3700	0	1
Estonia	3390	1	37
Lithuania	2440	1	30
Latvia	2430	1	22
Russia	2300	2	44
Belarus	2200	1	22
Romania	1390	6	39
Kazakhstan	1310	5	62
Bulgaria	1230	2	15
Uzbekistan	870	24	39
Ukraine	850	2	63
Turkmenistan	760	12	57
Moldova	410	4	66
Kyrgyzstan	350	12	86

[a]World Bank, *Entering the 21st Century: World Development Report 2000.* (New York: Oxford University Press 2000), 230–31 (U.S. dollars).
[b]Household Budget Survey, data cited in Milanovic: 68–69.
[c]Data based on income per head, cited in Milanovic: 75.

(columns 3 and 4) illustrates the incidence of poverty in the different countries in 1987–1988 and 1993–1995. The data define poverty at an income of less than U.S. $120 per person per month. The second column is GDP per capita in 1998. The table shows the clear division between three sets of countries: first with average GDP per head of over $4000 per annum, and with levels of poverty affecting less than 3 percent of the population, come Slovenia, the Czech Republic, and Hungary; at the other end of the scale comes the bottom cluster of Turkmenistan, Ukraine, Moldova and Kyrgyzstan, with average GDP below $1000 per annum per capita and levels of poverty between 39 and 86 percent of the population.

On chart 1.6, we combine the two sets of data from chart 1.5 and table 1.2: income inequality is plotted on the vertical scale and the extent of poverty on the horizontal. We may distinguish four East European societies with low levels of income inequality and poverty (Slovenia, Slovakia, Hungary and Czech Republic) and three countries of the former USSR with high levels of both (Russia, Krygyzstan and Ukraine).

On the basis of this analysis we may conclude that overall by 1998, most citizens in the former state socialist countries were worse off financially; there was greater poverty in all the countries and differentials between rich and poor had

Chart 1.6. Distribution of Income Inequality and Poverty by Countries

Income Inequality	High	Medium	Low
Low			Slovenia Slovakia Hungary Czech Republic
Medium	Romania Estonia Uzbekistan Moldova Turkmenistan Kazakhstan	Lithuania Bulgaria	
High	Kyrgyzstan Russia Ukraine		

Extent of Poverty

widened considerably. Five countries (Slovenia, Czech Republic, Hungary, Slovakia and Poland) had made good recoveries; Russia, Azerbaijan, Tajikistan, Armenia, Ukraine, Georgia and Moldova had all suffered severe decline and had grossly increased differentials between rich and poor.

These comparative data of the rich becoming richer and of the growth of a large underclass of very poor people provide the backdrop to the revival of the fortunes of the postcommunist parties discussed below by Stephen White and Paul Lewis, to the claims on the welfare state outlined by Linda Cook and Ray Taras, and to the adaptation of many women to provide sex services depicted by Louise Shelley. We now turn to the second aspect of transformation, which is to consider whether these changes are correlated with the transformation to pluralism and capitalism.

OUTCOMES OF TRANSFORMATION: PLURALISM AND CAPITALISM

Transformation was to herald a shift in organizing principles: politically, from hegemonic party control to political pluralism and polyarchy, and economically from central planning and state-owned assets to the economic market and private property. In scope, this was a revolutionary transformation.

Two major indexes of economic and political transition are widely used to compare the extent of marketization and political pluralism. The Fraser Institute's *Economic Freedom of the World 2000 Index*[36] ranks countries on a 10-point scale (0 the least free, 10 the most free).[37] This index is quite sensitive to different elements in the development of capitalism.[38] The extent of private sector share of GDP is regularly monitored by the EBRD.[39] On the development of political pluralism, Freedom House has devised two measures of "freedom" in terms of levels of political rights and civil liberties. Political rights include the prerogative of adults to vote and compete for public office and for "elected representatives to have a decisive vote on public policies." Civil liberties include the rights to "develop views, institutions and personal autonomy" independently of the state.[40] These data are collected in table 1.3.

The trajectory of transformation has led to three main groups of countries in terms of economic and political freedom. Those with political rights and civil liberties with an index of 6 or more on both criteria represent a regime sharing many features in common with advanced Western societies. One could say that

Table 1.3.   Political and Economic Freedoms

	Political Rights Scale	Civil Liberties Scale	Economic Freedom Scale	Private Sector GDP 1999
Hungary	7	6	7.4	80
Czech Republic	7	6	7.1	80
Estonia	7	6	6.8	75
Latvia	7	6	6.7	65
Lithuania	7	6	6.6	70
Slovenia	7	6	6.3	55
Poland	7	6	6	65
Slovakia	6	6	6.1	75
Romania	6	6	4.6	60
Bulgaria	6	5	5.3	60
Mongolia	6	5		
Moldova	6	4		45
Macedonia	5	5		
Ukraine	5	4	4.5	55
Georgia	5	4		60
Russia	4	4	5.4	70
Croatia	4	4	4.7	60
Armenia	4	4		60
Albania	4	3	4.3	75
Bosnia	3	3		35
Kyrgyzstan	3	3		60
Tajikistan	3	3		30
Azerbaijan	2	4		45
Kazakhstan	2	3		55
Belarus	2	2		20
Yugoslavia	2	2		
China	1	2	6.2	
Uzbekistan	1	2		45
Cuba	1	1		
North Korea	1	1	1	
Turkmenistan	1	1		25
Vietnam	1	1		

a transition to capitalism had been successful for these countries. At the other end of the scale are those with scores less than 4 on the political scales. These are regimes having a one-party political regime and (with the exception of China) a state-owned and planned economy—failures with respect to political and economic transformation. An intermediary group of countries has made some progress towards political liberalization. However, they have been unable to create a robust political shell for the development of capitalism, and the type of "transition" to capitalism therefore remains uncertain.

Along the vertical axis on chart 1.7 is the ranking on the political transformation index. Plotted on the other axis is the extent of economic liberalization on the Fraser scale and the level of gross domestic product originating in the private sector.[41] The top group is constituted of those countries with an index of 6 or more on the Fraser and the GDP scales, and the bottom group with an index under 4 on both. Study of chart 1.7 shows a very high correlation between economic and civil freedoms. (The economic freedom scale may appear to outstrip the political in places; this is partly because the latter is on a 7-point scale, the former on a 10-point scale.) Only one country stands out with an asymmetric relationship between economic and political; that is China. In the top right-hand corner are the countries that have made a successful transition: Hungary, the

Chart 1.7. Political and Economic Transformation

Great			Romania	Hungary Czech Republic Estonia Latvia Lithuania Slovenia Poland Slovakia
Partial	Mongolia Macedonia		Bulgaria Ukraine Georgia Russia Croatia Armenia Moldavia	
Little	Bosnia Yugoslavia Cuba Vietnam	North Korea Turkmenistan Belarus	Tajikistan Kyrgyzstan Uzbekistan Kazakhstan *Azerbaijan*	China
	No Data	*Little*	*Partial*	*Great*

Extent of Political Transformation (vertical axis label)

Extent of Economic Transformation

Czech Republic, Estonia, Latvia, Lithuania, Slovenia, Poland and Slovakia. On the bottom left are the failures—those with very little reform: North Korea, Turkmenistan and Belarus.

The data we have considered so far would suggest that the transition to markets, private property and pluralistic polyarchy and transparency has differed remarkably between the different countries of Eastern Europe—points that are taken up below by Paul Lewis. Some have had a fairly successful transition to capitalism with a firm political shell of democratic competitive institutions. A legal framework[42] providing for the ownership and transfer of property and for the legitimate control of the proceeds of production has been successfully constructed. Others, however, as detailed for Russia in the chapters by Stephen White and Lynn D. Nelson and Irina Y. Kuzes, have failed.

How then can we explain these differences and to what extent does our theoretical discussion point to significant causal relations?

Political Cohesion: Support for and Opposition to Transformation

First, we consider the political culture variables as defined in chart 1.1, and second, we shall turn to the preconditions in terms of level of modernization. One way to operationalize the political culture variable is to consider the political outcomes of the first election at the beginning of transition.[43] The extent to which countries had strongly politically embedded communist parties and/or publics that solidly supported radical policies for reform may be measured by combining the proportion of seats won by the largest noncommunist party with the share of seats gained by the successor communist party in the first postcommunist elections. We might focus on three major types of political consensus and dissensus[44]:

1. Strongly unitary and pro-radical reform: These countries are defined by having less than 25 percent of the seats for the communists *and* one noncommunist party having more than 40 percent seats.
2. Divided: These countries are defined by the major noncommunist party having over 25 percent of the seats *and* the communists having over 25 percent of them.
3. Strongly unitary and procommunist: Less than 25 percent held by one pro-reform party *and* more than 60 percent of the seats held by the communist party.

The post-transition countries are grouped by these criteria on the vertical axis on chart 1.8.[45] Plotted on the horizontal axis are their respective achievements by political and economic freedoms taken from chart 1.7. The groupings would suggest that there is a clear relationship between a unitary political movement for reform during the collapse of communism and subsequent successful economic and political transformation. The "successful" transformers are located at

Chart 1.8. Initial Political Cohesion and Political and Economic Transformation

Unitary– *Radical Reform*			Georgia Croatia	Latvia Czech Republic Estonia Hungary Slovakia
Divided			Bulgaria Ukraine Georgia Russia	Lithuania Poland
Unitary– *Procommunist*	Turkmenistan Belarus	Tajikistan Kyrgyzstan Uzbekistan Kazakhstan Azerbaijan		

Political Cohesion (vertical axis label)

Little	*Little/Partial*[a]	*Partial*	*Great*

Measure of Subsequent Political and Economic Transformation

[a]Little political transformation, partial economic transformation.

the top right-hand sector of the chart, the failures to the bottom left. The election results suggest that the absence of traditional communist opposition is an important variable in determining the success of a transition to markets, private property and polyarchic politics. The different levels of support for different parties in turn needs to be explained. (See the chapters by White and Lewis.)

The legacy of state socialism is also reflected in popular attitudes to politics. In the years following the collapse of communism, surveys have shown important differences in attitudes towards the market economy and the role of government in the economy. Miller, White, Heywood and Wyman[46] found that in Hungary and the Czech Republic there was less support for state involvement in the control of economic institutions than in Russia and Ukraine, as shown in table 1.4. Clearly, people in Hungary and the Czech Republic were less enthusiastic about state-run enterprises than those in Russia and Ukraine.

SOCIAL AND ECONOMIC PRECONDITIONS

Can we go further than this and link a successful revolution to the economic and social preconditions discussed above? We noted that traditional theories of revolution link political elites to the level of modernization and the rise of classes. In the shift to capitalism from feudalism, the bourgeoisie is stipulated

Table 1.4.   Public Attitudes to State, Return to Communist Power and Parliamentary Democracy

	Percent of Respondents in Favor of State-Run Enterprises (December 1993)[a]			
	Russia	*Ukraine*	*Hungary*	*Czech Republic*
Farms	58	42	45	55
Car Factories	79	73	56	38
Newspapers	79	73	47	33
TV Programs	84	76	58	37

Percent Who Favor Return to Communist Rule[b]				
Russia	*Ukraine*	*Hungary*	*Czech Republic*	*Belarus*
—	25	18	7	34

"Best get rid of Parliament and elections and have a strong leader who can decide things quickly"				
Russia	*Ukraine*	*Hungary*	*Czech Republic*	*Belarus*
—	55	18	16	44

[a]B. Miller, S. White, P. Heywood and M. Wyman, "Democratic, Market and Nationalist Values in Russia and East Europe: December 1993." Paper presented at 1994 Annual Conference of Political Studies Association, March 1994. Table 10.
[b]Data for 1993, R. Rose, W. Mishler, C. Haerpfer, *Democracy and Its Alternatives*. (Baltimore: Johns Hopkins University Press 1998), p. 111.

as the social actor underlying the sociopolitical changes that took place. In the period of *perestroika,* an ascendant bourgeoisie was lacking and qualitative studies point to the urban intelligentsia as being a major class in the reform process.[47] The question here is: how far the socioeconomic legacy of different state socialist countries was determinant to the introduction of successful policies of transition. Can we discern any relationship between level of development in the period of Soviet hegemony to the types of developmental strategies introduced and the subsequent, if relative, success of transition?

For a measure of level of industrial development, I have taken the amount of electrical energy produced per head of the population in 1987. (See column 1 of table 1.5.) As far as the level of industrialization is concerned, there appears to be no consistent relationship to the outcomes of transition in the European and post-Soviet countries. Hungary, Uzbekistan, Kyrgyzstan, Belarus and Poland all have lower-than-average levels of energy produced but have very different transition outcomes. At the other end of the scale, Russia, Lithuania, the Czech Republic and Ukraine have high outputs and also different outcomes.

As to class background, it might be hypothesized that the higher the density of intellectuals, the more favorable would be the support for, and the effect on, marketization and privatization. Persons with a higher education would be disposed to the market because it would further the valorization of labor and legitimate executive strata, extending their control over production to ownership of industrial assets. Marketization would be likely to increase earning differentials to their advantage. To measure the demographic density of the "intelligentsia," I considered (a) the numbers of people in employment with higher education and specialist secondary education as a proportion of the urban population (see column 3 of table 1.5), and (b) the number of people in employment with higher education only as a proportion of the urban population. (See column 4 of table 1.5. The total number of people employed in the economy at various dates between 1983 and 1986 is shown in column 2.)

The urban population is taken for these calculations, as rural actors played a small part in the reform movement and the change to capitalism.

Table 1.5. Electrical Power per Capita, Higher- and Middle-Specialist Education in State Socialist Societies (1983–1985)

	1(N)[a]	2(N)[b]	3(%)[c]	4(%)[d]
Moldova	4317	206	22	13
Kyrgyzstan	2780	172	19	12
Uzbekistan	2752	743	17	11
Belarus	3632	604	20	11
Lithuania	6222	228	18	11
Estonia	12,000	102	18	10
Ukraine	5332	2868	17	9
Kazakhstan	5318	753	16	9
Latvia	2000	166	16	9
Turkmenistan	3757	127	14	9
Russia	6889	8468	17	8
Hungary	2632	434	14	7
Poland	3746	1057	16	5
Czech Republic	5451	556	19	5
Bulgaria	4673	324	16	5
Vietnam	91	252	6	2
China	427			
Romania	3306			

[a]Electric energy output per capita, 1987. Figures relate to the per capita output of electricity (million kilowatt hours per head) in 1987. *Narodnoe khozyaystvo SSSR za 70 let.* M. 1987. 162, 658. Author's calculations of output divided by population.

[b]Total number of persons with higher education engaged in the national economy in 1987 former USSR, other countries 1983–1986 (000s). *Statisticheski ezhegodnik stran-chlenov soveta ekonomicheskoy vzaimopomoshchi 1988.* (Moscow 1988), 422. (Data for 1983–86). Trud v SSSR. Moscow 1988. 118. (Data 1997).

[c]Persons with higher and specialist secondary education in employment in national economy as percentage of urban population. Data for 1979 to 1983. *Statisticheski ezhegodnik stran-chlenov soveta ekonomicheskoy vzaimopomoshchi 1988.* (Moscow 1988), 422, 17. Narkhoz . . . za 70 let. 374,419.

[d]Persons with higher education (column 2) as proportion of the urban population. For sources, see column 2.

24 *David Lane*

There is no clear relationship between the countries that have had a successful transition and a high stock of people with higher education and specialized secondary education. Hungary, Poland and the Czech Republic have an average education/urbanism index of 16.6, whereas Russia, Ukraine and Kyrgyzstan averaged 17.6. Even when one disaggregates the higher educational stock from the specialized secondary, there is again no clear relationship between the successful countries and urban density of people with higher education. Poland, Hungary and Czechoslovakia come at the bottom of the table and Moldova, Kyrgyzstan, Belarus, Lithuania and Uzbekistan at the top.

The approach of Rueshemeyer and others who see democracy as a device mediating the interests of the working class and bourgeoisie under nascent capitalism would not seem to be relevant in the postcommunist societies. The bourgeoisie had little class presence and the working class could only be said to have been a significant mover in the transition in Poland.

The table also includes partial data from two non-European state socialist survivors, Vietnam and China. These states are clearly in a different league from the European countries, which suggests that there is a minimum threshold both of levels of industrialization and of an upper-middle-class formation, which are necessary conditions for a movement to political pluralism and to provide an impetus for market reform.

CONCLUSION

We may distinguish three different sets of countries. First, Poland, Hungary, the Czech Republic and Slovenia have relatively successfully extricated themselves from state socialism. These countries have founded pluralistic political regimes, have restructured their economies in the direction of private ownership and marketization and, in doing so, have achieved modest though positive rates of growth. Second, at the other end of the scale, are those countries that have retained, or reconstituted, in one form or another, previous habits of state socialism: Krygyzia, Yugoslavia, Turkmenistan and Belarus, and they have had relatively poor rates of growth and recovery. Third, there is a group of countries that falls between these that share some, but not all, of the features of Western-type societies, but have been relatively unsuccessful in achieving a transition to capitalism. They have encountered severe economic and social deterioration. These include the countries of the former USSR, which have experienced high levels of poverty, excessive income differentials and low levels of per capita income. They also have weak pluralistic political structures.

Two observations might be made about the character of those states that have successfully consolidated capitalist revolutions: first is their level of income per capita and, second, is their proximity to Western Europe. Data show quite conclusively that the richest countries are the ones that have taken the greatest strides to capitalism and pluralism. (Slovenia, $9760 per head, followed by the Czech Republic, $5040; Hungary, $4510; and Poland, $3900.)[48] These countries are also the ones with borders contiguous with the European Union. They have the highest levels of foreign direct investment (FDI). Hungary by far outstrips FDI per capita of other East European countries: for the period 1989–98, Hungary received $1652 per head, followed by the Czech Republic with $968; Estonia, $947; Latvia, $634; and Slovenia, $596. Ukraine received only $54 and Russia $60.[49] The very great disparity between the first two countries and the others suggests that there is something about their proximity to the West that may account for such differences. But one must guard against a "geographical determinism" that equates location with economic advance or decay. It is what is contingent on location that is important. Kaliningrad oblast of Russia, for example, bordering on Poland to the west and the Scandinavian countries to the north, is one of the most backward areas of the Russian Federation. Cultural and political traditions enable possibilities for investment and transfer of goods, which, in combination, make these countries more open and more likely to prosper under a capitalist regime; this prosperity, in turn, facilitates the give and take required in a parliamentary-type democracy. This in turn impacts on the acceptability of these countries to the global market: it gives confidence to Western investors to invest, which in turn incorporates the receiving countries into the capitalist world market.

Geographical proximity to the West enabled institutional diffusion to spread more rapidly to the central and eastern European countries. The political culture and popular orientations in Hungary and Czechoslovakia were more fitting to a move to capitalism and polyarchy than in other countries. (This point is also taken up in the chapter by Paul Lewis.) Hungary, the Czech Republic, and Slovenia in particular have historical links with the West. They are small countries and are able to exploit their economic comparative advantage by becoming closely integrated into the economies of the West. They also have had a longer period of exchange with the capitalist countries.

Hungary and Poland had a tradition, and political culture, opposed to communism and Russian hegemony. Hungary, Poland and Czechoslovakia had had significant reforms well before 1989. In Hungary, the New Economic Mechanism increased the autonomy of enterprises from 1968 and, as early as 1974, legislation allowed joint ventures to be established. By 1987, 35.8 percent of Hungary's exports (value terms) were with developed capitalist countries—the highest of any of the state socialist societies—and the same was true of imports of which 41 percent originated from developed capitalist countries.[50] Economically, state socialism was unsuccessful in Hungary in the period immediately prior to reform and support for communism was weak: in both Hungary and Poland there had been significant political demonstrations against the Communist governments.[51] The population was therefore more prone to accept radical changes. The Law on Enterprise Councils of 1984 decentralized the public sector and delegated property rights to the enterprise level.[52] An economic reform had already preceded a political reform. Russia and most of the countries of the former USSR did not have this affinity with capitalism and Western-type democracy.

In the concluding chapter of this book, Michael Cox points to the disappointment in the United States with the political development in Russia in the period of Eltsin's rule and the revision of American foreign policy. He locates the changing American position with respect to Russia in terms of the United States seeking to maintain hegemony in a stable global order, the promotion of liberal democracy and human rights, and the extension of market capitalism to be part of America's "strategic mission in the 1990s." The "flawed transition" has led to a greater American foreign policy concern with central and Eastern Europe, with the enlargement of NATO. However, he points out that a "return to the past" is unlikely, a view shared by all the chapters in this book. Putin's policy of Russia "regaining its strength" is exceedingly limited in the context of geopolitical pluralism, which has been established in the area of the former Soviet bloc. As Cox points out, many policy makers in the West share Vaclav Havel's sentiment that chaos in Russia may be bad for Russians but may perhaps be a good thing for other countries.

The "legacy" of communism, even in the central and eastern European states, has contradictory influences. The legacy of the "double rejective revolution" in Eastern Europe—rejection of communism and the hegemony of the USSR—has had a positive effect on the development of national consciousness in those countries. In the postcommunist states of the former USSR, as Ray Taras shows in his chapter in this book, the Soviet legacy promoted the development of a native language, media and history, which are positive for nation building, for self-identification and also for the definition of outsiders. State socialism ended up by making nations within its own political body—in both the USSR and Eastern Europe. However, as Linda Cook points out, the "long-established rights and patterns" make it difficult to implement the neoliberal policies advocated by Western advisers. Similarly, the legacy even of the relatively successful Soviet space industry is ambiguous. To succeed, Russian space companies need to be embedded in the global market to exchange scientific and technological results and this is furthered by the neoliberal reforms, as Stefanie Harter makes clear. On the other hand, the "deskilling" and the "unlearning" of previous skills found in the defense and space industries is clearly detrimental to further technological and economic advances. Advanced technologically based industries, such as space, are dependent on the advancement of science in general as well as on a firm financial base: both are unlikely to be delivered in Russia.

The countries of eastern Europe and the former USSR had different histories and traditions of which the "communist" legacy was only one part. The hegemonic Communist Party was embedded to varying degrees in the political structures and political support system, and the aspirations of populations for transformation and reform differed. In terms of the determinant role they play in Marxist and modernization theory, social class or level of economic development are not good predictors of a successful move to capitalism. The successful states are those with borders contiguous to the prosperous European states; they have a history of opposition to Soviet hegemony and a longer period of economic and political reform. They have a political elite structure more homogeneous and in support of capitalism and polyarchy and a population more ideologically opposed to communism. It is not surprising that they have carried out a successful capitalist revolution, whereas countries like Russia have not.

NOTES

1. Garton Ash described the 1989 revolutions as "refolution"—a mixture of reform and revolution. T. Garton Ash, *The Uses of Adversity*. (New York: Random House 1989), 276.

2. The question of democratization and revolution has been pertinently posed by Valerie Bunce, "The Political Economy of Postsocialism," *Slavic Review*, Vol. 58, no 4, Winter 1999, 792. See also her discussion of a revolution approach in: Valerie Bunce, "Lessons of the First Postsocialist Decade," *East European Politics and Societies* Vol. 13, no 2, Spring 1999, 2.236–243. On the absence of revolutionary goals and the atheoretical nature of the transition, see C. Offe, *Varieties of Transition*. (Cambridge: Polity 1996), especially chapter 3.

3. S. Bauman, "Social Dissent in the East European Political System," *European Journal of Sociology*, Vol. 12, 1971.

4. A revolutionary coup has low mass participation, a short to moderate duration, low to moderate domestic violence and the intentions of the insurgents are to achieve "fundamental changes in the structure of political authority and possibly some change in the social system." R. Tanter and M. Midlarsky, "A Theory of Revolution," *Conflict Resolution*, Vol. 11, no 3, 265.

5. Tanter and Midlarsky, 265.

6. For discussion of methodology, see also: Michael McFaul, "Lessons from Russia's Protracted Transition from Communist Rule," *Political Science Quarterly*, Vol. 114, no 1. 1999: 103–130.

7. See particularly Harry Eckstein, F. J. Fleron Jr., et al, *Can Democracy Take Root in Post-Soviet Russia?: Explorations in State-Society Relations*. (Lanham and Oxford: Rowman and Littlefield 1998). See especially the articles by F. J. Fleron Jr., "Congruence Theory Applied: Democratisation in Russia" (35–68), P. G. Roeder, "Transitions from Communism: State-Centred Approaches" (201–228) and W. M.Reisinger, "Transitions from Communism: Putting Society in its Place" (229–248).

8. The literature on early-twentieth-century transitions focused on the shift from feudalism to modernity in terms of democracy and dictatorship, the best-known approaches here being those of Samuel Huntingdon and Barrington Moore. The concern with shift from autocracy to democracy involves modernization theories of the 1960s and 1970s associated with the work of Lipset, Smelser, Rustow and Almond and Verba. More recent

developments of this form of change are associated with the writing of Przeworski and Schmitter and O"Donnel.

9. Valerie Bunce has posed the question of whether one should use democratization or revolution as a frame for the analysis of transition. She points to the incomplete nature of the revolutions in some postcommunist countries. Valerie Bunce, "The Political Economy of Postsocialism," *Slavic Review*, Vol. 58, no 4, Winter 1999: esp. 762, 791.

10. I have adopted here some of the categories used by Reisinger and Roeder; see William M. Reisinger, "Transitions from Communism: Putting Society in Its Place" in H. Eckstein et al, *Can Democracy Take Root in Post-Soviet Russia?* (Lanham: Rowman and Littlefield 1998), 231.

11. Valerie Bunce, in taking a revolutionary perspective, is concerned with the scale and process of change but she does not define actors in this sense. She sees revolutionary change stemming from within system elites—there was a "regime-in-waiting." Bunce, "Lessons of the First Postsocialist Decade," 241.

12. Weber's idea of a "protestant ethic" as a precipitant for the rise of capitalism is an early example of this approach and has been developed with respect to the nature of political culture by Almond and Verba. See G. Almond and S. Verba, *The Civic Culture*. (Princeton, NJ: Princeton University Press 1963). The major thrust of these theories is the idea that stable democracies such as the United States and the United Kingdom are sustained by the participatory orientations of the mass of the people. Such "democratic" attitudes are socialized from an early age and linked to historical traditions. S. M. Lipset, "Some Social Requisites of Democracy, Economic Development and Political Legitimacy," APSR LIII, March 1959. See his classification of stable and unstable democracies and stable and unstable dictatorships, 342. This line or argument is developed in *Political Man* (London: Mercury 1963).

13. "The elite variable in democratic transitions and breakdowns." ASR. Vol. 54, 1989, 17–32.

14. Guillermo O'Donnell and Philippe C. Schmitter, *Transitions from Authoritarian Rule: Tentative Conclusions about Uncertain Democracies*. (Baltimore: Johns Hopkins University Press 1986).

15. G. Di Palma, *To Craft Democracies: An Essay on Democratic Transitions*. (Berkeley: University of California Press 1990). J. J. Linz and A. Stepan, *Problems of Democratic Transition and Consolidation*. (Baltimore: Johns Hopkins University Press 1996).

16. D. Stark and L. Bruszt, *Post Socialist Pathways*. (New York: Cambridge University Press 1998). D. C. North, *Institutions, Institutional Change and Economic Performance*. (New York: Cambridge University Press 1999).

17. Here I am referring to the Marxist literature, others, such as Arendt, have interpreted insurgents in a nonclass framework and have viewed revolution as restoration. The American Revolution is interpreted as revolt of insurgents against a colonial elite. Hannah Arendt, *On Revolution*. (New York: Viking 1963), 34–40.

18. Barrington Moore, *Social Origins of Dictatorship and Democracy*. (London: Penguin Press 1967).

19. D. Rueschemeyer, E. H. Stephens, and J. D. Stephens, *Capitalist Development and Democracy*. (Cambridge: Polity Press 1992), esp. 300.

20. A. Callinicos, *The Revenge of History: Marxism and the East European Revolutions*. (Cambridge: Polity Press 1991), 56.

21. This is quite a different category to that of Moore and Rueschemeyer et al. See D. Lane and C. Ross, *From Communism to Capitalism: Ruling Elites From Gorbachev to Yeltsin*. (New York: St. Martin's Press; London: Macmillan 1998).

22. See, for example, David Lipton and Jeffrey Sachs, "The Strategy of Transition" in David Kennett and Marc Lieberman, *Economic Transformation in Eastern Europe and the Former Soviet Union*. (Fort Worth: Dryden Press 1992), 350–354. Originally published as "Creating a Market Economy in Eastern Europe: The Case of Poland," *Brookings Papers on Economic Activity*, Vol. 1. (Washington D.C.: Brookings Institution 1990).

23. Zbigniew Brzezinski, *The Grand Failure*. (New York and London: Macmillan 1989), 232. He points out that five countries are in "grave crisis" and another six in "crisis"; four (including China and East Germany) were not in crisis. 234.

24. J. Kornai, *From Socialism to Capitalism*. (London: The Social Market Foundation 1998), 2, 40

25. B. Kaminski, *The Collapse of State Socialism*. (Princeton, N.J.: Princeton University Press 1991), 16, 3.

26. Ludwig von Mises, "Economic Calculation in Socialism" in Kennett and Lieberman, *The Road to Capitalism: Economic Transformation in Eastern Europe and the Former Soviet Union* (Fort Worth: Harcourt Brace Jovanovich 1992), 37. Originally published in *Socialism: An Economic and Sociological Analysis*. (New Haven: Yale University Press, 1951).

27. Klaus von Beyme, for example, claims that the "process of transformation was so unique that the old notions of *revolution* and *reform* tend to be inappropriate." Klaus von Beyme, *Transition to Democracy in Eastern Europe*. (New York: Macmillan 1996), p. 18. He suggests "system's change" as an approach.

28. M. Gorbachev, *Perestroika*. (London: Collins 1987), 49–59.

29. Von Beyme, for example, emphasizes that the state socialist societies were "*a uniform socialist political system* which was unique in European constitutional history." ibid. 20.

30. A good example of this is Stark's account of privatization. See: David Stark, "Recombinant Property in East European Capitalism," AJS, 101, no 4, Jan 1996, 993–1027.

31. Ken Jowitt, *New World Disorder: The Leninist Extinction*. (Berkeley: University of California 1992), espec. 285–7.

32. *Transition Report 1999*. (London: EBRD 1999), 73.

33. Branco Milanovic, *Income, Inequality, and Poverty during the Transition from Planned to Market Economy*. (Washington, D.C.: World Bank 1998), 45.

34. Milanovic, 160.

35. Milanovic, 67.

36. www.fraserinstitute.ca accessed 12 Feb 2000. Another index, using a five-point scale, is that of the Heritage Foundation: see G. P. Driscoll, Jr., K. R. Holmes, M. Kirkpatrick, *2000 Index of Economic Freedom*, Wall Street Journal, Heritage Foundation, 2000.

37. This index considers government consumption as a proportion of total consumption, the ratio of transfers and subsidies to GDP, the number, composition and share of output by state-operated enterprises, government investment as a share of total investment, the use of price controls, the rates of top marginal tax thresholds, duration and use of military conscription, growth rate of money supply, level of inflation, access to foreign currency bank accounts, exchange rate controls, risk of property confiscation, risk of government canceling contracts, revenue derived from taxes on international trade, variation on tariff rates, share of trade sector covered by nontariff restrictions, size of the trade sector, percentage of bank deposits held in privately owned banks, share of total domestic credit allocated to the private sector, determination of interest rates by market forces, access to the country's capital markets by foreign capital. Summarized from Appendix 2, Explanatory Notes and Data Sources.

38. Philip G. Roeder has also constructed an index of national, democratic and capitalist transformations, 1999: see Philip G. Roeder "The Revolution of 1989: Postcommunism and the Social Sciences." *Slavic Review*, Vol. 58, no 4, 1999, 743–755. His economic data are derived from the Heritage Foundation and Wall Street Journal index, Bryan T. Johnson, Kim R. Holmes and Melanie Kirkpatrick, *The 1999 Index of Economic Freedom*. (Washington, D.C. 1999).

39. EBRD, *Transition Report 1999* (London: EBRD 1999), 24. In interpreting these data, one should note that in some countries, privately owned companies may still have considerable state ownership, especially in large-scale industry.

40. Freedom House, Freedom in the World 1998/99, Website www.freedomhouse. org. Accessed 11 Feb 2000. Rankings (on a 1–7 point scale) are shown on table 1.3 I have reversed the rankings given by Freedom House to make symmetric with the economic ratings; hence the higher the rank, the higher the level of freedom.

41. EBRD, *Transition Report 1998* (London: HMSO), table 2.1.

42. The Czech Republic, Estonia, Hungary, Slovenia, and Slovakia were the countries that had made the most progress towards levels of transparency (lack of corruption) and economic well-being. See *1999 Transparency International Corruption Perceptions Index*. http://www.transparency.de/documents. This survey is based on interviews with 770 senior executives at major companies; they were asked about the propensity to bribe senior public officials by corporations.

43. See M. Steven Fish, "The Determinants of Economic Reform in the Postcommunist World," *East European Politics and Societies*, Vol. 12, no 1, Winter 1998, 31–78; and his "Postcommunist Subversion: Social Science and Democratisation in East Europe and Eurasia," *Slavic Review*, Vol. 58, no 4, Winter 1999, 794–823.

44. Data on extent of political consensus taken from calculations made in EBRD, *Transition Report 1999* (London: EBRD 1999), 108.

45. Not shown in the chart are Slovenia, which had less than 25 percent of the seats for both the largest pro-reform party and the communists—it came in the top reform group with great political and economic transformation—and Romania, which came in strongly unitary and procommunist group (3 above)—it subsequently had a great political transformation, but only a partial economic one.

46. William L. Miller et al., *Values and Political Change in Post Communist Europe*. (New York: St. Martin's Press, 1998).

47. See discussion in David Lane, *The Rise and Fall of State Socialism*. (Oxford: Polity Press 1996), 168–170 and G. Schopflin, *Politics in Eastern Europe*. (Cambridge, Mass.: Blackwell 1993).

48. World Bank, *Entering the 21st Century: World Development Report 1999/2000*. (New York: Oxford University Press 2000), 230–31.

49. *Transition Report 1999 Update*. (London: EBRD 1999), 12.

50. *Statisticheski ezhegodnik stran-chlenov soveta ekonomicheskoy vzaimopomoshchi 1988*. (Moscow: 1988), 342.

51. Taking the index of real wages of manual and nonmanual workers, it fell from 100 in 1980 to 96 in Hungary in 1985 and to 81 in Poland; in Czechoslovakia there was only a slight rise to 101. *Statisticheski ezhegodnik . . . 1988*, 81.

52. Laszlo Urban, "Hungarian Transition from a Public Choice Perspective," in A. Bozoki, A. Korosenyi and G. Schopflin, *Post Communist Transition: Emerging Pluralism in Hungary*. (New York: St Martin's Press 1992), 92.

2

Party Systems and the State Socialist Legacy in Eastern Europe

Paul G. Lewis

Democratic parties and their institutional development are important not only—or even primarily—in their own right but rather because of their relation to one another. Their capacity to represent distinctive segments of society and pursue the particular interests associated with them, and on this basis to seek power through competitive elections, is the very raison d'être of political parties in a democratic system. From this point of view, parties operating within a pluralist order are fundamentally different from the monopolistic party that dominates under communism. They constitute a central part of the "firm political shell of democratic competitive institutions" identified by David Lane in chapter 1 as characteristic of the former socialist countries that have undergone a full political transformation. The contrast between state socialist regimes and those fully adapted to the world of liberal capitalism is a particularly strong one in this area.

Postcommunist party politics is not only radically different in theory from the undifferentiated sphere of communist politics and the monolithic structures of one-party rule but is, in most views, also critically burdened by the legacy they have imposed. Participation rates have, indeed, often been low in postcommunist eastern Europe and the new parties are largely catch-all organizations that do not function well as participatory institutions, although it is by no means clear how far this is "a legacy of communism, an imitation of political life in some Western states . . . or a reemergence of the interwar pattern."[1] The Leninist legacy, from another perspective, consisted of a "large number of new parties scrambling desperately to achieve a niche in the new democratic environment" and was, at least in the short term, equally negative for postcommunist political development.[2] The influence of strongly politically embedded communist parties is also seen by Lane[3] as one of the key cultural factors impeding the successful transition to a market system, private property and polyarchic politics. On the face of it, then, the legacy of state socialism has not been positive for party development although it is recognized in chapter 1 that the influence of the former regime is more complex when different theoretical perspectives are brought into play, questions of path dependence are raised[4] and due attention is paid to the different character of the communist establishment in the various eastern European countries.

A distinction should also be drawn between the competitive party as such and the idea of a party system, and it is the association of parties and their agglomeration to form the "political shell" of competitive democracy that is most significant. In the democratic context, indeed, it only makes sense from some points of view to judge the overall significance of a party in terms of its relations with others and to evaluate its position within the broader political framework. Parties are, in short, particularly interesting to the extent that they make up a party *system*. Study of the development of democratic party systems in eastern Europe therefore involves investigation of the emergence of political parties in relation to others and the crystallization of a pattern of relations between them—primarily in the context of electoral competition and the democratic struggle for power. As Giovanni Sartori has emphasized, parties only make a system when they are part of a coherent whole: a party system is "the system of interactions resulting from inter-party competition."[5] Discussion of party systems directs attention to a different level of analysis from that of the individual party. Strictly speaking, the concept of system is meaningless unless it has properties that are distinct and separate from those of its constituent elements, and any system results solely from the patterned interactions of the parts that make it up. In practice, though, the individual party and the system formed by a number of them are confused, and discussion of emerging party systems is often conducted in terms of the nature, organization and electoral clout of the few leading parties in a particular country.

Party systems and their stabilization are generally understood to play an important role in the consolidation of all new democracies.[6] Developments in eastern Europe so far have not provided signs of major steps in the direction of strong party system development or much suggestion of stability in this area.[7] Three reasonably standard elections have now been held in many parts of eastern Europe and, while levels of electoral volatility and party instability have been high, something like viable two-party systems can be identified in at least the more developed countries. But even this really concerns little more than the emergence of identifiable right- and left-wing blocs. Only in the Czech Republic have the leading contenders for power actually been the same parties in the last two elections, and after the unconvincing victory of the Social Democrats in the 1998 elections, interparty relations there have shown strong corporatist tendencies and stimulated such public disillusion that surveys showed support for the unreconstructed—and formerly marginalized—Communist Party, reaching 23 percent in October 1999.

In both Poland and in Hungary the basic constituents of the systems—the parties themselves—showed a high degree of fluidity. Solidarity Election Action only came into existence little more than a year before its election victory in Poland during 1997, while Fidesz suddenly became the dominant opposition force in Hungary during 1998 and rather unexpectedly replaced the Democratic Forum as the leading right-wing party. It is hardly possible to discuss party systems, though, when the stable units out of which they might be constructed do not really exist. The outcome of the elections during 1997 and 1998 even in east-central Europe was not so much the emergence of party systems as such as the structuring of the political space into identifiable left- and right-wing segments, which reasonably well organized parties could then be expected to fill. Nevertheless, like most other observers, I shall often refer to party systems in the rather loose suggestive sense of political structuring and interparty relations, even if the formal conditions for "systemness" do not yet exist.

In east-central Europe the political space was at least opened up by a clear break from the communist regime, generally in terms of one or more changes of government following fully competitive democratic elections. A low vote for politically embedded communist parties and a substantial victory for noncommunist forces in the first competitive elections is seen by Lane as a prime marker for the movement towards pluralism and the rapid transformation of the state socialist system.[8] As much as the formation of governments by freely elected parties, this confirmed the importance of the emergence of effective oppositions for the development and stabilization of a democratic order.[9] In broad terms, of course, this signalled a major break from conditions of state socialism and the rejection of its political legacy. But in less formal terms such developments built on specific regional legacies in terms of political culture and popular orientations to communist rule,[10] which had in turn been a basis for national policies of reform communism and forms of proto-pluralism within the socialist establishment. But this only concerned developments in east-central Europe. Elsewhere in eastern Europe there have been less favorable conditions for the development of organized opposition and correspondingly fewer signs of party system emergence or even the proper structuring of a democratic political space.[11] In the Balkans, the leadership-dominated parties that ruled in Serbia and Croatia throughout the 1990s in particular still lacked much of an organized or stable opposition and both stayed well in the train of the democratization process, while the breakthrough from a minimally reconstructed postcommunism in Romania at the end of 1996 led to little more than a weak coalition government blocked both by a postcommunist opposition and the conflicting demands of its own constituents.

The results of the 1998 elections in Ukraine also showed few signs of the country moving much beyond the stage of tentative postcommunist change, as forces close to the former establishment retained much of their existing dominance, although greater prospects for change were apparent following the

Moldovan vote the same month. It would not be realistic to expect very much in terms of a stable and clearly differentiated party system so soon after the collapse of the strongly entrenched form of authoritarian rule seen in the Soviet Union, but the signs of such patterns developing have been very limited indeed in most of the countries concerned. Many deputies in Ukraine remain unaffiliated to any party, and the notion of an independent parliament in which parties could begin to develop a clear identity is currently still a distant prospect in Belarus.

The establishment of a reasonably open democratic space is the basic pre-condition for the operation of the competitive processes that underlie the development of any party system, and this by no means exists everywhere in eastern Europe. Indeed, none of the former "patrimonial" communist countries, where much of the old political apparatus maintained much of its control, could be described as an unambiguous democracy, a condition that characterized virtually the whole of the Balkans and the non-Baltic post-Soviet area (see table 2.1).[12] For such reasons, it has been argued, most east European systems are likely to be considerably weaker and more fragile than those seen in other recently democratized regions of the world.

In terms of party development, as Peter Mair has suggested, in eastern Europe patterns of democratization are different, the electorate is different, and both the context and pattern of party competition are different. At the present stage parties are unstable and their social roots quite shallow and, while political preferences do seem to be settling into more of a stable pattern, electoral volatility (the degree to which voters switch party preferences in successive elections) has understandably reached high levels. In the light of broad comparative estimates, the average electoral volatility in western Europe between 1960 and 1989 was 8.4 percent (although under the different conditions prevailing between 1918 and 1930 it had stood at 12.3 percent), while the equivalent value for the first elections in postcommunist east-central Europe was 25 percent.[13] The significance of such indicators should not be exaggerated though, and this degree of volatility is not out of line with that seen in other democratizing regions and was, for example, exceeded by five out of twelve Latin American countries in legislative elections held between 1978 and 1993. It can nevertheless be concluded that the proximity of the more successfully transformed state socialist countries to western Europe, as well as the reasonably high levels of overall modernization noted by Lane,[14] did not provide sufficient conditions for effective party system development in a broader comparative context.

Latin American experience also contains some parallels with eastern Europe in terms of particular models of transition and the evolution of certain types of authoritarian party. Mexico and Paraguay were, for example, ruled for decades by "single parties fused with the state" in ways similar, though not identical, to those of communist Europe. On this basis the idea of "hegemonic party systems in transition" emerges as one denoting structures that were not fully institutionalized but more developed than those classified as by Sartori as simply "in-

Table 2.1. The Countries of Contemporary Eastern Europe

Freedom House Ranking, 1998–1999	Political Order	Party System
Free		
Czech Republic	Largely competitive	Emerging two-bloc system
Estonia		
Hungary		
Latvia		
Lithuania	Partly competitive	Authoritarian legacy, weak party development
Poland		
Slovenia		
Slovakia		
Romania		
Bulgaria		
Partly Free		
Albania	Semi-authoritarian	Largely hegemonic, little pluralism
Bosnia		
Croatia		
Macedonia		
Moldova		
Ukraine		
Not Free		
Yugoslavia (Serbia/Montenegro)	Authoritarian	Hegemonic
Belarus		

Source: Column 2 categories from A. Karatnycky, ed. *Freedom in the World: Annual Survey of Political Rights and Civil Liberties,* New York: Freedom House, 1999.

choate." This type of party system indeed raises questions about the appropriateness of any uniform scale of institutionalization, and the degree to which it can be identified with broader processes of democratic development. Due to their longevity and particular features, it is indeed more accurate to refer to such hegemonic systems as part of a separate category rather than a point on some continuum of institutionalization.[15] Such problems loom even larger in the context of eastern Europe than in Latin America, and here the status of communist successor parties has been a major source of controversy as well as prime area for investigation in terms of the legacy of state socialism.

But there is not necessarily a difficulty with the idea of communist successor parties within a pluralist party system per se, and the institutional transfer from one regime to another does not in itself cast doubt on the political credentials of new social democratic institutions in Poland, Lithuania, and Hungary where the parties were voted into power and left office according to the rules when they lost a subsequent election. Complaints about their modus operandi, the bureaucratic mentality of their leading staff and continuing links with elements of the former establishment may not be irrelevant, but there is little serious doubt that the reconstituted parties now operate as part of a developing pluralist system. The same is broadly true of Bulgaria, although the early electoral victories of the socialists there was achieved in the face of a very weak opposition and in a barely developed democratic context.

More serious questions arise about other east European countries, where parties were renamed and reorganized as some elements of pluralist democracy were introduced around them while their communist leaders and their supporters never really lost power or had their dominant influence within the political system interrupted. A major aspect of the change was the introduction of competitive elections, whose impact and full systemic implications were nevertheless vitiated by the fact that former incumbents never left major offices of state and maintained control over much of the political—and indeed economic—infrastructure. Serbia and Ukraine thus provided equivalent examples to the "hegemonic party systems in transition" identified by Mainwaring and Scully in the Latin American context. Less closely associated with the old political establishment but similarly distant from a full liberal democracy with a pluralist party system were the national-populist, semi-authoritarian polities of Slovakia and Croatia. Outside the track of democratization and party development altogether lies the personal dictatorship of Aleksandr Lukashenka in Belarus who has shown a growing distaste for parties and all semblance of independent parliamentary activity in general.

Classification of party systems by any criterion thus requires conditions of relatively free political competition and a reasonable length of time for patterns to become apparent. Only then can the "political shell" of democratic institutions be said to be fully formed. Time has certainly been limited in this sense, although some kind of emerging multiparty pattern can be identified in the more developed countries of east-central Europe. Signs of any democratic party system are fewer elsewhere in eastern Europe where progress in the transition from authoritarian communist rule has been more limited and the institutional legacy of state socialism has been carried forward in more direct fashion. But there has has also been considerable variation in east-central Europe and different ways in which the institutions and practices of state socialism have been built upon.

COMPETITIVE POLITICS AND PARTY SYSTEMS IN EAST-CENTRAL EUROPE

Regional diversity has always been strong in eastern Europe and has become yet more pronounced since the end of communist rule.[16] To some extent, as already suggested, the different parts of the region can be broadly identified with different types of party system. Only the countries of east-central Europe and the Baltic states possess anything like the competitive systems associated with modern liberal democracies, an association recognized by Charles Gati[17] and later affirmed more formally by the decision of the European Union in 1997 to intensify negotiations on integration with five of the more advanced postcommunist states, all of them located in this region. But even in these cases it is only in an approximate sense that anything like a party system can be identified. Comparison of the range of electoral outcomes gives a broad indication of the level of party system development.

In each of the five countries of east-central Europe at least three competitive elections had been held by the end of 2000. Table 2.2 shows the range of parties represented in the parliaments over that period, and makes clear the fact that new parties were still gaining entry to parliament in the third sequence of elections. The smallest number of parliamentary parties overall was in Hungary, where only seven were elected during this period and six of these played a part in government in one or more of the three parliaments. They were therefore, in Sartori's terms, the "relevant" parties in terms of his model and could be seen as the components of what seemed to be the most viable party system in eastern Europe. But even in Hungary the Democratic Forum was almost completely replaced by Fidesz as the leading right-wing force between 1990 and 1998, and any "system" that could be identified was not made up of quite the same components over the whole period. The presence of six relevant parties in the legislature for most of the time also placed Hungary in the high fragmentation pattern identified by Sartori, and denoted the polarized pluralism associated with unstable polities and weakly rooted democratic system.[18]

Although no more than six relevant parties (or party groupings) were present in the parliaments of Poland and the Czech Republic between 1993 and 1998 at any one time, there was already more variation in the particular organizations involved overall in these countries during this period than in Hungary and thus even less "systemness." Nine parties gained parliamentary representation in the Czech Republic between 1992 and 1998 compared with seven in Hungary, while as many as twenty-four electoral committees (but hardly parties) were represented in the fragmented Polish parliament of 1991. Nevertheless, by 1998 something like a bipartisan legislature had developed in all three countries.

This pattern was not followed in the two other countries of east-central Europe. The overall number of parties during the 1990s in Slovakia and Slovenia (ten and twelve, respectively) was again higher than Hungary's, but their parliaments were nowhere near as fragmented as that in Poland between 1991 and 1993. Slovenia also developed a rather different form of party government, in that new coalitions were formed after the elections of 1992 and 1996 with the Liberal Democracy Party continuing on both occasions as their central component. It had come to the fore after a change of prime minister in 1991, and the party

Table 2.2. Party Representation in Successive East-Central European Parliaments

	First: 1990–1992	Second: 1992–1996	Third: 1997–2000
Hungary			
Hungarian Democratic Forum	X	X	X
Hungarian Socialist Party	X	X	X
FIDESZ	X	X	X
Independent Party of Smallholders	X	X	X
Alliance of Free Democrats	X	X	X
Christian Democratic Peoples Party	X	X	
Hungarian Justice and Life Party			X
Czech Republic			
Czech Social Democratic Party	X	X	X
Civic Democratic Party	X	X	X
Christian Democratic Union	X	X	X
Communist Party	X	X	X
Civic Democratic Alliance	X	X	
Association for the Republic	X	X	
Moravian Silesian Movement	X		
Liberal Social Union	X		
Freedom Union			X
Poland			
Democratic Left Alliance	X	X	X
Democratic/Freedom Union	X	X	X
Polish Peasant Party	X	X	X
Confederation for Independent Poland	X	X	
21 other committees represented	X		
Union of Labor		X	
Non-Party Bloc for Reform		X	
Solidarity Electoral Action			X
Movement for Reconstruction of Poland			X
Slovenia			
Liberal Democracy	X	X	X
Social Democratic Party	X	X	X
Slovenian National Party	X	X	X
United List of Social Democrats	X	X	X
Slovene Peoples Party	X	X	X
Slovene Christian Democrats	X	X	X
			(with SPP)
Democratic Party	X		
Greens	X		
Democratic Party of Retired		X	X
New Slovenia (Christian)			X
Party of Youth			X
Slovakia			
Movement for Democratic Slovakia	X	X	X
Hungarian Coalition	X	X	X

Table 2.2.   (Continued)

Slovakia, continued			
Slovak National Party	X	X	X
Party of Democratic Left	X	X (as Common Choice)	X
Christian Democratic Movement	X	X	
Democratic Union		X	
Association of Workers		X	
Democratic Coalition			X
Party of Civic Understanding			X

continued as the main governing force for much of the 1990s. But Slovenia was far from showing signs of becoming what Sartori called a predominant party system, in which a given party was able to amass an absolute majority in three consecutive elections.[19] There was also a dominant party in Slovakia for most of the time between 1992 and 1998, but its authority was considerably less secure and the overall level of democracy in the country less advanced than in Slovenia. Mečiar's Movement for Democratic Slovakia (MDS) was as clearly dominant over all competing parties in both the 1992 and 1994 elections, with a lead of 22.5 percent in terms of total vote over its nearest rival in 1992 and 25.3 in 1994. This was far higher than the lead of any other victorious party in postcommunist east-central Europe over its competitors. But the MDS was even further away than Slovenia's Liberal Democracy from developing as the institutional core of a predominant party system. The party lost overall parliamentary control in 1998, but had already found it difficult to preserve its dominant position in Slovakia's generally fragmented pattern of party relations at an earlier stage. In 1994 it failed to maintain relations with any viable coalition partner, lost control of the government and had to face a further election less than two years into the life of the independent Slovak republic. The MDS was dominant over other parties in terms of the number of parliamentary votes it controlled but able to find few partners with whom a governing coalition could be formed. It survived for the full life of the parliament elected in 1994 partly because other Slovak parties were also divided and did not form a coherent opposition, although one was finally put together to contest the 1998 elections that succeeded in defeating the MDS.

Elements of party competition finally prevailed, but for much of the 1990s Slovakia appeared to be governed by something very much like the "hegemonic party system in transition" identified in Latin America.[20] The major problem faced there in terms of democratic party system development, therefore, was less the lack of institutionalization commonly diagnosed in postcommunist eastern Europe than the residual institutional strength of a transitional power structure based on the MDS with strong roots in the former regime. Slovakia was the country in the region where the legacy of state socialism could most clearly be seen in institutional terms. The main issue was, as in other parts of the postcommunist

world, less one of party system development and more the patchy nature of democratization and failure to develop the conditions for party competition. To the
extent that we can talk at this stage of institutionalization and democratic consolidation in terms of party systems at all, then, it is the other countries of east-
central Europe (Hungary, Poland, Slovenia, the Czech Republic) that best represent it.

The summary view taken here is also based on the number of parties con-
testing elections and gaining representation in parliament, processes that by no
means determine the nature of party system dynamics once a legislature is constituted. Hungary's relative stability in the east European context, for example,
is cast in a somewhat different light by further understanding of relations within
the country's parliament. In some contrast to the set of six parties that contested
the 1990 and 1993 elections, for example, the Hungarian parliament in October
1993 contained as many as seventeen distinct political groupings.[21] Prior to the
1998 elections the Democratic Forum, the leading force in the 1990–94 parliament, had largely self-destructed as had the Christian Democrats.[22] Although
the HDF survived to gain a small number of votes in the subsequent elections
and became part of the government coalition, it achieved this solely by coming
to an agreement with the victorious Fidesz. It therefore still counted as a "relevant" party according to Sartori's classification.

Judgments on system structure and party institutionalization even in east-central Europe under these conditions must therefore be somewhat conjectural.
But the notion of an emerging structure provides some perspective on party development in eastern Europe and sheds light on the nature of the institutional
framework that has developed in the countries furthest along the road of postcommunist transformation. It helps demarcate the more developed democracies
from other postcommunist countries, and defines major characteristics of inter-
party relations.

EXPLAINING PARTY SYSTEM EMERGENCE

In association with continuing fluidity and the general weakness of party structure or overall "systemness," it is by no means easy to arrive at an explanation of
how the degree of party system formation that does exist has come about or the
precise part that any state socialist legacy might have played. Accounts of why
established party systems differ generally emphasize the importance of institutional factors, like the electoral system and the structure of the state institutions
within which the parties operate, or they take a more sociological approach and
trace the structure of party systems to underlying social cleavages.[23] In the context of postcommunist eastern Europe other major approaches direct attention
to the legacy of the former regime, the impact of the pattern of transformation
itself or the nature of the conflict between the authoritarian regime and the

democratic opposition. The influence of the latter factor, however, is generally regarded as being of only temporary significance, particularly as democratization progresses and patterns of political competition become established.[24]

Institutional variables offer the first possible explanation for the emergence of different types of party system. It is difficult, however, to establish any direct relation between the electoral mechanism applied and the party systems that have emerged in eastern Europe. A plurality system, based on a simple electoral majority, has generally been held to encourage the formation of a two-party system, while proportional representation favors the development of multipartism. Nearly all east European states, however, have adopted some form of proportional representation for the main parliamentary chamber, not least because there was no way in which two relatively well-balanced party antagonists could be expected to present themselves to the electorate at the beginning of the post-communist period. So the differences in eastern Europe that can be detected are hardly due to this difference in the form of election. One country in which a plurality system was applied—Ukraine, where some (1998 elections) or all (1994) candidates had to gain 50 percent of the vote—was certainly not successful in producing a balanced or effective party system. The requirement that successful candidates needed to gain the vote of half of all those entered on the electoral register in Belarus just made it extremely difficult to elect a quorate parliament at all—which was surely the objective underlying the regulation in any case. The poorly developed party system in such countries was as much due to the incompleteness of the democratization process as to any single electoral mechanism.

Within the basic system of proportional representation there are also variations in terms of whether two-stage elections are held (with the leading candidates in the first round proceeding to a run-off in the second as in France, which gives voters a chance to switch to a second choice), more complex systems in which multiple votes can be cast in different constituencies (for example, at local and regional levels), or various mixtures of different systems to achieve elements both of proportionality and an effective majority. There were also regulations of varying strictness on coalitions and election alliances (in which parties standing in an electoral coalition may be required to form a single party fraction in parliament if successful), and thresholds set at different levels (generally from 3 to 5 percent) to exclude very small parties from the legislature. A threshold, generally of 3 to 5 percent for individual parties, has been applied in most countries and has helped facilitate the emergence of moderate pluralism in terms of party systems.

Comparison of the 1991 election in Poland (when there was no barrier to parliamentary entry) with later ballots in 1993 and 1997 (where a 5 percent threshold was imposed) certainly shows the threshold having had some effect in countering the fragmentation of the party system (twenty-four parliamentary groups gaining representation in 1991 compared with six parties in 1993 and five in

1997) and assisting the formation of stable government coalitions. The cost of achieving this degree of moderate pluralism was graphically shown in the 1993 election when much of the right wing (34 percent of the electorate) failed to gain representation. Whatever the immediate effect in terms of exclusion from parliament, though, there was no doubt that the introduction of a threshold made a lasting impact on the process of party system formation. Changes in electoral institutions in the Baltic states have also prompted moves towards party system consolidation, and the abolition of electoral coalitions (or *apparentements*) in Estonia and Latvia has helped moderate fragmentation in those countries.[25] The outcome of any particular electoral mechanism is, though, by no means automatic and a sequence of elections is necessary for any systemic impact to take firm effect. Political cultures must also change for political institutions to have common consequences.[26]

A second approach to party system emergence is sociological, one particularly influential variant of which has been the model of multiple cleavages constructed by S. M. Lipset and S. Rokkan.[27] In this formulation modern European party systems are seen as the product of a number of historic social conflicts and cleavages that developed over the centuries. It therefore involves a broad and very significant conception of social legacy, one that stretches back centuries in the case of western Europe. The lines of cleavage comprise: one originating as far back as the Reformation and Counter-Reformation in the sixteenth and seventeenth centuries and focusing on conflicts of the center and periphery, another stemming from the French Revolution and concerning state-church relations, and later cleavages originating in relations between forces deriving from land and industry or between the owner and industrial worker. This pattern of four major social cleavages has, it is argued, fed directly into the way in which political forces are organized in contemporary democracies and has determined the different form taken by party systems in modern industrial societies.

On this basis it was observed that the modern party systems of the 1960s were remarkably similar to those of the 1920s, and thus concluded that the lines of political cleavage that emerged in the 1920s became "frozen" in a form that survived as the organizational template for the pattern of party relations in contemporary democracies. The validity of the "freezing" hypothesis and its status some thirty years on is the topic of much debate and it remains a central point of reference for the understanding of modern democracies and their party systems.[28] But one of its major implications seems to be that established party systems have very deep social and historical roots indeed, and that new democracies might not have such good chances of replicating their experience.

Such a perspective even raises the question of whether postcommunist eastern Europe can develop anything resembling a fully structured party system at all. It is certainly clear that the "frozen cleavage" hypothesis in its original form is not directly applicable to eastern Europe—although views differ on whether this is because the cleavages are different, due rather to their not freezing or freezing in ways that do not produce a clearly structured political space in which party systems can form, or because all of the east European regimes have been subject to more than one fundamental discontinuity and have just not experienced the stable conditions under which "freezing" can take place. But observers at least agree that postcommunism produces a relatively unstructured political field in which the conditions for party system formation are open rather than tightly constraining.

This does not mean that contemporary east European party systems are unstructured or that they will not develop a clearer pattern of relations. The idea that the postcommunist political landscape is a *tabula rasa* lacking structure and perceived in relatively random ways by its active constituents is certainly not generally confirmed.[29] New social cleavages have developed and there are limited signs of these being reflected in party alignments, but the question of their "freezing" in the line with the model advanced by Lipset and Rokkan must wait for some time before any clear answer is possible. Cleavages, indeed, appear to be more numerous than those commonly identified in the west and vary in the degree to which they fissure the politics of the region. Eight separate cleavage dimensions have been identified by Klaus von Beyme: those of center-periphery, religious-secular, rural-urban and capital-labor in line with established west European patterns—but also some arising from the eastern experience and more recent developments, for example: bureaucratic-libertarian, materialist-postmaterialist, nationalist-westernizing, and centralist-decentralizing.[30] Major cleavages also arise directly in terms of conceptions of the communist past, and this turns attention to the view of party system formation that bears directly on the issues of transformation dealt with in this book.

This third approach directly confronts the legacy of state socialism. One variant has counterposed "legacies of the past" with the "imperatives of liberalization" and suggests that, while the "Leninist" period expunged much of the legacy of an earlier past, structures of the communist period affected subsequent developments in a variety of ways although the interaction of different factors was more important than the contribution of particular elements differentiated by time period.[31] The length of the communist period and its far-reaching social impact have also been considerably more important for emerging party systems than the particular mode of regime transition.[32] The idea that the recent communist past has exerted a stronger influence on postcommunist politics, including any emerging party systems, is more intuitively convincing than the supposition that some deep-rooted social cleavages are likely to freeze into new structures of party relations under the fluid political conditions of the early twenty-first century. The more clearly defined party structures of east-central Europe compared with the Balkans and the FSU also suggest that the longer experience of communist rule (in the latter case) and the more entrenched forms of authoritarianism (in the former) exert some kind of influence over contemporary developments. These observations are also very much in line with Lane's argument for the importance of political culture in explaining the different levels of political transformation in eastern Europe.[33]

One problem with a general view being taken of the legacy of state socialism, though, is that the experience of communist rule was itself significantly differentiated. The legacy of both Hungary and Poland (as well as Slovenia) was marked by a higher degree of liberalization throughout much of the communist period, dating back to the shared experiences of 1956, whose consequences were, nevertheless, rather different in concrete terms. The Czechoslovak bid for reform in 1968 echoed these earlier events, but again prompted a different resolution. The reform experiences of these countries within state socialism were diverse in both content and outcome, but the fact that they had at times dominated the political agenda and remained to a greater or lesser extent present as policy options were important determinants of the nature of the state socialist legacy in those cases.[34] Further, differences in both the communist and postcommunist periods can be linked with contrasts in precommunist experience such as the democratic experience of interwar Czechoslovakia and the more limited, but still significant, elements of constitutional and representative government in Hungary and Poland.

The precise meaning of any single state socialist legacy thus remains open to some doubt. It is often used to suggest that the Balkans and FSU have in some way a "larger" inheritance that weighs more heavily on the democratization process and has thus held back party development, but it is really the nature and makeup of any legacy that is at issue. It is an approach to postcommunist development that has raised certain doubts. The validity any blanket explanation of postcommunist party development in terms of old regime legacies has been subject to considerable question and the dichotomy of explanations in terms of indivisible "legacies" and "institutions" not regarded by some analysts as useful for empirical analysis.[35]

That, of course, is not to say that former practices and perceptions of political life do not have any consequences for contemporary developments. But it does suggest that the legacy is a highly differentiated one that may explain the differing levels of postcommunist structural development in quite different ways. Legacies may be distinguished, then, not just by weight or intensity but also their nature and the level at which they can be understood to operate. An initial distinction may be drawn between legacies operating at institution and regime level. Former ruling parties in east-central Europe may not have been, as noted in chapter 1, "politically embedded"[36] to the extent they were able to block radical policies of transformation but they often bequeathed major resources that gave the postcommunist successor parties significant advantages in the new arena of competitive politics. This concerned material resources like money, property and equipment as well as a broader organizational legacy in terms of structure, membership and political skills. The former ruling parties were significantly disadvantaged for some years after 1989 in terms of lack of legitimacy and popular support in a context of electoral competition, but their successor socialist organizations in both Poland and Hungary were well endowed in material and organizational terms to confront incumbent liberal-conservative parties as their early popularity began to fade in the early to mid-1990s.

Distinctive legacies of state socialism can also be observed at regime level in terms of overall political culture and the nature of political practices in different east European countries. An openness to reform has already been noted in Hungary and Poland (a category to which Slovenia can be added) in a situation where the communist regime enjoyed limited popular support and authoritarian rule proved increasingly difficult to sustain. Similar tendencies could be detected in Czechoslovakia during the 1960s, but a different strategy was followed there following the Soviet invasion of 1968. This openness was associated with a greater tolerance of political diversity in east-central Europe than in the countries of the Balkans and the former Soviet Union, less emphasis on ideological orthodoxy and a de facto acceptance of elements of pluralism both in the communist party and the political system more generally. These relatively "soft" regimes provided positive conditions for more overt pluralism, competitive politics and party development when the regional situation permitted during the late 1980s. The origins of the relatively mature party system in contemporary Hungary can in this respect be traced to their early origins in 1987 during the late communist period, a development quite out of the question in orthodox Czechoslovakia but also not seen in Poland where opposition was channelled within the relatively monolithic Solidarity movement. Conditions in those two countries were relatively conducive to postcommunist pluralist development, but less so for the emergence of clearly defined party systems.

A further legacy of state socialism in terms of the development of party systems can be seen in their developing relationship with the postcommunist electorate and the way in which the communist experience impinges on the social cleavages that can be understood to underpin divisions between the major parties. While the "frozen" cleavages identified by Lipset and Rokkan may have only limited relevance to the emerging party systems of east-central Europe, the more fluid social divisions of postcommunist society may have more direct significance. Three distinctively postcommunist dimensions of cleavage formation have been identified by Herbert Kitschelt.[37] One relates to resource allocation and distinguishes advocates of political principles of distribution (populism) from those committed to the market; a second concerns the extent and nature of democratic participation and differentiates modern libertarians from traditional authoritarians; while a third contrasts those holding a universal conception of citizenship rights from others making them contingent on ethnic, religious or national identity. Initial investigation confirmed that the tabula rasa view taken of the party systems in eastern Europe was indeed misleading—although the view taken here of party system was considerably more complex than that based on just the number of parties and concerned the establishment of congruent relations between voters and party elites. It also demonstrated, on rather a different basis, the distinction already drawn between the increasingly pluralist countries of east-central Europe from the hegemonic systems of the Balkans. Bulgaria thus "represents a different political world than the Central European countries" and was characterized by a legacy of the overwhelming strength of the communist elite during the transition. Party systems in east-central Europe were quite different, with that in the Czech Republic giving voters the most distinctive choice of alternatives.[38]

In more concrete terms, most writers see a primary cleavage in postcommunist society developing around the economic dimension and a recognizable left-right axis emerging as the major structuring agency in east European party systems.[39] It varies in strength and takes particular forms in different countries, being most clearly articulated in the Czech Republic where it is as sharply defined as in western Europe.[40] While four distinct kinds of party have been identified by one analyst of contemporary east-central Europe (liberal, liberal-traditional, tradition/state-oriented, liberal/state-oriented), there are quite striking differences across the region as to where they are located on the political spectrum.[41] Cleavages other than the socioeconomic are also highly influential and the significance of religious issues has, for example, been considerable in Poland. This in turn is closely linked with the continuing division seen between those who maintain a consistently negative view of the communist regime, and those associated with it, and groups that take a more pragmatic and nuanced view of the communist period. While observable to varying degrees elsewhere, this line of division is particularly prominent in the Polish electorate. It represents a social cleavage that goes furthest to explain the party system that has emerged in Poland and persists as a particularly distinctive legacy of state socialism in that country.[42]

The division between those associated with the former regime and anticommunist Solidarity forces has been particularly strong in Polish presidential contests and was a prominent factor in the 1997 Polish elections, although the second victory of Aleksander Kwaśniewski on behalf of left-wing forces in the presidential election of October 2000 may show that the influence of this legacy is finally beginning to reduce. The part it plays in defining electoral cleavages varies considerably within the east European region. In the Czech Republic decommunization has been found to have a low salience for politicians as a whole. It was an issue whose salience had also greatly declined in Hungary. Only in Bulgaria, where democratization and the crystallization of party positions is less advanced, were struggles over contemporary economic issues also strongly linked with issues and individuals directly representative of the old regime.[43] The profound experiences of the region in terms of communist rule thus impinge on emerging party structures in a variety of ways and with a varying degrees of intensity in the different countries. In some situations, too, the practice of communist authoritarianism in the national context, particular inheritances from the period of Soviet domination and the resonance just of specific events continue to play a highly significant part. One singular example has been the prime importance of the 1956 revolution in subsequent Hungarian developments.[44]

CONCLUSION

While generalization about the influence of the state socialist legacy on patterns of party system development in east-central Europe may have only limited relevance in broad terms, then, its utility is considerably greater when due attention is paid to national context and the level at which the legacy operated. Distinctions may be drawn at regime level between the precommunist legacy, the inheritance of the years of communist rule (and of the different phases of communist rule), and the ways in which these experiences may reinforce one another in terms of forming overall postcommunist legacies. The less positive impact of the Czechoslovak communist legacy in comparison with Hungary or Poland on subsequent democratic developments has thus been moderated by the more positive pluralist experience of the interwar years. Authoritarian rule in the Balkans, however, both in the pre-1939 years and during the communist period, produced a far less positive legacy for postcommunist development. Linked with the regime legacies are those associated with specific political institutions, and here the relative weakness of the communist parties in the "softer" regimes of Hungary and Poland became the bases for major sources of organizational strength in the postcommunist period. The diverse legacies of east-central Europe thus combine in some cases at least to strengthen the process of postcommunist democratic development and provide more positive conditions for party-system formation.

NOTES

1. I. Volgyes, "The Legacies of Communism: An Introductory Essay," in *The Legacies of Communism in Eastern Europe* (ed. Z. Barany and I. Volgyes), Baltimore: Johns Hopkins University Press (1995), 15.

2. B. Geddes, "A Comparative Perspective on the Leninist Legacy in Eastern Europe," *Comparative Political Studies* vol. 28, 2 (1995): 269.

3. See this collection Chapter 1, section 4.

4. See this collection Chapter 1, section 1.

5. *Parties and Party Systems: A Framework for Analysis,* Cambridge: Cambridge University Press (1976), 44.

6. M. Cotta, "Building Party Systems after the Dictatorship," in *Democratization in Eastern Europe* (ed. G. Pridham and T. Vanhanen), London: Routledge (1994), 100.

7. P. G. Lewis, *Political Parties in Postcommunist Eastern Europe*, London: Routledge (2000), 150–55.

8. Chapter 1, section 4.

9. See R. A. Dahl (ed.), *Political Oppositions in Western Democracies*, New Haven: Yale University Press (1966). His conclusion suggests a view of party systems that gives this dimension particular prominence.

10. Chapter 1, section 5.

11. P. G. Lewis, "The Repositioning of Opposition in East-Central Europe," *Government and Opposition* vol. 32, 4 (1997): 628–29.

12. H. Kitschelt, Z. Mansfeldova, R, Markowski, and G. Tóka, *Postcommunist Party Systems: Competition, Representation, and Inter-party Cooperation*, Cambridge: Cambridge University Press (1999), 14, 40.

13. P. Mair, *Party System Change: Approaches and Interpretations*, Oxford: Clarendon Press (1997), 175, 183. Different estimates of volatility levels have been produced by a range of analysts, and those cited here in fact suggest a lower level of volatility than some others.

14. Chapter 1, section 5.

15. S. Mainwaring and T. R. Scully (eds.), *Building Democratic Institutions: Party Systems in Latin America*, Palo Alto, Calif., Stanford University Press (1995), 20–21.

16. G. Wightman, "Parties and politics," in *Developments in Central and East European Politics* (ed. S. White, J. Batt and P. G. Lewis), London: Macmillan (1998), 147.

17. "The Mirage of Democracy," *Transition* vol. 2, 6 (1996).

18. *Parties and Party Systems*, 127. The "relevance" of parties is carefully defined in pp. 121–24.

19. Ibid., 199.

20. Mainwaring and Scully, *Building Democratic Institutions*, 20.

21. P. G. Lewis, "Democratization and Party Development in Eastern Europe," *Democratization* vol. 1, 3 (1994): 393.

22. G. Schopflin, "Hungary's Elections: The Dilemma of the Right," *RFE/RL Newsline* 29 April 1998.

23. A. Ware, *Political Parties and Party Systems*, Oxford: Oxford University Press (1996), 190–96.

24. W. Merkel, "The Consolidation of Post-autocratic Democracies: A Multi-level Model," *Democratization* vol. 5, 3 (1998): 50–51. A. Ágh also identifies the conflict between forming ruling parties and new opposition groups as one of three dominant cleavages in his genetic typology of east European parties (*The Politics of Central Europe*, London: Sage, 1998, 115–21), but similarly suggests that this cleavage line has limited contemporary significance.

25. V. Pettai and M. Kreuzer, "Institutions and Party Development in the Baltic States," *Party Development and Democratic Change in Postcommunist Europe—the First Decade* (ed. P. G. Lewis), London: Frank Cass (2001), 112–14.

26. R. Taagepera, "How Electoral Systems Matter for Democratization," *Democratization* vol. 5, 3 (1998): 86, 88.

27. Lipset, Seymour L. and Stein Rokkan (eds.) *Party Systems and Voter Alignments: Cross National Perspectives*, New York: Free Press (1967), 1–64.

28. P. Mair, "Party Systems and Structures of Competition," in *Comparing Democracies: Elections and Voting in Global Perspective* (ed. L. LeDuc et al.), London: Sage (1996), 102–3.

29. R. Markowski, "Political Parties and Ideological Spaces in East Central Europe," *Communist and Postcommunist Studies* vol. 30, 3 (1997): 221–22.

30. *Transition to Democracy in Eastern Europe*, London: Macmillan (1996), 128–30.

31. B. Crawford and A. Lijphart, "Explaining Political and Economic Change in Post-Communist Eastern Europe," *Comparative Political Studies* vol. 28, 2 (1995): 171–99. This draws on Geddes's work on the Leninist legacy in the same volume.

32. S. W. Rivera, "Historical Cleavages or Transition Mode? Reflections on the Emerging Party Systems in Poland, Hungary and Czechoslovakia," *Party Politics* vol. 2, 2 (1996): 177–208.

33. Chapter 1, sections 4 and 5.

34. Chapter 1, section 5.

35. Kitschelt, *Postcommunist Party Systems*, 12.

36. Chapter 1, section 4.

37. "Party Systems in East Central Europe: Consolidation or Fluidity?", University of Strathclyde Studies in Public Policy 241 (1995), 55.

38. Ibid, 3–4, 80–82, 98.

39. J. Bielasiak, "Substance and Process in the Development of Party Systems in East Central Europe," *Communist and Postcommunist Studies* vol. 30, 1 (1997): 39.

40. Markowski, "Political Parties," 229.

41. R. Herbut, "Systemy partyjne krajów Europy Centralnej i Wschodniej oraz wzorce rywalizacji politycznej," in *Demokracje Europy Środkowo-Wschodniej w perspektywie porównawczej* (ed. A. Antoszewski and R. Herbut), Wrocław: Wydawnictwo Uniwersytetu Wrocławskiego (1997), 144–47.

42. T. Zarycki, "Politics in the Periphery: Political Cleavages in Poland Interpreted in Their Historical and International Context," *Europe-Asia Studies* vol. 52, 5 (2000).

43. Kitschelt, *Postcommunist Party Systems*, 261.

44. A. Bozoki, "Party Formation and Constitutional Change in Hungary," *Journal of Communist Studies and Transition Politics* vol. 10, 3 (1994): 54.

II

POLITICAL CHANGE

3

Russia: The Revenge of the Superstructure

Stephen White

The Soviet system was—above all—a system that claimed no mandate from a mass electorate. The party supposedly represented the best interests of working people, and its mandate came from the ideology that gave it that role, not from a competition for the popular vote. Elections were held regularly, and in 1936, when a new constitution was adopted that incorporated a secret ballot, Stalin went so far as to predict a "very lively electoral struggle."[1] Another member of the leadership, Andrei Zhdanov, warned the Central Committee the following year that there might be "hostile agitation and hostile candidacies" in the elections that were about to take place to the new Supreme Soviet, particularly from religious organizations.[2] In the event, the "bloc of Communists and non-party people" won an impressive 97.8 and 98.6 percent, respectively, in the elections to each of the two chambers, and up to the end of the 1980s there was no departure from a system that recorded near-unanimous support for a slate of candidates that had effectively been chosen by the regime itself.

Elections, however, were just one of the ways in which regime and society interacted. There was no suggestion that (for instance) Soviet foreign policy was a matter for public debate, let alone contestation, but on other issues in which the regime had no particular interest, particularly at local level, it could afford to be at least consultative. Equally, it could often allow a popular role in the implementation of decisions even if it was reluctant to concede a role in their formulation. Conversely, the introduction of fully competitive elections after 1991 was not as radical a change as is sometimes supposed. Elections in which the great majority of seats were contested had already taken place in the spring of 1989, and again a year later. And the evidence of early postcommunist Russia was that even more genuinely competitive elections, with a choice of party and not just of candidate, did not necessarily represent a shift in the locus of political authority from regime to citizens. Indeed, if anything, Russians felt they had even less influence over government in the postcommunist years than they had enjoyed in the later years of the Soviet period.

For an optimistic Boris Yeltsin, speaking just afterwards, the defeat of the attempted coup was proof that Russians had at last thrown off the "fetters of seventy years of slavery."[3] Even at the time this seemed an extravagant verdict. Thousands of Muscovites had taken to the streets in defense of their parliament and president, both of them still communist; but few took any notice of Yeltsin's call for an all-out national strike, and the collapse of the regime itself at the end of the year was the result of elite maneuvers, in a decision that was thoroughly deplored by ordinary citizens. There were at least two senses in which this was less of a transition, still less a "revolution," than the replacement of an entire system by mass action that had taken place in most of Central and Eastern Europe. In the first place, it gave too little weight to the evidence that ordinary citizens, in the late Soviet period, had ways of advancing their interests that did not depend on the existence of competitive elections. And it exaggerated the difference that could be made by the formal institutions of democracy in the absence of a wider change in the political culture: in tolerance, respect for law and the capacity to work together as citizens. Considered over a much longer term, was this the "end of history," a decisive break with centuries of authoritarianism, or a more limited change that showed the continuing importance of the legacy of Soviet rule, and of Russian history before it?

STATE–SOCIETY RELATIONS IN THE LATE-SOVIET PERIOD

Those who lived under the Soviet system were sometimes described as "subject parochials," a term made popular in Almond and Verba's work on political culture. Such people were aware of developments in political life and had a view of the legitimacy of government, but had no means of influencing the policy making process. Their relationship with the political system was "passive," in that they were expected to carry out the decisions of government but had no means of influencing them. In the words of a representative study that was based directly on this conceptualization, the USSR had a dominant political culture, which was the culture of its party elite. There was participation, but it was directed from above by the party bureaucracy. And ordinary citizens, for their part, were suspicious, apathetic, and given to dysfunctional behavior such as hooliganism and crime. All of this was based around an "ideologically indoctrinated, hierarchically-centralist organizational complex—the CPSU—claiming a monopoly of legitimate policy initiative, interest aggregation, and control, but demanding participation in the fulfilment of its objectives not only by its members but by all Soviet citizens."[4]

The idea that ordinary citizens might lack political influence was, of course, dismissed out of hand by Soviet spokesmen; and within the framework of official orthodoxy there could certainly be wide-ranging exchanges. The Stalin constitution, published in draft for national discussion, involved nearly 34 million members of the public who among them suggested over 150,000 amendments.[5] The new family legislation of 1936, however, was a better indicator of the use that was made of communications from ordinary people at this time. A sharply retrogressive measure, it was intended to strengthen marriage, and (among other things) outlawed abortion. A few letters appeared pointing out that "lack of living space" was often the real problem; but the published correspondence as a whole, together with the editorial coverage, was overwhelmingly favorable. It later emerged that the great majority of letters had in fact opposed the new law but that only a few had been published, while every single communication in favor had been selected. "The Boss says we must have more children" was the simple explanation.[6]

The constitution of 1977 was also the subject of an extensive national consultation. Leonid Brezhnev, chairman of the commission responsible for its preparation, was able to report that more than four-fifths of the adult population—about 150 million people—had taken part in the discussion. Letters had arrived in an "unending flow" at party headquarters, Brezhnev reported; they had overwhelmingly affirmed that "yes, this is the Basic Law we have been waiting for."[7] The final text, approved in October 1977, incorporated 110 amendments and one new article. For Brezhnev, the discussion had shown how "firm and creative [wa]s the unity of all classes and social groups, all nations and nationalities, and all generations of Soviet society around the Communist Party."[8] Only in 1990 was it disclosed that the letters that reached the constitutional commission and the press had raised all kinds of other issues. Why, for instance, was there no choice of candidate at elections? Why had the CPSU been given a political monopoly in Article 6? And why had Brezhnev been given two Hero of the Soviet Union awards thirteen years after World War II had ended?[9]

Political activity, under such circumstances, tended to be covert rather than overt: the use of bribery, connections or legal or semi-legal means of influencing a government that could not be influenced through the ballot box. But this did not mean it could not be influenced at all. Under Soviet conditions there was a big difference between the world of "high politics," where decisions were made by the party elite, and "low politics," which were much less closely regulated by the central authorities.[10] For many citizens, high politics was "none of my business—that's up to the Central Committee." But low politics gave individuals the opportunity to pursue a variety of strategies in dealing with local authorities that involved the use of ethnic or family relations, the trading of favors, or straightforward corruption. Under democratic centralism, government directives could not be openly opposed; but interpersonal relations at the local level were normally of little interest to the regime, and individual citizens could negotiate their own forms of accommodation.

There were many ways in which the exercise of political power could be mediated in such circumstances. One of the most important was covert participation in the implementation of central policy directives, involving the "interaction between the citizen as client or supplicant looking for private benefit and the representative of the system interpreting and implementing policy for this individual."[11] Soviet citizens, on the evidence of emigre interviews, had relatively high levels of political knowledge but were reluctant to discuss issues openly, and had little faith in their ability to influence government decisions. Participation, it emerged, was "direct and personalized," and more likely to emphasize personal or family connections than regular forms of group action. Bribery was an important part of this pattern of interaction and was accepted as a "common way of handling difficult situations," particularly where employment, housing, or university admission was concerned.[12]

Official mechanisms could also be adapted to local purposes. Voting, for instance, had little to do with the choice of an alternative government. But there were other ways in which it could be used to signify the preferences of voters. There was the threat not to vote, which was not illegal in itself but which could embarrass local officials who were expected to secure the highest possible turnout. According to the testimony of emigres who had worked as canvassers, the threat not to vote could be used to ensure that housing repairs were carried out, or that a local church was reopened.[13] Comments could also be written on the ballot paper itself, all of which were gathered up and analyzed after the exercise had been completed. Many could be accommodated with little difficulty. "Had I a hundred votes to cast," wrote a fervent Muscovite in 1970, "they would all be cast for the Party of Lenin which led a weak, illiterate Russia out of her darkness and made her a rich and mighty power." Remarks of this kind, the newspaper added, were "too many to list."[14]

In a rather different case quoted by Solzhenitsyn, an engineer just after the war had "given vent to his feelings and on his ballot paper had applied an obscene epithet to the Genius of Geniuses himself." Despite the shortage of labor, several detectives spent a month examining the handwriting of local residents before the offender was identified and imprisoned.[15] In a still more disagreeable case, the central authorities identified some "brown-coloured matter . . . giving off a strong smell" in an envelope directed to Comrade Stalin in the mid-1930s, which was later checked out by the NKVD laboratories and confirmed as excrement "probably of animal origin."[16] It was more common in the later Soviet period for communications from the voters to be considered by the local party committee and then passed to appropriate administrative agencies. Comments were also considered by the police and KGB, which evidently found them a useful form of feedback.[17]

It was easier and generally more effective to send a letter to a party committee or to the press. A tradition of this kind went back to early tsarist times, when a basket was lowered from a window in the Old Kremlin Palace in which petitioners could place their grievances.[18] Communications were discouraged during the Stalin years, but even at this time regional party first secretaries "were often quite responsive to appeals from ordinary people."[19] Under Khrushchev and Brezhnev much greater emphasis was placed on letters from the public as well as other forms of within-system participation. More than half a million letters reached party headquarters every year during the 1970s, and the flow of letters to the central press was an estimated 60 to 70 million.[20] Few of them, obviously, could be published, but many more were investigated by the paper's own staff, and full analyses of the flow of correspondence were sent to the party and state authorities. Ordinary members of the public appear to have regarded letters, at this time, as the best means at their disposal of influencing the decisions that were taken in their local area.[21]

Gorbachev had given particular attention to letters from the public during his party career and he made frequent references to them after he had been elected general secretary, sometimes quoting directly. In April 1985, for instance, he mentioned that party members had been asking why officials held the same posts for years on end, and in Kiev in early 1989 he quoted from some of the complaints that had reached him about the food supply.[22] Gorbachev was asked, during a visit to Leningrad in October 1987, if letters from ordinary people actually reached him. Yes, they did, he replied; he tried to read as many of them as possible, and took some home for further study.[23] A substantial part of Gorbachev's postbag came from abroad, particularly from Germany, Sweden and the United States.[24] Gorbachev responded to an appeal from a retired U.S. admiral when he announced his moratorium on nuclear testing; and he used his correspondence once more when seeking to end the Soviet military presence in Afghanistan, circulating his Politburo colleagues with a "flood of letters" from soldiers asking why they had been sent, and from mothers pleading to have their sons brought home.[25]

To what extent did ordinary people feel that these opportunities—clearly some distance short of fully competitive elections—gave them an influence over those who ruled in their name? How "free" did they feel in the late Soviet period, and how far did their perceptions diverge from those who lived in liberal democracies? The evidence, in fact, is that in the last years of Soviet rule Russians felt "remarkably free." In a survey of European Russia in May 1990, James Gibson found that a majority of respondents did not believe the Soviet government would prevent them from making a speech that was critical of its activities, or that it would prevent them from publishing their criticisms. Majorities, certainly, believed the government would not permit them to organize nationwide strikes—but the same was true of a majority of Americans. A majority, again, thought they would not be allowed to organize public meetings of an anti-government character; black Americans, however (not whites), took the same view. Generally, Gibson concluded, "white Americans perceived[d] the least amount of government repression, black Americans the most, with Soviet people in between."[26]

Other inquiries suggested that participation, even in the Brezhnev period, was some distance from the image of "undifferentiated, ritualistic participation in state organizations" that predominated in the literature. Nor was it accurate to see the Soviet citizen as "psychologically disengaged, mobilized to take part in public life by a simple desire to get ahead or to avoid conflict with the authorities." Ordinary citizens, on the contrary, "made choices whether or not to participate in most types of activity, choices that reflected their attitudes as well as their social position."[27] Friedgut found similarly that those who took part in residential and neighborhood activities "enjoyed a sense of community with their neighbors and valued the tangible benefits of their work"; citizens who contacted local officials, moreover, had opportunities for "cooperative and active" work within the system. Interviews with ordinary citizens, and with deputies, also suggested a real sense of civic competence at the level of local government, with a widely distributed belief that contacts with officials could have a real influence on the decisions they took.[28]

The same conclusions are suggested by the development of national politics during the last years of Soviet rule. When elections were opened to independent candidates in 1989 and the vote became a genuine choice, the result was that more Communist Party members were elected to the new Soviet parliament than ever before—87 percent. In the Russian elections of March 1990, another record proportion of the successful candidates—86 percent—were members of the CPSU. In March 1991, when they were asked to express a view on the continuation of the USSR as a "renewed federation," 78 percent of those who voted—on a turnout of more than 80 percent—declared in favor. The dissolution of the USSR, when it took place at the end of 1991, did not reflect the wishes of ordinary people (who continue to regard it as a great misfortune), nor did it reflect the original intentions of the republican leaders who took part in the final negotiations. Yeltsin himself was so drunk he fell out of his chair; he later insisted that if there had been no coup a new union treaty would have been signed and the USSR would have survived.[29]

STATE–SOCIETY RELATIONS IN POSTCOMMUNIST RUSSIA

What, a decade or more after the collapse of communist rule and of the USSR itself, did ordinary Russians make of it all? How much, and in what ways, did they think the political system in which they lived had changed since 1991? And to what extent had their new institutions provided them with the kind of empowerment they had been denied in the Soviet period? The evidence of the survey that was conducted for the present author and associates in the early months of 2000 by the All-Russian Centre for the Study of Public Opinion (VTsIOM) was that a majority of Russians were prepared to settle for the system they now had, as compared with a number of alternatives (table 3.1). But a substantial minority had no objection to the suspension of the Duma they had elected hardly a month earlier, and as many as 40 percent supported a return to communist

Table 3.1.   Support for Alternatives to the Present Regime (percentages)

	Strongly Approve	Approve	Disapprove	Strongly Disapprove
Suspension of the Duma	11	26	44	14
Return to communist rule	18	22	29	29
Military rule	3	8	35	53
Monarchy	3	7	29	58
Dictatorship	11	18	30	39

Source: Derived from a nationally representative survey, fieldwork January–February 2000, n = 1,940, conducted for the author and associates by VTsIOM, Moscow.

rule. Nearly a third, indeed, were prepared to support dictatorship. Patience, moreover, was not unlimited, and support for the postcommunist system was not unconditional. More than half of our respondents, for instance, agreed entirely (23 percent) or in general terms (34 percent) that another form of government should be considered if the present regime was unable to resolve the country's problems in the reasonably near future.[30]

What, then, about the changes that had taken place since 1991? How significant were they, and how welcome? Basic liberties, certainly, were much better protected (figure 3.1). There was more freedom of conscience, more freedom to travel abroad, more freedom to say what you thought, more freedom to join any organization you wanted, and more freedom to take part in politics—or (just as important in the postcommunist context) *not* to take part in politics. But when it came to relations between government and citizen the position was much less clear, indeed inverted. Russians, compared with the late communist system, were hardly less likely to believe they were better protected from the risk of arbitrary arrest. And they were actually *less* likely to think they were able to influence the government that spoke in their name (larger numbers thought there had simply been no change). A majority (51 percent) thought similarly that they were *less* likely to be treated fairly and equally by government than in the Brezhnev years. There was a welcome, in other inquiries, for many of the postcommunist changes: freedom of speech, the freedom to travel abroad, and to engage in business; but there was much more limited support for the right to strike, and a majority thought multiparty elections had actually brought more harm (50 percent) than good (21 percent).[31]

How, then, did Russians think of the postcommunist system in which they lived in the 1990s, as compared with the Soviet system of the 1970s and 1980s? I have set out the evidence in table 3.2, which is based upon data gathered and published by the All-Russian Centre for the Study of Public Opinion. As table 3.2 makes clear, the communist system, in spite of its lack of fully or—for most of its existence—even partly competitive elections, was regarded first of all as "close to the people" and "familiar," a formulation not very different from the relationship that the Soviet authorities had claimed themselves. It was also "strong" and "authoritative," and at the same time "honest" and "legal" (its main

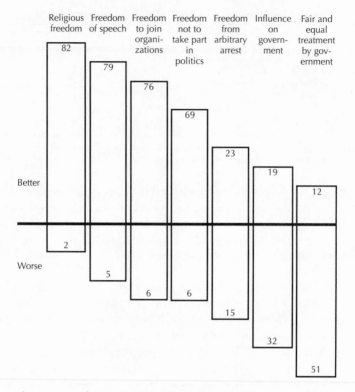

Figure 3.1.   Changes in Basic Liberties since 1991

fault was that it was "bureaucratic"). Postcommunist rule, by contrast, was not simply "weak," "irresolute" and "incompetent," but also "criminal," "remote" and even "illegal," even though its constitutional status was formally beyond reproach. And it was hardly any less "bureaucratic" or "short-sighted."

Conventionally, elections have been regarded in the West as all but the defining characteristic of a democracy. Russians, and many East Europeans,[32] do not necessarily take the same view. The All-Russian Centre asked Russians at the end of 1999 and the start of 2000 what they themselves understood by "democracy." The responses are set out in table 3.3. Civil liberties came first, but is closely followed by economic prosperity and state control. The elective nature of state office, still more so minority rights, were accorded less importance. And there were many who associated democracy with disorder, empty talk and licence. The same emerged from other inquiries. Russians, in one such investigation, were reasonably willing to support democracy in abstract terms. But nearly two-thirds (63 percent) were also prepared to agree that democracies were "indecisive" and that they tended to indulge in "too much squabbling"; and there were far more positive assessments of the communist system (55 percent thought it "good" or "very

Table 3.2. The "Most Characteristic" Features of Communist and Postcommunist Rule (percentages)

Soviet Rule, 1970s–1980s		Postcommunist Rule, 1990s	
Close to the people	36	Criminal, corrupt	63
Legal	32	Remote, alien	41
"Our own," familiar	32	Irresolute	32
Bureaucratic	30	Weak, powerless	30
Strong, firm	27	Short-sighted	28
Short-sighted	23	Bureaucratic	22
Authoritative, respected	21	Parasitic	18
Secretive, closed	17	Illegal	12
Just	16	Unprofessional	12
Honest, open	14	Incompetent	11

Source: *Ekonomicheskie i sotsial'nye peremeny*, no. 3, 1998, 57 (national representative survey, February–March 1998, n = 1,500)

good") than of the system that had been established after 1991 (91 percent though it "bad" or "very bad"). Russians, in fact, were decidedly ambivalent: a minority supported democratic values as they would be understood in the West, but an equally substantial minority favored a "strong hand."[33]

Our own survey, carried out in the early months of 2000, found a similar distribution of opinion. The most widely shared view was that equality before the law was an essential characteristic of democracy (87 percent); but the "economic prosperity of the country" counted for almost as much (83 percent), and a guaranteed level of income was an essential characteristic of democracy for a very substantial 73 percent. Rather fewer (63 percent) associated democracy with the existence of competitive elections; and fewer still (51 percent) associated it with the ability to criticize the government. It is difficult to resist the conclusion that for Russians, as for perhaps a large part of the postcommunist world, democracy is defined in terms not very different from those of the Soviet period: formal procedures are important, but still more important is the way that people live, and the extent to which government is concerned about their welfare and able to do something to improve it.

Even within conventional terms Russian political development since the end of communist rule has given rise to some misgivings. As noted in chapter 1 by David Lane, one measure of Russia's democratic performance is provided by the "Comparative Survey of Freedom," sponsored by Freedom House of New York.[34] There has been no dramatic improvement in civil and political rights following the end of communist rule. The USSR, in the Brezhnev years, had been "unfree" in terms of Freedom House criteria, but by the start of 1991, while still under communist rule, it was already "partly free." The new union treaty that was under consideration at this time, Freedom House considered, was based on human rights, and a democratic state was being established on the basis of the principles of popular sovereignty and the rule of law. All the union republics had

Table 3.3.   Russian Perceptions of "Democracy" (percentages)

Freedom of speech, press and religion	37
Economic prosperity of the country	33
Strict legality	29
Order and stability	28
Election of all high state officials	15
Possibility for all to do as they please	10
Empty talk	10
Anarchy and lawlessness	6
Domination of the minority by the majority	6
Guarantees of the rights of minorities	5
Other	1
Don't know	8

Source: Nationwide VTsIOM poll, 30 December 1999–4 January 2000, n = 1,600, accessed at www.russiavotes.org/Mood_rus_cur. More than one answer could be given.

declared some form of sovereignty, reformers had been successful in local elections in many parts of the country, Gorbachev's directives were being routinely disregarded, and the Soviet parliament had adopted laws guaranteeing freedom of the press and freedom of conscience, both of them in 1990.[35]

Postcommunist Russia was initially placed much higher than its Soviet predecessor, though still "partly free." Ten years on it was still "partly free," but at a much lower level. Postcommunist Russia, in the year 2000, was rated no more "free" than the USSR had been during the last year of Soviet rule (see figure 3.2). Freedom House had several concerns about the quality of democracy and human rights in early postcommunist Russia. Economic life, they pointed out, in an "alarming trend," was increasingly dominated by the major energy and industrial corporations, which had been privatized by their *nomenklatura* that had managed them in the past, and who continued to enjoy substantial privileges. By contrast, a nascent private sector of small businesses and entrepreneurs had made very little headway; and the media were increasingly dominated by harassment, violence against journalists, and the disproportionate influence of financial and industrial interests connected with the government.[36]

An influential school of thought has distinguished in this connection between "electoral democracies" and more broadly based "liberal democracies." Democracy, for such scholars, involves more than competitive elections. It means a government that is limited by law, and one that is accountable to the electorate directly or through representative institutions. It is also important, from this perspective, to establish if the rights of ordinary citizens are respected, whether or not they are seeking to influence government. Can they travel freely, and express their views in the media without undue restriction? Do they have freedom of worship, and the right to assemble peacefully? Is there, finally, a "democratic society," including a network of groups and associations, economic institutions

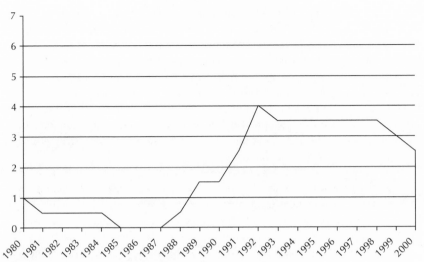

Figure 3.2. Freedom House Ratings, USSR/Russia 1980–2000

that are accountable to those who work within them as well as to the public, and a "culture of tolerance and civic responsibility"?[37]

Turkey, for instance, is an electoral democracy in that there are regular opportunities to choose among competing parties and candidates, and government itself has changed hands at regular intervals. But there are restrictions on the basic rights of Kurds (who account for about a tenth of the population), and there are extrajudicial killings and attacks on the rights of assembly.[38] Russia, for bodies like Freedom House, occupies a similar position in the hierarchy of democratic performance. There are certainly competitive elections, but the regime itself enjoys an undue degree of influence upon the whole process through its control of the media, particularly television. And there have been disturbing signs, in some of the regions, that local officials are continuing to control the electoral mechanism in much the same way as they were able to do in the Soviet period. How else was one to explain the presidential election in Bashkortostan in the summer of 1998, for instance: the main opposition candidates were kept off the ballot paper, the Supreme Court called for their reinstatement but was ignored, and the incumbent won election with more than 70 percent of the vote? Or a by-election in neighboring Tatarstan in which the republic's prime minister took 99 percent of the vote and his opponent a modest 0.72 percent?[39]

Certainly, there were forces that were pulling Russia towards more pluralist forms of politics at the start of a new century. Many new freedoms were securely established, including religious liberty and the freedom *not* to take an interest in political life. Almost anything could be published. A large part of the economy was, at least nominally, outside the direct control of the state. But there were enduring weaknesses in terms of popular control over executive action; and an increasing disposition, on the part of figures like the newly elected president, to seek to resolve the country's problems by the reimposition of a Soviet-style discipline. Clearly, there was no inevitability about "democratization": a few of the former Soviet republics had established market economies and liberal democracies, but others had regressed to forms of personalist rule that were more repressive than the system that had preceded them. Russia, entering a new century, was somewhere in between: it seemed likely to retain its basic liberties, but its political system increasingly reflected the Soviet and prerevolutionary tradition of executive authority rather than the Western tradition of limited and accountable government based upon the consent of a mass electorate.

This suggested still wider conclusions about the explanation of political change. For neoinstitutionalists, in politics as in economics, there were no "special countries." Russians were "economic men" who rationally responded to incentives; they were just as keen to take risks and work hard as anyone else, and they would find a market was as natural a vehicle for them to do so as it was in other countries.[40] This made it difficult to explain how it was that democracy and the market had taken such peculiar forms in postcommunist Russia, and why there were such sharp differences between the course of reform in the post-Soviet republics and in Central European countries like Poland and the Czech Republic—differences that would become institutionalized as these countries became members of NATO and the European Union. For a different school of economists, there could be no adequate explanation that did not take into account the "particularity of the culture of different types of civilization";[41] in this case, factors such as geography, and Russia's lack of a developed legal system even before the Bolsheviks had come to power.

CONCLUSION

Democracy, as Huntington has reminded us, is a product of very specific circumstances. It had originated in the West, in northeastern Europe, not in Eurasia. It was here, not in Russia, that there had been a separation of spiritual and temporary authority, a rule of law that had laid the basis for the protection of human rights, a social pluralism that had encouraged the formation of representative institutions, and a "tradition of individual rights and liberties unique among civilized societies."[42] Many of these developments had found expression at various times in Russia, but they had rarely been as influential as in Western Europe. There had been no feudalism, at least in the form of a balance of interests regulated by law. Social classes had been defined by service to the state. The Orthodox Church was an extension of government rather than a rival source of authority; and government itself accepted no legitimate limit to the scope of its decisions. Russia, in other words, had little experience of the "defining historical phenomena of Western civilization," and lacked almost every one of its defining characteristics. As a consequence, popular and elite identities were torn between the secular Western values of which Marxism-Leninism had been a part, and older, Slavophile values that celebrated their many differences.[43]

None of this meant that Russians were condemned to a future as authoritarian as their past had been. But it exposed the limitations of any framework that was not informed by an understanding of the culture within which institutions had necessarily to operate. And it pointed up the weakness of some of the triumphalist accounts that had appeared as the Cold War ended in what appeared to be a Western victory. There had been no "end of history" in Russia; liberal ideas had shallow roots, relations with the West continued to be difficult, and there was strong support for the idea that Russia should develop according to its own traditions without recapitulating the patterns of other countries. This, in fact, was what was meant by the "revenge of the superstructure." Russia's early postcommunist years had been dedicated to a demonstration of the validity of liberal ideas, in politics as in economics. But as those values lost favor and as their assumptions were increasingly questioned, a rather different framework emerged in their place that drew upon collectivism, patriotism and social justice. Entering a new century, this was a framework within which communists and nationalists could both be comfortable; and within which a newly elected president and a mass electorate could at last find common ground.

NOTES

1. I. V. Stalin, *Sochineniya*, vol. 1 (Stanford, Calif.: Hoover Institution, 1967), 129–30.

2. *Voprosy istorii*, no. 5, 1993, 4.

3. *Izvestiya*, 12 August 1991, 1.

4. Frederick C. Barghoorn, *Politics in the USSR*, 2nd ed. (Boston: Little, Brown, 1972), 20–25, 260. See also Gabriel A. Almond and Sidney Verba, *The Civic Culture: Political Attitudes and Democracy in Five Nations* (Princeton, N.J.: Princeton University Press, 1963), 19.

5. E. B. Pashukanis and P. V. Tumanov, eds., *Vsenarodnoe obsuzhdenie proekta Konstitutsii Soyuza SSR* (Moscow: Partizdat, 1936), 5. For a more recent discussion, see Ellen Wimberg, "Socialism, Democratism and Criticism: The Soviet Press and the National Discussion of the 1936 Draft Constitution," *Soviet Studies*, vol. 44, no. 2 (1992), 313–32.

6. Robert C. Tucker, *Stalin in Power: The Revolution from Above, 1928–1941* (New York: Norton, 1990), 357–8.

7. L. I. Brezhnev, *Leninskim kursom. Rechi i stat'i*, vol. 6 (Moscow: Politizdat, 1978), 518. The number of proposals that had been received in the course of the discussion was rather arbitrarily determined: Supreme Soviet staff thought it was about 300,000, Central Committee staff thought it had been 600,000, and Brezhnev simply decided "Let's say 400,000" (Yuri Korolev, *Kremlevskii sovetnik* [Moscow: Olimp, 1995], 197).

8. Brezhnev, *Leninskim kursom*, vol. 6, 518–19, 537.

9. *Voprosy istorii KPSS*, no. 10, 1990, 73–7

10. Seweryn Bialer, *Stalin's Successors* (New York: Cambridge University Press, 1980), 166–7.

11. Wayne DiFranceisco and Zvi Gitelman, "Soviet Political Culture and 'Covert Participation' in Policy Implementation," *American Political Science Review*, vol. 78, no. 3 (September 1984), 604.

12. Ibid., 611.

13. Victor Zaslavsky and Robert J. Brym, "The Functions of Elections in the USSR," *Soviet Studies*, vol. 30, no. 3 (July 1978), 365, 367.

14. T. H. Friedgut, *Political Participation in the USSR* (Princeton, N.J.: Princeton University Press, 1979), 112–13.

15. Alexander Solzhenitsyn, *V krugom pervom* (London: Collins, 1968), 51.

16. *Istochnik*, no. 3, 1993, 126–7.

17. Ronald J. Hill, "The CPSU in a Soviet Election Campaign," *Soviet Studies*, vol. 28, no. 4 (October 1976), 597.

18. *The Times*, 12 July 1982, 1.

19. Sheila Fitzpatrick, "Supplicants and Citizens: Public Letter-writing in Soviet Russia in the 1930s," *Slavic Review*, vol. 55, no. 1 (Spring 1994), 104.

20. Stephen White, "Political Communications in the USSR: Letters to Party, State and Press," *Political Studies*, vol. 31, no. 1 (January 1983), 51–2.

21. Ellen Mickiewicz, *Media and the Russian Public* (New York: Praeger, 1981), 69. The overall tenor of letters from the public, in the late 1980s, was that society needed "not radical reform, but only a few changes" (*Svobodnaya mysl*,' no. 7, 1993, p. 80); the archives similarly suggested that there had been "few" letters in support of Solzhenitsyn after the 1974 decision to expel him from the country (ibid., no. 6, 1992, 81).

22. M. S. Gorbachev, *Izbrannye rechi i stat'i*, 7 vols (Moscow: Politizdat, 1987–90), vol. 2, 164; and *Pravda*, 24 February 1989, 2.

23. *Pravda*, 13 October 1987, 1.

24. *Izvestiya*, 7 August 1991, 1.

25. See, respectively, Lloyd S. Fischel, ed., *Dear Mr. Gorbachev* (Edinburgh: Canongate, 1990), xv–xvi, 6; Diego Cordovez and Selig S. Harrison, *Out of Afghanistan: The Inside Story of the Soviet Withdrawal* (New York: Oxford University Press, 1995), 247.

26. James L. Gibson, "Perceived political freedom in the Soviet Union," *Journal of Politics*, vol. 55, no. 4 (November 1993), 947–8.

27. Donna Bahry and Brian D. Silver, "Soviet citizen participation on the eve of democratization," *American Political Science Review*, vol. 84, no. 3 (September 1990), 837.

28. Ibid., 823. Jeffrey Hahn found, similarly, on the basis of his interviews with deputies, that "Soviet citizens, either as deputies or through them, can and do participate effectively in their local government" (*Soviet Grassroots: Citizen Participation in Local Soviet Government* (Princeton, N.J.: Princeton University Press, 1988), 261.

29. David Remnick, *Resurrection: The Struggle for a New Russia* (New York: Random House, 1997), 27; and *Izvestiya*, 10 January 1995, 1. Yeltsin's bodyguard and confidant Alexander Korzhakov confirmed in his memoirs that there had been no prior agreement to dissolve the USSR: *Boris El'tsin: Ot rassveta do zakata* (Moscow: Interbuk, 1997), 127.

30. Fieldwork was conducted by the All-Russian Centre for the Study of Public Opinion (VTsIOM) between 13 and 29 January 2000 (n = 1940). A full account, including details of sample construction, is available in Richard Rose, *Russia between Elections: New Russia Barometer VIII* (Glasgow: Centre for the Study of Public Policy, University of Strathclyde, SPP 328, 2000).

31. *Ekonomicheskie i sotsial'nye peremeny: monitoring obshchestvennogo mneniya*, no. 6, 1999, 87.

32. For an exploration of these issues, see Janos Simon, "Popular Conceptions of Democracy in Postcommunist Europe," in Samuel H. Barnes and Simon, eds., *The Postcommunist Citizen* (Budapest: Erasmus Foundation and Institute for Political Science of the Hungarian Academy of Sciences, 1998), 79–116.

33. Elena Bashkirova, "Value change and survival of democracy in Russia," paper presented to the XVIII World Congress of the International Political Science Association, Quebec City, August 2000, accessed at www.romir.ru/eng/valuechange.htm.

34. *Journal of Democracy*, vol. 11, no. 1 (January 2000), 189–90.

35. *Freedom Review*, vol. 22, no. 1 (January-February 1991), 8.

36. Ibid., vol. 27, no. 1 (January-February 1996), 10, and Adrian Karatnycky, ed., *Nations in Transit: Civil Society, Democracy and Markets in East Central Europe and the Newly Independent States* (New Brunswick, N.J.: Transaction, 1997), 439.

37. See Stuart Weir and David Beetham, *Political Power and Democratic Control in Britain* (London: Routledge, 1998), 10. The distinction between "electoral" and "liberal democracy" is explored in Larry Diamond, *Developing Democracy: Toward Consolidation* (Baltimore: Johns Hopkins University Press, 1999).

38. This passage is based upon the U.S. State Department Country Reports on Human Rights for 1999 (accessed at www.state.gov/www/global/human.rights).

39. See, respectively, *Izvestiya*, 16 June 1998, 1, and 5 November 1998, 2.

40. See, respectively, Petr Aven in *Nezavisimaya gazeta*, 27 February 1992, 5; and Maxim Boycko et al., *Privatizing Russia* (Cambridge, Mass.: MIT Press, 1995), 9.

41. *Voprosy ekonomiki*, no. 9, 1998, 150.

42. Samuel Huntington, *The Clash of Civilisations and the Remaking of World Order* (London: Simon & Schuster, 1997), 71.

43. Ibid., 143–4.

4

Russia's Federal Legacy and Democratization

Cameron Ross

Many authors have alluded to the unique nature of Russia's transition and its difficult task of simultaneously reforming its economy and polity.[1] But there is in fact a third transition under way in Russia that is of no less importance: the need to reconfigure central-local relations and to create a stable and viable form of federalism. Forging a federal system at the same time as privatizing the economy and radically overhauling the political system has made Russia's transition triply difficult. In this chapter I argue that Russia's weak and asymmetrical form of federalism has played a major role in thwarting the consolidation of democracy. Just as founding elections and the "freezing" of party systems are highly important for the subsequent trajectory of transitional societies, I would argue that the "freezing" of a particular set of federal (both constitutional and unconstitutional) relations over the period 1990–1993, has been of no less importance in shaping the present contours of Russia's semi-authoritarian form of governance. The result has been the formation of a highly asymmetrical federation with a weak federal state and powerful federal subjects. I discuss four major factors that have been instrumental in bringing about the current chronic weakness of "state capacity" at the federal level and which, in turn, have thwarted the development of democracy in Russia.

1. The negative impact of the hybrid ethno-territorial principle of federalism that was bequeathed to Russia from the Soviet regime
2. The weak legitimacy of the December 1993 Constitution
3. The challenge of ethnic secessionism
4. Bilateralism and the development of "contract federalism"

RUSSIAN FEDERALISM AND THE SOVIET LEGACY

According to the 1977 Constitution, "the Union of Soviet Socialist Republics" was a "unified, federal, multinational state formed on the principle of socialist federalism." The federation, which was established according to the dual principles of ethnicity and territory, encompassed fifteen *ethnically* defined union republics, twenty autonomous republics, eight autonomous oblasts, ten autonomous okrugs, and 159 *territorially* based regions. But if we define a federal state as one in which,

> (a) "neither the federal nor the constituent units of government are constitutionally subordinate to the other," (b) "each order of government has sovereign powers defined by the constitution," (c) each subject is empowered to deal directly with citizens in the exercise of its legislative, executive, and taxing powers, and (d) "is directly elected by and accountable to its citizens."[2]

then on all these counts the USSR was not an authentic federation. For although the Constitution proclaimed the republics' rights of sovereignty (Article 76), and secession (Article 72), the right to enter into treaties with foreign powers (Article 80), and local control over economic developments (Article 77), such rights were heavily qualified in practice, by the provisions of other articles,[3] which in practice made a mockery of the sovereign powers granted to the republics. And, in any case, although the state was supposedly based on federal principles, the party, which declared itself to be "the leading and guiding force in society," was a unitary body. Moreover, party and state bodies operated under the principle of "democratic centralism," whereby each administrative level was subordinate to the level above it and centralized control from Moscow. In 1989 Gorbachev publicly admitted that the republics' rights of sovereignty were largely formal in nature, "Up to now," he noted, "our state has existed as a centralized and unitary state and none of us has yet the experience of living in a federation."[4]

This is not to say that the federal subjects in the USSR were totally powerless and subservient to the central authorities or that nationalist demands had been quelled when Gorbachev took over the reins of power in 1985. For paradoxically, the very policies that the communists had used to placate nationalism ended up giving it succor. As Bialer notes, the concept and reality of Soviet federalism contained a dangerous dualism,

> On the one hand it granted to formed nations cultural autonomy, territorial integrity, and symbols of statehood; on the other hand it insisted on the supremacy of the central state and government and strove for a state of affairs where national separateness and ethnic identity would ultimately wither away.[5]

The USSR's adoption of an "ethno-territorial" form of federalism was originally designed as a temporary measure, adopted to entice the non-Russian nationalities to join the Union. But as Gleason notes, such a principle entailed a recognition of the "national statehood" of the constituent republics.[6] Under Soviet federalism, ethnicity

> was institutionalized both on the individual and on group levels. On the individual level, nationality was registered on each person's internal passport. . . . At the group level, the ethno-territorial basis of political organization established firm links between national groups, their territories, and their political administrations.[7]

In addition, according to Stalin's formula "national in form, socialist in content," the nations of the Soviet Union were supposed to develop to the point where all national groups would be equal. But as Zwick notes,

> In its attempt to neutralize tribal, ethnic and religious identifications and replace them with socialist norms, the Soviet regime awakened national feelings among its population, and then, by promising to equalize all nations, made the people acutely aware of the differences that had always existed between Russians and non-Russians.[8]

Soviet nationality policies even promoted nation building for national communities that had "not yet achieved ethnic awakening in the pre-revolutionary period."[9] And far from withering away, the administrative organs of the republics gradually developed a sense of "proprietary bureaucratic self-interest."[10]

FEDERALISM AND NATIONALISM UNDER GORBACHEV

Gorbachev's policies of perestroika, glasnost, and democratization, opened up the nationalities and federal question to nationwide debate. Gorbachev's dilemma was how to reform simultaneously the Soviet economy and polity, while maintaining the unity of the communist party and state. In the end, Gorbachev failed on all counts. His acknowledgment of the legitimate demands of the republics for greater economic and political autonomy, and his proposals for a revived "Union of Soviet Sovereign States," came far too late to save the Union. The rise of Russian nationalism coupled with the collapse of the communist party over the period 1990–1991 finally propelled the Soviet Union into the abyss.

Gorbachev's reluctant acceptance of the need for an asymmetrical form of Soviet federalism, mixing confederal relations for some (the three Baltic republics, Georgia, Moldova and Armenia) with varying degrees of federal relations with the others, stemmed from a genuine belief on his part in the economic benefits to be gained in preserving the Union. Gorbachev repeatedly stressed the interdependent nature of the Soviet economic system and the fact that the republics,

> rely on a division of labour in a highly institutionalised, integrated national economic complex; depend on the central authorities for resource allocations, investments, subsidies, and grants-in-aid; and enjoy the diplomatic, economic, and

military advantages that accrue to a superpower. To cut such ties would mean to "dissect a living body."[11]

But economic decentralization soon led to calls for political decentralization. Once the CPSU began to fragment along political and ethnic lines there was nothing left to hold the Union together. Elections for republican parliaments in 1990 inflicted heavy defeats on the communist party candidates in the majority of the republics. In April 1990, Yeltsin gained the chair of the Russian (RSFSR) parliament, and in June Russia made its historic declaration of sovereignty, whereby it proclaimed,

> full power of the RSFSR in decisions on all questions of state and public life . . . ; the priority of the RSFSR's Constitution and laws on the entire territory of the RS-FSR; the exclusive right of the people to ownership, use and disposal of the national riches of Russia, and the right of free exit from the USSR.[12]

The Russian government under Yeltsin's leadership now began to champion the rights of other republics. And between "June and October, Uzbekistan, Moldova, Ukraine, Belorussia, Turkmenistan, Tajikistan and Kazakhstan declared their sovereignty, while Armenia . . . took the further step of declaring its independence."[13] Yeltsin also entered into negotiations with these "sovereign republics," and even signed a number of bilateral treaties with them.

Over the Autumn-Winter period of 1990–91 Gorbachev appeared to have abandoned the "democratic" camp and to have moved to the "right." It appeared as if he was determined to save the Union at all costs. But after the failure of Soviet OMON troops to set up "national salvation fronts" in the Baltics in January of 1991, Gorbachev tried another tact, seeking instead to gain approval for his Union Treaty through a nationwide referendum. But the result of the referendum, held in March 1991, was inconclusive, and at best represented a pyrrhic victory for Gorbachev: for although 76.4 percent of those participating supported "a renewed federation of equal sovereign republics," six of the fifteen republics refused to participate in the ballot (Estonia, Latvia, Lithuania, Armenia, Georgia and Moldova).[14] As Lapidus notes,

> Faced with the choice between the hardliners' pressure to maintain the Soviet Union through force by imposing a new Union Treaty from above and the democratic demands to concede real sovereignty to the republics, Gorbachev struck a deal with Yeltsin and the leaders of those nine republics which participated in the March 1991 referendum.[15]

According to the provisions of this so-called 9+1 Agreement, signed on April 23, 1991, the three Baltic republics, Armenia, Georgia, and Moldova, were to be allowed to secede from the USSR and a new fourth version of the Union Treaty was to be concluded in the summer. As John Miller notes, "Implicit in this was recognition by the Union administration of the sovereignty of the union-republics; and that the federation inaugurated by the Union Treaty should be a very weak one in which the Centre would retain only a minimum of power."[16] It was the plan to sign the Union Treaty on August 20, 1991 that sparked off the attempted coup. The failure of the coup, in turn, accelerated the demise of the USSR, leading to its total collapse by December.

As we noted above, Russia's Declaration of Sovereignty in June 1990 was a major catalyst in the collapse of the USSR. But the RSFSR was itself a quasi-federation comprising sixteen ethnically defined Autonomous Soviet Socialist Republics (ASSRs), ten national okrugs (districts) and five autonomous oblasts. And seven other such "autonomies" were trapped inside a further four Soviet republics.[17] If Russia could declare its sovereignty, then why should the autonomous republics within Russia not follow suit? After all, some of these ASSRs (e.g., Tatar and Bashkir) were actually larger and more populous than some of the Soviet republics (e.g., Estonia, Latvia, Moldova). Whereas Gorbachev's policies had led to the rise of nationalism in the USSR, Yeltsin's policies were in danger of leading to a similar rise of national sentiment in the RSFSR. As Aleksandr Tsipko warned,

> the stronger the striving of the RSFSR to free itself from the centre, the stronger will be the desire of the autonomous formations to free themselves from Yeltsin. And in their own way they are right. The relations of Russia to the autonomies is constructed on the same principle as that of the Union to the RSFSR.[18]

Over the period 1990–1991 the ASSRs became embroiled in the wider struggle between Yeltsin and Gorbachev. In an attempt to weaken Russia's role in the negotiations over the Union Treaty, Gorbachev began to espouse the need to raise the status of the autonomies. In the All-Union "Law on the Delimitation of Powers between the USSR and the Subjects of the Federation" of April 26, 1990, the autonomous republics, were described as "subjects of the federation," thus recognizing their right to equal representation with the union-republics, in the negotiations over the Union Treaty.[19] In reply, Yeltsin, on a nationwide tour of the Russian Federation in August 1990, urged the ASSRs to "take as much sovereignty as they could swallow." Furthermore, he proclaimed, "if this meant full independence from Russia your decision will be final."[20] And it was not long before the ASSRs took Yeltsin at his word, and unilaterally declared their sovereignty. On August 30, 1990, Tatarstan declared itself the sixteenth republic of the USSR,[21] and by the end of the year almost every other autonomy had likewise declared its independence from its host union republic.

On December 15, 1990 the Russian Congress of People's Deputies adopted a series of amendments to the RSFSR constitution, which raised the status of its sixteen ASSRs to constituent republics of the Russian Federation. In addition, in July 1991, the Russian Supreme Soviet adopted a number of decrees that "elevated the status of four of Russia's autonomous oblasts, Adygeya, Gornii Altai, Karachevo-Cherkessiya, and Khakasiya (with the exception of the Jewish Autonomous Oblast in Siberia), to constituent republics of the federation."[22] This brought the total number of ethnic republics within Russia to twenty. After the collapse of the USSR, the number of republics within Russia increased to twenty-one, when the Checheno-Ingush Republic was separated into the Chechen and Ingush republics in the summer of 1992. Thus, the Soviet Union's hybrid ethno-territorial principle of federalism was bequeathed to Russia. In addition to the twenty-one *ethnically* defined republics, the Russian Federation comprises ten autonomous okrugs and one autonomous oblast, and there are fifty-seven *territorially* defined regions.[23]

THE WEAK LEGITIMACY OF THE DECEMBER 1993 FEDERAL CONSTITUTION

The founding constitutional arrangements of any regime must surely be considered as one of the most vital factors determining the future trajectory of the state. The tragedy for Russian federalism and Russian democracy is based on the following four developments:

1. The collapse of communism in the USSR was at best an incomplete "revolution," which largely witnessed the replacement of one set of Soviet leaders headed by Gorbachev, by another set of Russian elites under Yeltsin. Although it could be argued that over the period 1991–93 a "circulation of elites" took place within the central organs of power, there was only a partial circulation in the regions where "nomenklatura continuity" has been the norm rather than the exception.[24] Russia's postcommunist elites, particularly in the ethnic republics, soon turned to nationalism and separatist demands, rather than democracy, to legitimate their rule. In a short space of time many of Russia's republics were headed by "elective dictatorships" or "delegative democracies."
2. A new alliance of regional political and economic elites soon took hold of power in the regions, as Russia embarked on a massive privatization program in 1992–93. These groups were the first to be given access to the rich pickings of the regional "privatization troughs." Both of these groups had a vested interest in demanding economic and political sovereignty for their territories, and it was not long before they proclaimed their outright control of the vast natural resources and the wealth of their regions.
3. Over the period October 1991 to October 1993 the federal authorities in Moscow were engaged in a "civil war," which pitted the Russian presidency and government against the Russian parliament. For two years the central powers in Moscow were paralyzed by this all-encompassing battle. During this period of weak central power, the republics became es-

pecially vociferous in their demands for national autonomy. In the absence of a new federal constitution (until December 1993), many of the ethnic republics unilaterally abrogated to themselves a whole series of rights and privileges. The republics and regions were also wooed by representatives of both the parliament and president, who promised the regions ever greater degrees of autonomy. Making the best of the political impasse in Moscow, regional elites scored a great victory when Yeltsin signed the 1992 Federal Treaty.

The Federal Treaty

The Federal Treaty of March 1992 created an "asymmetrical federation" with the rights granted to the ethnic republics far outweighing those given to the territorially based regions.[25] The republics were recognized as sovereign states with rights of national self-determination and, by implication, the right to secede from the Union. They were awarded citizenship rights and ownership of their land and natural resources. The republics were also granted their own constitutions and powers to elect their own executive heads. The regions were given no such rights of ownership, nor were they allowed constitutions. Instead the regions were permitted to draw up local charters, and their top executives were to be appointed from above. Two republics, Tatarstan and Chechnya, refused to sign the treaty and Bashkortostan and Sakha signed only after they were granted special concessions. Tatarstan later held a referendum on its state sovereignty, which was supported by a majority of its citizens. Only Chechnya went so far as to declare its outright independence.

It was not long before this two-class federal system came under attack from the regions that demanded parity with the ethnic republics. As Lapidus and Walker note, "Why should the inhabitants of Kareliya, where the Karelians make up only ten percent of the population and Russians almost seventy five percent, enjoy special economic privileges simply because they live in a region arbitrarily designated an autonomous area?"[26]

Indeed, a number of regions were so incensed by their second-class status within the federation that they unilaterally elevated their status to that of republics. Thus, in July 1993, Sverdlovsk Oblast and Primorskii Krai declared themselves republics, and Chelyabinsk Oblast declared its intention to become a republic of the Southern Urals.[27] Republics and other bodies also began to withhold their tax revenues, refusing to give them up to the federal authorities.

The December 1993 Constitution

The 1992 victory of the republics over the federal authorities appeared to come to an end with Yeltsin's dissolution of the Russian parliament in October

1993 and the adoption of his presidential Constitution in December 1993. To the dismay of the republics, the text of the Federal Treaty was not incorporated into the federal Constitution. The Constitution now proclaimed that all components of the federation were equal (Article 5), thus rejecting the special privileges that had been granted to the republics in March 1992. The Constitution clearly sets out the respective powers of the federal authorities and its subjects. Thus, Article 71 defines those powers exclusively allotted to the federal government, while Article 72 is devoted to those powers that are to be shared and come under the joint jurisdiction of the federal authorities and federal subjects. But there are no specific powers set down for the regions, although Article 73 does concede that any powers not covered by Articles 71 and 72 rest with the federal subjects. Rather confusingly, Article 11 also states that central-periphery relations are to be determined "by the Federal Treaty and other treaties," which suggests that the Federal Treaty and the Constitution are both still valid today—a position defended by many of the republics who have refused to relinquish the powers given to them in March 1992. Another important article in the Constitution is the so-called "flexibility clause" (Article 78), which allows the center to transfer "the implementation of some of its powers" to the federal subjects and vice versa.[28] As Lapidus and Walker rightly note, "this leaves open the possibility of bilateral agreements between Moscow and the subjects and the further development of an "asymmetrical federation," discussed below.[29]

Support for the Constitution

Although the Constitution was supported by 58.4 percent of the voters nationwide (according to official statistics), it was rejected by a majority of voters in sixteen regions, and in eight of the twenty-one republics. Additionally, in eleven regions and six republics the Constitution failed to be ratified, as turnout was below the required 50 percent. And the Constitution was boycotted altogether in Chechnya. Surely, an essential attribute of any democratic federation is the voluntary membership of its subjects. But in Russia the Constitution failed to be ratified in forty-two of the eighty-nine regions.[30]

It was not long before a number of those republics whose citizens had rejected the Constitution declared that the federal Constitution was not valid in their territories, and that their own constitutions were to take precedence.[31] Those constitutions (Chuvashiya, Yakutiya-Sakha, Chechnya, Tatarstan and Tyva) ratified between the signing of the Federal Treaty in March 1992 and the ratification of the Russian Constitution on December 12, 1993 were the most radical, granting the republics rights of self-determination, sovereignty and secession. Indeed, a number of republics (Tatarstan, Bashkortostan, Sakha, Tyva, Ingushetiya and Buryatiya) have gone so far in their rejection of the federal Constitution that their relations with the center are more typical of those in a confederation than a federation.[32] Thus, for example, Article 1 of the Constitution of Tyva states that as a sovereign state, Tyva is a member of the Russian Federation on the basis of a Federal Treaty and as such Tyva has the right to self-determination and the right to secede from the Russian Federation.[33] Tatarstan's Constitution (Article 61) stipulates that it is an "*associate member* of the federation" on the basis of a treaty and the mutual delegation of powers, and that it is a subject of international law. Similarly, Article 70 of Bashkortostan notes that the republic is a member of the Russian Federation on a contractual or treaty basis.[34]

A number of republic constitutions have also unilaterally abrogated to themselves jurisdiction over policy areas that rightfully belong to the federal government. Thus, for example: the Constitution of Tyva grants the republic the right to decide issues of war and peace; some constitutions allow the republics to adopt laws about military service (Bashkortostan, Sakha, Tyva); establish procedures for declaring a state of emergency in their territory (Buryatiya, Komi, Tyva, Bashkortostan, Kalmykiya, Kareliya, North Osetiya, Ingushetiya); the exclusive right to engage in foreign relations and foreign trade, and to sign international treaties (Dagestan, Tatarstan, Bashkortostan, Tyva, Ingushetiya, Komi).[35] And a majority of the republics, in contravention of the Federal Constitution, grant their citizens dual citizenship.

In the Russian Constitution, in distinction from the Federal Treaty, it clearly states that the ownership, use and disposal of land and minerals is under the joint jurisdiction of the federal authorities and federal subjects (Article 72). But only two republic constitutions (Komi and Kareliya) conform in this respect with the federal Constitution. In particular, Sakha, Tatarstan, Bashkortostan, Tyva and Buryatiya, all state that such natural resources belong to the inhabitants of their republics. In Article 5 of the Constitution of the Republic of Sakha, it is even stated that the, "air space, and continental shelf of the territory is the inalienable property of the citizens of the Republic."[36] Several republics also give themselves the right to decide questions regarding the federal budget. In the Constitutions of Sakha and Bashkortostan it is stated that their legislative organs have the right to define the volume of payments to the federal budget—a provision that clearly contradicts Article 71 of the Russian Constitution.

The Ethnic Challenge

It is of course much more difficult to build democracy where ethnic conflict is endemic and there are demands for separatism. The Chechen model is an extreme case of sovereignty claims being taken up to the point of demanding independence. But there are demographic and economic factors that have stifled other separatist movements from gaining support: (1) Nationality based entities (including autonomous regions) occupy 53 percent of the country's area, but only 18 percent of the population lives in those regions;[37] (2) According to a microcensus carried out in 1994, Russians make up the overwhelming majority of the population (82.95

percent);[38] (3) Of the 172 ethnic groups, the largest—the Tatars—make up only 3.8 percent of the population (followed by the Ukrainians (2.3), Chuvash with (1.2), Bashkirs (0.9), Belorussians (0.7) and the Mordvinians (0.6); all the others comprise less than 1 percent;[39] (4) Russians predominate not only in the Russian Federation as a whole, but also in most of its regions—in seventy-four of the eighty-nine members of the federation;[40] (5) Of the twenty-one republics, the eponymous population comprises a majority in only seven and a plurality in two,[41] whereas Russians have an absolute majority in nine, and a plurality in three.[42]

One would imagine that demands for secession are likely to be strongest in those republics situated in the outer rim of the federation, which border on foreign states and where a majority of the population is eponymous. The subjects that qualify on these grounds are mainly to be found in the North Caucuses (the republics of Chechnya, Dagestan, Ingushetiya, Kalmykiya, and North Osetiya) and indeed this has proven to be the most volatile area of the federation.[43] But these republics are also some of the poorest in the federation and are highly dependent on subsidies from the federal budget.

BILATERAL TREATIES AND THE FORMATION OF A TREATY-BASED FEDERATION

The authority of the Constitution has also been fundamentally weakened by the Yeltsin regime's propensity for signing special bilateral deals. Forty-six treaties have been signed to date. These bilateral accords often give the local signatories substantial rights over the disposition of natural resources on their territory, special tax concessions and other economic and political privileges. For example, special tax agreements with Tatarstan, Bashkortostan and Sakha, in 1996 alone, cost the federal treasury 3.5 trillion rubles.[44] Other agreements have given republics the right to conduct their own independent relations with foreign states, set up their own national banks, and create their own political and administrative organs.[45] The treaties and accompanying agreements were generally signed for a period of between two and five years.

The first step on this path to an "asymmetrical federation" was the landmark treaty signed with the Republic of Tatarstan on February 15, 1994. The treaty, which took nearly three years to work out, to all intents and purposes, created a "state within a state," and came as close as one could possibly come to giving Tatarstan real sovereignty over its economic and political affairs, including foreign trade and foreign policy. Twelve agreements were signed between the governments of Russia and Tatarstan regulating relations in the spheres of trade, property, budget, finance, the banking system, the military, the military industrial complex, customs, foreign economic ties, higher education, ecology and the coordination of the legal and security services.[46]

But political factors have also helped to determine who will be the lucky beneficiaries. In 1996 there were no less than eighteen treaties that were signed in the run up to the presidential elections. Yeltsin used the treaties to bribe regional elites into supporting his presidential campaign. The President was also able to capitalize on the fears of regional elites, who believed that if the communists or the nationalists came to power they would call a halt to the treaties.[47] The last treaty to be signed, to date, was in June 1998, with Moscow City.

The legal basis for the treaties are to be found in Articles 11 and 78 of the Constitution, and in the Presidential Decree (No. 370) of March 12, 1996.[48] According to this decree, "the treaties and accompanying agreements are (1) not to violate the Constitution of the Russian Federation; (2) cannot change the status of a subject of the federation; (3) cannot add to or change what is enumerated in Articles 71 and 72 of the Constitution; and (4) must respect the supremacy of the Constitution."[49] But, as we illustrate below, these provisions have simply been ignored.

As Umnova demonstrates, the treaties have significantly widened the number of areas coming under joint jurisdiction as stipulated in Article 72: "In Tatarstan there are 17 new spheres, in Bashkortostan and Sakha 11, in Kabardino-Balkariya 8, in North Osetiya 14; Buryatiya 3. With Sverdlovsk Oblast 8, with Kaliningrad Oblast 11 and Udmurtiya 11."[50] Thus the following areas were transferred from the exclusive authority of the federal authorities to joint jurisdiction: state defense (Tatarstan, Bashkortostan, Kabardino-Balkariya, North Osetiya); introduction of a state of emergency (Kabardino-Balkariya); conversion of defense industries to domestic production (Tatarstan, Bashkortostan, North Osetiya, Udmurtiya, Sverdlovsk and Orenburg oblasts); coordinating of military production complex (Tatarstan and Bashkortostan); management of the defense industry (Sverdlovsk oblast, Udmurtiya); the citing of military forces (Bashkortostan); arms sales (Tatarstan); coordination of budget finance, money-credit and pricing policy and the administration of public energy, transport, and communications (Tatarstan, North Osetiya, Kabardino-Balkariya).[51] In other cases constitutional powers exclusively reserved for the Russian federation government have been transferred to the sole jurisdiction of the federal subjects; international relations (Tatarstan); national banks (Tatarstan, Bashkortostan); republican citizenship (Tatarstan, Kabardino-Balkariya, Bashkortostan).[52]

A more recent law[53] adopted by the Duma on June 30, 1999, now stipulates, that in the future all bilateral treaties will have to be approved by the Federal Council. But this law has come too late. As Stoner-Weiss observes, "contractual federalism" has now replaced "constitutional federalism" as the basis of centre-periphery relations.[54]

Legal Separatism

For many regions a more realistic option than outright secession has been the development of "economic" and "legal" separatism or what Khemkin terms "internal separatism," the process whereby a number of subjects have withdrawn themselves from the legal and economic orbit of the federation and have become de facto autonomous islands within the Russian state.[55] According to an analysis by the Ministry of Justice, of the 44,000 regional acts adopted over the period

1995–97, almost half were in violation of the Russian Constitution and federal legislation.[56] What we are witnessing is a new "war of laws" between the federal authorities and the regions reminiscent of the struggle between the union-republics and the federal authorities during the Gorbachev period.

The ability of the regions to opt for legal separatism has been increased by the fact that the top executive and legislative bodies are now elected from below, rather than appointed from above. Up until the gubernatorial elections of 1995–97 the majority of regional chief executives were appointed to their posts by the president. The fact that regional leaders now come to office through the ballot box has significantly enhanced their local powers. No longer can the Russian president simply appoint loyal supporters to rule the regions.

The weakness of strong nationwide integrative parties has also had a negative impact on Russian federalism. As Alfred Stepan observes, "No other federal system has a party system that to date has contributed so little to producing polity wide programmatic discipline."[57] The vast majority of regional assemblies are partyless as are the majority of elections for regional governors. Thus, for example, of the 3,481 deputies elected to Russia's eighty-nine republics and regional assemblies, in post, as of January 1998, only 635 (18.4 percent) were elected on a party ticket.[58] It is very difficult to consolidate parties in weak and fragmented federal systems, but it is even more difficult to build federal systems in the absence of strong and territorially comprehensive parties. Regionally based parties such as "Voice of Russia," "Fatherland" and "All-Russia" have recently emerged with the aim of capturing seats in the lower house of the parliament. The new "party of power" headed by Vladimir Putin also includes a large number of regional leaders. As Daniel Slider notes, these governors' blocs are in effect, "anti-party parties" that have been set up specifically to preclude effective national party building in the regions.[59]

Regional executive heads and the chairs of regional assemblies are also ex-officio members of the federal council and the new elections have thus led to changes in its composition. The current president can no longer dictate the membership of the council as did Yeltsin via his powers of appointment. More recently the council has begun to flex its muscles, blocking or vetoing any legislative initiatives challenging its authority and jealously guarding the powers of regional elites.

We should also add that elites in rich and financially independent republics, such as the so-called "donor regions"[60] (regions that pay more into the federal coffers than they receive back) have been far more successful than the poverty-stricken regions in their bid for "legal separatism." As Stroev (former chair of the federation council) stresses,

> "We now have a situation whereby some poor regions are totally dependent on the centre and no real federal relations exist whilst a second stronger group has the trappings of federalism and finally the most powerful autonomous entities such as Tatarstan, coexist with Moscow as part of an exclusive club of confederative states."[61]

FEDERALISM AND DEMOCRATIZATION

According to Ronald Watts, *federalism* "refers to the advocacy of multi-tiered government combining elements of shared-rule and regional self-rule. It is based on the presumed values of achieving both unity and diversity by accommodating, preserving and promoting distinct identities within a larger political union."[62] Scholars of federalism have also stressed the positive relationship between federalism and democratization. Thus, for example, Daniels argues that "by distributing power, federalism curbs arbitrary rule, both at the centre and locally. It decentralizes responsibility while providing a mechanism to restrain potential local conflicts and abuses. It provides a school of democracy, and it quite literally brings government closer to the people."[63]

For Preston King, federation and democracy are but two sides of the same coin, and for true federalism to function relations between the center and regions must be grounded in constitutional law and democratic representation. In particular, the constituent units of the federation must be incorporated into the decision-making procedures of the central government on some "constitutionally entrenched basis."[64] For King then, only liberal democracies can be truly federal.[65]

Such theories are fine for liberal democracies, but what of Russia, where it could be argued that the relationship between federalism and democratization has been wholly negative? Russia's unique brand of "asymmetrical federalism," far from promoting democracy, has bolstered authoritarian regimes in the regions. High levels of regional autonomy have led the regions more often in the direction of dictatorship than democracy. Local democracy is surely a necessary prerequisite for democratization at the national level. And the provision of certain basic democratic procedures should, in a democracy, be universally available to all citizens across the federation regardless of their place of residence. However, as Przeworski rightly observes,

> Citizenship can be universally exercised only when the normative system is guided by universal criteria, when the rule of law is effectively enforced, when public powers are willing and able to protect rights, and when all individuals enjoy some social and economic prerequisites [and] governments and officials . . . act in accordance with the constitution and the laws.[66]

In Russia this has been far from the case, and there are wide regional variations in the development of civil society, electoral practices and adherence to constitutional norms and the exercise of human rights. The Constitutions of the republics and the charters of the regions have been forged out of fire and the struggle for power between regional executive and legislative bodies of power. Whoever wins the struggle imposes their form of political system. Indeed, there would appear to be as many forms of federal relations as there are subjects of the federation. As O'Donnell observes, when democratic institutions are weak and inchoate their place is soon taken over by informal practices, such as clientelism, patrimonialism and corruption.[67] The chronic weakness of parties has left open the door for other groups to enter politics. Two of the most powerful are industrial executives and state bureaucrats. In a new postcommunist corporatist alliance, regional economic and political elites have joined forces to plunder the wealth of their regions.

In many regions governors and presidents have been able to violate electoral rules with impunity. The inability or the unwillingness of the Russian Constitutional Court, the Central Electoral Commission and other federal law enforcement agencies to step in and declare such elections null and void has fundamentally undermined the Constitution and set back the development of a "legal culture" in Russia. The "politicization" of the judiciary, electoral commissions and the courts is a particularly worrying development. Regional electoral commissions, for example, are formed by regional elites—half of the members coming from nominations from the regional executive body, and half from the regional assembly.[68] The unwritten message from the Yeltsin administration to the Russian Central Electoral Commission, and to other bodies charged with implementing federal laws, was to turn a blind eye, if those infringing such laws were supporters of the Russian president.

For Montesquieu, large states must choose between tyranny and federalism. But as Petrov stresses, "True to its habit of choosing both evils, Russia has taken the path of building a 'federation of tyrannies.'"[69] Federalism and democratization in Russia exist in contradiction rather than harmony. In a vicious circle, authoritarianism at the center has been nourished by authoritarianism in the regions and vice versa.

THE SOVIET FEDERAL LEGACY

As we have shown, one of the most destructive legacies that Russia inherited from the Soviet Union was the ethno-territorial form of federalism. The "dual nature" of Russian federalism, which grants different constitutional rights and powers to subjects of the federation, has from the outset created major tensions and divisions within the state. The challenges of ethnic secessionism, the demands for legal separatism, and the development of bilateralism are but logical responses to the constitutional inequalities inherent in the system.

Over the period August 1991 to the storming of the Russian parliament in October 1993, Yeltsin had to grapple with the same dilemma that Gorbachev had faced only a few years earlier, namely, how to democratize the political system, and decentralize the economy, while maintaining the unity of the state. Fearful of the disintegration of the Russian Federation, Yeltsin was forced to concede major powers to the twenty-one ethnic republics in the Federal Treaty of March 1992. Much of the subsequent history of the Yeltsin period can be seen as one of trying to regain those powers, which he was forced to relinquish at a time of presidential weakness. In his "Presidential Constitution" of December 1993 Yeltsin attempted to level out the powers of the regions and republics. However, the Constitution was fundamentally weakened by its failure to be ratified in forty-two federal subjects. The ethnic republics now declared their own constitutions as legally binding in their territories and a "new war of laws" between the center and the regions quickly took hold. Chechnya demanded outright secession and Tatarstan continued to declare that it was only an "associate member" of the federation.

Russia's "dual federalism" as we have seen, is by its very nature, asymmetrical, and Yeltsin's promotion of bilateralism was another logical response to this asymmetry. But bilateralism also undermined the authority of the Constitution and it soon encouraged a number of regions to push for "legal separatism." Yeltsin's response to such demands was to try and buy off regional elites, conceding even greater powers to them, in return, for their pledges of economic and political support.

In the end, Yeltsin succeeded, where Gorbachev had failed, in maintaining the "unity" of the state, but only at the sacrifice of democratization. And as President Putin embarks on a major overhaul of the federal system, in his attempt to grapple with the Soviet federal legacy, it is unlikely that the consolidation of democracy will be very high on his agenda.

NOTES

1. See, for example, J. J. Linz, and A. Stepan, *Problems of Democratic Transition and Consolidation* (Baltimore: John Hopkins University Press: 1996).

2. Ronald L. Watts, "Models of Federal-Power Sharing," paper presented to the Forum of Federations International Conference on Federalism, Ontario, Canada, (October 1999): 1–9; 1.

3. See, in particular, articles 73 and 134.

4. "Draft Nationalities Policy of the Party under Present Conditions," adopted by the CPSU Central Committee Plenum, September 20, 1989, quoted in Stephan Kux, "Soviet Federalism," *Problems of Communism* (March-April, 1990): 1–20; 2.

5. Seweryn Bialer, Stalin's Successors: Leadership, Stability and Change in the Soviet Union (New York: Cambridge University Press, 1980), 210–211.

6. Gregory Gleason, *Federalism and Nationalism: The Struggle for Republican Rights in the USSR* (Westview Press: 1990), 3.

7. Philip Goldman, Gail Lapidus, and Victor Zaslavasky, "Introduction: Soviet Federalism—Its Origins, Evolution and Demise," in Gail Lapidus, Victor Zaslavsky with Philip Goldman (eds.) *From Union to Commonwealth: Nationalism and Separatism in the Soviet Republics*, (New York: Cambridge University Press, 1992), 2.

8. Peter R. Zwick, "Soviet Nationality Policy: Social, Economic, and Political Aspects," in Gordon Smith (ed.), *Public Policy and Administration in the Soviet Union* (Praeger: 1980),142–171; 149.

9. Goldman et al., op. cit. 2.

10. Gleason, op. cit., 3.

11. Kux, ibid, 6–7.

12. See articles 5 and 7.

13. Archie Brown, *The Gorbachev Factor* (Oxford: Oxford University Press: 1997), 287.

14. See Brown, op. cit. 256.

15. Goldman, Lapidus, Zaslavsky, op. cit. 15.

16. John Miller, *Mikhail Gorbachev and the End of Soviet Power* (New York: St. Martin's Press: 1993), 175.

17. There were two ASSRs in Georgia and one each in Azerbaijan and Uzbekistan. There was also one autonomous region in the republics of Azerbaijan, Georgia and Tadjikistan.

18. John B. Dunlop, *The Rise of Russia and the Fall of the Soviet Empire* (Princeton, Princeton University Press: 1993), 64.

19. Ann Sheehy, "Russia's Republics: A Threat to Its Territorial Integrity?" *RFE/RL Research Report*, Vol. 2, No. 20 (May 14, 1993): 34–40; 36.

20. John B. Dunlop, op. cit., 62.

21. Mikhail Filippov and Olga Shevtsov, "Asymmetric Bilateral Bargaining in the New Russian Federation: A Path-Dependence Explanation," *Communist and Postcommunist Studies*, 32 (1999): 61–76; 70.

22. John T. Ishiyama, "The Russian Proto-parties and the National Republics," *Communist and Postcommunist Studies*, Vol. 29, No. 4: 395–411 (1996): 397.

23. Including six Krais, forty-nine Oblasts and two cities of federal significance with the status of an Oblast (Moscow and St. Petersburg).

24. See David Lane and Cameron Ross, *The Transition from Communism to Capitalism: Ruling Elite from Gorbachev to Yeltsin* (New York: St. Martin's Press: 1999).

25. There were actually three federal treaties, with separate agreements for the republics, the autonomies and the regions.

26. G. W. Lapidus and E. W. Walker, "Nationalism, Regionalism, and Federalism: Center-Periphery Relations in Postcommunist Russia," in G. W. Lapidus (ed.), *The New Russia: Troubled Transformation* (Boulder, Colo.: Westview Press: 1995), 96.

27. John Lowenhardt, *The Reincarnation of Russia: Struggling with the Legacy of Communism* (Essex, England: Langman: 1995), 125.

28. See C. Ross, "Federalism and Regional Politics," in Bowker M. and Ross C. (eds.) *Russia After the Cold War* (Essex, England: Langman: 2000); C. Ross, "The Republicanisation of Russia: Federalism and Democratisation in Transition," in C. Pierson and S. Tormey (eds.) *Politics at the Edge* (New York: Macmillan: 2000) and R. Sakwa, "The Republicanisation of Russia," in the same collection.

29. Lapidus and Walker, op. cit., 102.

30. Leonid Smirnyagin (ed.), *Rossiiskie Regiony Nakanune Vyborov* (Moscow: Yuridicheskaya Literatura: 1995), 7–43.

31. Nineteen of Russia's twenty-one republican constitutions (all except Kalmykiya and Kareliya) contain provisions that violate the Federal Constitution.

32. I. A. Umnova, *Konstitutsionnye Osnovy Sovremennovo Rossiiskovo Federalizma* (Moscow: Delo: 1998), 110.

33. S. V. Alekseev, V. A. Kalamanov, A. G. Chernenko, *Ideologicheskie Orientiry Rossii*, (Moscow: Kniga i Biznes: 1998): Vol 1. 392.

34. Umnova, op. cit., 106.

35. Ibid., 108.

36. Ibid., 107.

37. Interview by N. Arkhangelskaya with Aleksandr Arinin, "The Problem of Separatism in Russia: Elitist Separatism Has Its Price," *Kommersant-Daily* (Nov. 29, 1996): 3. Translated in the *Current Digest of the Soviet Press* (hereafter, CDPSP), No. 48 (1996): 5–6.

38. Emil Pain and Andrei Susarov, "Line Five in the Mirror of Demography," *Rossiiskie Vesti* (October 30, 1997): 2, translated in the *CDPSP*, Vol. XLIX, No. 44 (1997): 10–12; 10.

39. Emil Paine and Andrei Susarov, "Line Five in the Mirror of Demography," *Rossiiskie Vesti* (October 30, 1996), *CDPSP*, Vol. XLIX, No. 44, 10–12.

40. Ibid., 11.

41. Chechnya, Chuvash, Ingushetiya, Kalmykiya, North Osetiya, and Tuva. To this we can add Dagestan, which is made up of thirty-three national groups and where Russians account for only 9.2 percent of the total population.

42. Those with an absolute majority of Russians are Adygeya, Buryatiya, Altai, Kareliya, Khakasiya, Komi, Mordova, Sakha-Yakutiya, and Udmurtiya, and those with a Russian plurality are Bashkortostan, Karachai-Cherkessiya and Marii-El.

43. Another region that may eventually secede is Kaliningrad, which is geographically cut off from the rest of the federation on the Baltic coast.

44. Aleksei Lavrov, "Asimmetriya Byudzhetnovo Ustroistva Rossii: Problemy i Resheniya," in Andrei Zakharov (ed.) *Asimmetrichnost' Federatsii* (Tacis: 1997): 99–122; 104.

45. Umnova, op. cit., 108–114.

46. Rafael Khakimov, "Asimmetrichnost" Rossiiskoi Federatsii: Vzglyad iz Tatarstan, in *Asimmetrichnost' Federatsii,* op. cit., 61–76; 68. In April 1999 the treaty was renewed and Moscow won back some of its powers, particularly over taxation.

47. Fillipov and Shevtsov, op. cit. 73.

48. "Ob utverzhdenii Polozheniya o poryadke raboty po razgranicheniyu predmetov vedeniya i polnomochii mezhdu federal'nymi organami gosudarstvennoi vlasti i organami gosudarstvennoi vlasti sub'ektov Rossiiskoi Federatsii i, o vzaimnoi peredache osushchestvleniya chasti svoikh polnomochii federal'nymi organami ispolnitel'noi vlasti i organami ispolnitel'noi vlasti sub'ektov Rossiiskoi Federatsii", *Sobranie Zakonodatel'stva Rossiiskoi Federatsii* (1996): No. 12, 1058.

49. K. Stoner-Weiss, "Central Weakness and Provincial Autonomy: Observations on the Devolution Process in Russia," *Post-Soviet Affairs*, Vol. 15, No. 1, (1999): 87–106; 91.

50. Umnova, op. cit., 112.

51. Ibid., 112.

52. Stoner-Weiss, op. cit., 92

53. "O printsipakh i poryadke razgranicheniya predmetov vedeniya i polnomochii mezhdu organami gosudarstvennoi vlasti Rossiiskoi Federatsii i organami gosudarstvennoi vlasti sub'ektov Rossiiskoi Federatsii." Adopted by the State Duma, June 4, 1999 and ratified by the president on June 24. *Rossiiskaya Gazeta* (June 30, 1999): 3.

54. Stoner-Weiss, op. cit., 87–106; 92.

55. S. Khemkin, "Separatizm v Rossii—Pozadi ili Vperedi?" *Pro et Contra*, Vol. 2, No. 2 (Spring 1997): 5–19; 18.

56. *Izvestiya* (March 4, 1997): 4.

57. Alfred Stepan, "Russian Federalism in Comparative Perspective: Problems of Power Creation and Power Deflation," paper delivered to the 31st National Convention of the AAASS, St. Louis, Missouri (November 18–21, 1999): 36.

58. Unpublished data from the Central Election Commission in Moscow.

59. Daniel Slider, "National Political Parties in Russia's Regions," paper delivered to the 31st National Convention of the AAASS, St. Louis (November 20, 1999): 6.

60. There were thirteen donor regions in 1999: St. Petersburg and Moscow cities; Moscow, Irkutsk, Lipetsk, Samara, Perm and Sverdlovsk oblasts; Republics of Bashkortostan and Tatarstan; Khanty-Mansi and Yamal-Nenets Autonomous Okrugs and Krasnoyarsk Krai (*IEWS: Russian Regional Report*), Vol. 4., No. 20 (May 27, 1999): 14.

61. V. Shpak, "Federalism Does Not Yet Exist in Russia—but Problems Do," *Kommersant Daily* (January 20, 1998): 4.

62. Ronald L. Watts, op. cit. 1.

63. R. V. Daniels, "Democracy and Federalism in the Former Soviet Union and the Russian Federation," in P. J. Stavrakis, J. DeBardeleben and L. Black (eds.) *Beyond the Monolith: The Emergence of Regionalism in Post-Soviet Russia,* (Baltimore: John Hopkins University Press: 1997), 233.

64. Preston King, *Federalism and Federation* (1982), 94, cited in M. Burgess and Alain-G. Gagnon (eds.) *Comparative Federalism and Federation* (Toronto: University of Toronto Press: 1993), 5.

65. See Graham Smith (ed.), *Federalism: The Multiethnic Challenge* (Essex, England: Langman: 1995).

66. A. Przeworskii (ed.), *Sustainable Democracy* (New York: Cambridge University Press, 1995), 34.

67. G. O'Donnell, "Delegative Democracy," *Journal of Democracy*, Vol. 5, No. 1 (January 1994): 55–69; 59.

68. See the Resolution of the Central Electoral Commission of the Russian Federation, "O Primernom polozhenii ob izbiratel'noi kommissii sub'ekta Rossiiskoi Federatsii," January 25, 1995, published in *Sbornik Zakonodatel'nykh i Inykh Pravovykh Aktov Po Voprosam Vyborov v Federal'nye Organy Gosudarstvennoi Vlasti i Referenduma Rossiiskoi Federatsii* (Moscow: "Ves Mir" 1997), 369–377; 371.

69. Nikolai Petrov, "Russia's Regions or Regions' Russia?: Prospective Realignment of the Nation's Political Subdivisions," *Carnegie Institute Briefing Papers*, No. 3 (March 1999): 1–6; 1.

5

Elites and Institutions in Russian Economic Transformation: The Case of Sverdlovsk

Lynn D. Nelson and Irina Y. Kuzes

Democratization is a key component of the Russian transformation away from Communist Party rule, and the trajectory of this transformation can be gauged by examining the extent to which centralized power is moderated by the influence of divergent interest groups that operate in a pluralist context. Regional-level developments provide good measures of the extent to which interest group activities are being encouraged that are fundamental to democratic decision making. In this chapter, we examine democratization trends since the demise of the Soviet Union by focusing on Sverdlovsk, a region we have been studying since mid-1992. As one of the "success stories" among Russia's regions, Sverdlovsk offers a striking example of how interests have coalesced around economic issues where the stakes are high and how power has been effectively concentrated in the hands of skillful regional leaders. These regional elites enjoy administrative authority that is largely unchecked while simultaneously acting as market agents in a context of abundant exportable commodities.

The Sverdlovsk oblast is situated in the Ural region just inside Asia. The oblast has 4.7 million inhabitants, 1.5 million of whom live in Yekaterinburg, the oblast capital. Sverdlovsk is one of only a few among Russia's eighty-nine administrative subdivisions that is a net contributor to the federal budget. A wealthy region because of its natural resources and manufacturing industries, Sverdlovsk has often attempted to chart its own course since the demise of the Soviet Union. The oblast's independence-minded governor Eduard Rossel has frequently clashed with Moscow authorities over questions about central oversight of the region's economic and political activities.

Because Sverdlovsk was an early center of political activism, we can graphically see in that oblast how the struggle has been played out between interests of industrial managers and those of democratically oriented reformers.

Sverdlovsk further illustrates the conflicts of interests between raw materials exporters and those who have wanted to strengthen domestic production. Sverdlovsk also offers insight into strategies that have been effective for both Boris Yeltsin and Sverdlovsk's current governor in their confrontations with diverse opposition groups, and into the shifting priorities that characterized political and economic trends at the regional level during Yeltsin's presidency.

In his introduction to this volume, David Lane discusses variables that are "the major building blocks" in analyses of the transformation process—key components being elites and institutions.[1] In Lane's characterization, elites and institutions can reflect divergent interests, and thus exert opposing pressures, in transformational developments. The activities of elites, who lead transformations, are grounded in values and norms. Institutions, which are embedded in the social structure, serve to constrain change actions. Thus, the analysis of both leadership, through elite pacts, and history, with attention to the effects of path dependence, can offer complementary insights into the pace and scope of democratization trends.

We employ three benchmarks for assessing progress toward democratization at the regional level—factors that stand out in the literature as being useful indicators of progress toward the consolidation of democracy in formerly authoritarian regimes. We phrase these factors for assessment as questions, and we return to them in the concluding section of the chapter. First, is substantial movement evident in the regions toward identifying and removing the authoritarian elements of the previous regime?[2] Gretchen Casper and Michelle Taylor suggest that, closely tied to the process of removing authoritarian elements is the position of actors in the new order who are carryovers from the authoritarian regime. They argue that "The more authoritarian actors maintain their ability to influence politics after their exit from office, the greater the chance that the new democracy will collapse."[3] This assumes, of course, that the leaders of the new regime are different individuals from those of the old order. Because in Russia most top political leaders after the USSR's demise were also leaders under the old regime, our focus was not on the actors themselves but their actions and the policies they have established.

Second, are institutions being strengthened in the regions that facilitate open expression of complaints and concerns, and that ensure governmental responsiveness? This factor is often phrased in terms of promoting civil society, creating mediating structures and building social capital. The utility of these latter concepts in measuring movement toward consolidation has been questioned, however. John Mueller considers the "civil society" concept to be "rather murky," and he agrees with Philippe Schmitter and Terry Karl that the "norms of a civic culture are better thought of as a *product* and not as a producer of democracy."[4] A focus on institution building that promotes citizen involvement in political issues and governmental responsiveness is fundamental, since, as Mueller notes, "In the end, most of what democratic governments actually do on a day-by-day basis is the result of pressure and petition."[5]

Third, once a democratic government has been installed at the regional level, do regional elites outside the government change "their political beliefs and tactics" in ways that support the new government?"[6] As Michael McFaul phases the broader problem for a country in the process of democratization, "If a transition from authoritarian rule is to succeed, all major political actors must agree to reject old political institutions and accept the new rules of the game."[7] This is no small task, of course, and even under optimal conditions, acceptance and support of democratic rules of the game by old-regime elites is likely to sometimes be grudging. In inquiring into the beliefs and tactics of regional elites, we wanted to examine "compliance with the democratic rules of the game" to be found "over time,"[8] across a broad spectrum of activities.

In the first section of the chapter, we examine features of the devolution of power away from the center that have been critical to the restructuring of political and economic life in Sverdlovsk. Next, we discuss coalition building by Soviet-era elites in Sverdlovsk—a process that accompanied the shifting locus of power that was a defining feature of Gorbachev's reforms. Tied to the coalition-building phase was a rapid and striking upsurge of grassroots activity in the waning days of Communist Party rule.[9] Then, we discuss three additional aspects of evolving political relations in Sverdlovsk that have fundamental implications for economic activity: opportunism and the vagueness of property and ownership rights, the reassertion of executive power and the preservation of monopolism.

THE DEVOLUTION OF POWER

The Transition to Relative Autonomy at the Regional Level

Beginning early during his tenure as general secretary, Gorbachev instituted a variety of procedures that would inevitably attenuate central power.[10] At first, these initiatives were aimed at improving efficiency. Later, as resistance to his reforms tightened among many state and Party elites, Gorbachev sought through decentralization to diminish the power of his opponents. The decentralizing theme had a regional dimension, in which the authority of regional Party bosses was weakened, with executive power that had been held by the Party hierarchy tending to flow into the hands of executive committees of local soviets—bodies which at that time did not function effectively as legislative bodies, as Gorbachev himself repeatedly noted. De facto power had already shifted in large measure out of Moscow's control and into the hands of regional and branch clans.[11]

The ideological underpinnings of the Soviet system were already being challenged during this period, and Gorbachev's decentralizing initiative further deepened the crisis surrounding the "unity of interests" doctrine. With the further lifting of restraints against the pursuit of interests below the societal level, region-based corporate-administrative clans were now able to begin operating with relative autonomy. One result of this autonomy has been that administrative market procedures, now transformed, have come to dominate mainstream economic relations. Below, we illustrate this process in Sverdlovsk.

The Creation of Private Wealth

There were also other regional-level effects of the devolution of power. As *obkom*s lost their coordinating function to executives of soviets, they began using the "administrative currency" at their disposal to create joint ventures, financial institutions and other businesses. This outcome was to be expected among enterprising members of the oblast Party committee apparatus and their close colleagues. The knowledge and ties that they had developed, in order to coordinate economic activities in their regions, had been a part of their expected Party work. Now that their roles were being redefined, many saw it as only natural to continue utilizing the networks that they had formerly been expected to organize and maintain.[12]

An additional effect of the devolution of power was that inadequate supplies of goods were further imperiled by the shift of power from first secretaries to Soviet executives, and by the diversion of resources to new structures that *obkom* apparatuses were creating. In the past, the shadow economy had filled the gaps between what was needed and what the state could supply. Now that the gaps were larger, and supply networks were being fragmented, the shadow economy was able readily to expand to take advantage of these new opportunities.

Conflicts of Interest within Clan Structures

Relative autonomy at the regional level did not mean unity. The demise of the "unity of interests" doctrine under Gorbachev[13] changed relations at every level of the society, and at the regional level one of the effects was that within corporate-administrative clans deep fissures soon developed. Before the transition began, diverse interests had been represented in regional clans; but all of the coalitions that had been formed were united in their common efforts to claim state resources and circumvent state power. Construction had different interests from high technology, for example, and sometimes these interests were in competition—as each interest grouping lobbied Moscow for resources and favorable decisions of all kinds.

At the start of the transition, clan participants were united in their efforts to maintain power and influence in the face of democratic opposition, which often directly opposed the existing clan structures. They also saw, better than most, the opportunities for personal gain that were being presented by perestroika, and they were determined to exploit them. Having won those battles, however, clan members increasingly became divided over conflicts of interest, and these struggles have expanded into new forms of criminality that were largely unknown within the ranks of *nomenklatura* elites previously. These activities have come to include participation of criminal groups and gangs that were earlier excluded from the dominating corporate-administrative clans.

COALITION BUILDING

Even radical change, Douglass North observes, "is seldom as discontinuous as it appears on the surface."[14] In Russian political and economic relations, the kind of path dependence that has been particularly problematic reflects a combination of the legacies of both Communism and the late Soviet-era shadow economy. An "historically derived continuity"[15] can be seen in patterns of both political decision-making and business activity as they have been practiced from the late Soviet era until now—continuity that helps to explain both the current malaise in Russian political life and the failure of economic reform initiatives until now. At the heart of this process have been the alliances that privatizing *nomenklatura* members formed with members of the shadow-criminal economy and that have broadened and deepened the scope of shadow economy activities well beyond their Soviet-era levels.

The Shadow-Criminal Connection

The solidification of corporatist-administrative clan structures from the 1960s onward meant that the preconditions for widespread economic criminality were already present when the Gorbachev reforms began. Putnam notes that "organized criminality . . . everywhere has a broadly similar structure," being "based on traditional patterns of patron-clientelism," and "the ancient culture of mistrust." It has historically "burgeoned," he observes, "in response to the weakness of the administrative and judicial structures of the state."[16] What had restrained Soviet patron-clientelism from the Khrushchev period onward had been the dominating administrative hand of the state and the party—a constraining force that was removed when the party ceased to oversee the clan structures.

Because the corporatist-administrative clan arrangements that were regional centers of power at the time Gorbachev took office operated outside the Communist normative-ideological system, clans pursued their interests through informal clientele connections. Although administrative market activities were officially prohibited, there was widespread public consensus that these arrangements were necessary to circumvent negative features of the Soviet system.

As momentum grew to create a legal second economy that would operate as an officially sanctioned supplement to the Soviet system, the shadow economy came to be viewed as a source of both political support and capital that could be useful as reform-oriented *nomenklatura* pursued transition initiatives. In the

"500 Days" proposal, Yavlinsky et al., estimated that shadow economy income then totaled 20 percent of the national GNP.[17] They believed that another benefit would also accompany the integration of shadow economy participants into the mainstream economy—the undermining of shadow activity itself. Since "the main cause of the existence of the shadow economy on this scale . . . is the absence of private property as a means of production," they reasoned, as well as "the predominance up to now of command and administrative methods," liberalization and privatization would themselves be effective in overcoming corruption and economic crime more generally.[18]

Executive Political Officials in Clan Structures

Sverdlovsk's clan structures, which today dominate a substantial proportion of the region's political and economic life, revolve around the activities of executive officials. Although it is widely acknowledged, even among officials, that illegal practices are widespread among executives, today there are no effective institutional constraints on their activities.

The reforms that were introduced in 1990 changed the role of local soviets from functioning as arms of the Party hierarchy to becoming major participants in policy making and overseers of executive actions. Soviet-era executives were unaccustomed to a system in which significant oversight authority was given to popularly elected legislative bodies, and in Sverdlovsk, as in Moscow at the federal level, efforts were soon undertaken to end this move by Gorbachev toward checks and balances. The failed August 1991 coup was one such attempt, as were Yeltsin's 1993 actions, which abolished not only the national parliament but also local soviets.

Eduard Rossel became the dominant figure in Sverdlovsk under the new conditions that were created through perestroika. In 1990, he left the directorship of Sreduralstroy, a vertically integrated consortium of construction operations and plants that manufactured building materials, to become chairman of the oblast soviet's executive committee (*ispolkom*) and of the Sverdlovsk oblast soviet. In 1991, a new administrative office was established in every region to circumvent Party oversight—that of head of the oblast administration. Yeltsin appointed Rossel regional head of administration in Sverdlovsk. Rossel was elected governor in 1995. He won reelection in August 1999 in a race that was not close.

The change in leadership that brought to the top of Sverdlovsk's corporate-administrative clan a person who had never been a party functionary meant few changes for the clan structure itself, however. Most key figures remained the same, as did their functions and their connections with one another. Further, economic and political relations under Rossel's leadership have continued to reflect defining features of the Soviet system in key respects. Executive-centered hierarchy remains the accepted approach to internal organization. As we will indicate later, property rights remain vague, and a substantial level of monopolism in economic relations continues to prevail. And "the implicit contract law" of the regional "firm" makes it inevitable that hierarchy would continue to be "its own court of ultimate appeal."[19]

The joint venture Interural provides an example. Founded in 1989, it was created as a Soviet-Swiss company out of Sreduralstroy, which was one of the largest construction enterprises in the Urals. Rossel was director general of Sreduralstroy at the time. Interural was created to link Sreduralstroy to foreign firms that could provide opportunities for capital investment and technology transfer, with a focus on construction and building materials. Soon, however, copper export had become a major focus of Interural's activity. By 1991, about 90 percent of all copper exports from the Sverdlovsk oblast were going through Interural, and the firm's principal work had shifted to export-import operations. Natural resources were the primary export, and foodstuffs were the chief import product. Decisions about who would have export licenses in such cases were made in Moscow, but only the best positioned firms were typically granted licenses. Support from the oblast administration was persuasive.

Interural has been able to work out notably favorable terms for its export-import activities—privileges so striking that they became a public issue in the early 1990s. But when a group of deputies attempted to launch an investigation into Interural's operations in 1993, the initiative was quickly stopped.[20] By that time, Rossel had been appointed head of administration (governor) by Yeltsin, having served since 1990 as chairman of the oblast soviet and of the executive committee (*ispolkom*). Rossel's daughter had been appointed a representative of Interural in Germany, and the son of the oblast Party first secretary who had succeeded Yeltsin in Sverdlovsk had become manager of the Interural office in England. Yeltsin's son-in-law had joined the company's Moscow headquarters. The director general of Interural since 1989 has been Aleksandr Tikhonov, who worked at the Ministry of Foreign Trade until that time.

Of course, many joint ventures and cooperatives that were organized during the late 1980s were not as closely tied to first-tier regional administrative elites and top-ranking Party leaders as Interural has been. Yet, *nomenklatura* involvement in this process was inevitable, because of the tight administrative control that existed over both resources and the right to conduct economic transactions in the Soviet economy. The pattern that is evident in Interural's evolution illustrates a process, then, that has been repeated many times over throughout Russia.

Numerous non-state firms were created out of state enterprises with the participation of managerial and administrative *nomenklatura*. Claiming for themselves the most lucrative niche that they could find, again and again they drew in relatives and influential officials who could promote their firms' interests effectively. This "pre-privatization stage" of economic restructuring, developing in production, distribution and financial institutions throughout the economic system, effectively divided the "cream of the cream" among the business opportunities that were manifest in Russia during that period. By the time that "people's privatization" was begun under Yeltsin, the consolidation of new economic arrangements was already well underway.

First- and Second-tier Elites

Another key coalition was formed between reform-oriented elites of the first tier with ambitious second-tier elites who had long been held back from assuming top posts in the Soviet system. Many of the elites who have taken vanguard positions among Russia's new business class have been second-tier *nomenklatura*—top figures in the RSFSR rather than the USSR, regional elites rather than republican elites, or vice-heads rather than heads of departments and agencies. We have pointed out elsewhere that a number of the USSR's highest ranking elites had come to favor deep reform in the Soviet system by the mid-1980s, but for notably different reasons.[21] Only some of them favored economic liberalization, and their cause was joined in the Gorbachev period by a large number of lower-ranking Party functionaries and sectoral and regional elites below the top level who saw opportunities for career improvement through liberalization.

Alliances with Democrats

Finally, the alliances that reform-oriented *nomenklatura* formed with Russian democrats outside the elite core was pivotal in overcoming barriers that were presented by Party ideology and many of the Party's top leaders. Gorbachev had attempted to undermine the authority of "obstructionist" high Party officials through democratizing initiatives, and this theme found natural supporters among many reform-oriented elites who hoped to see the Soviet system radically modified. Thus, ideologically driven elites were joined in these democratization efforts by a number of others who had more pragmatic concerns—individuals who were attempting, through the marshaling of public opinion, to discredit officials who were above them and in that way advance in the system.

Further, the democratic movement helped to legitimate the process of remaking the ground rules for economic activity, a key feature of which was the parceling out state-controlled property and privileges to favorably positioned *nomenklatura*. Gorbachev had pointed the way toward this development with his initial emphasis on interest diversity, which had quickly emerged as an alternative to the "unity of interests" theme. And just as *nomenklatura* elites were starting to taste the fruits of interest representation that benefited their own cooperatives and entrepreneurial ventures, Gorbachev was raising the stakes in his perestroika campaign by pushing for ever broader democratization.

In Sverdlovsk, Rossel was concentrating his power during 1990, at the time that democrats' public support was the highest. Although Rossel was the choice of local elites to head the oblast administration following the August 1991 coup, democratic movement participants in Sverdlovsk had overwhelmingly opposed the appointment. Their view was that Rossel was too closely connected with the shadow economy to be a suitable choice. Nor was Rossel popular with the electorate, overall, in the early 1990s. As late as March 1991, only five percent of Yekaterinburg[22] respondents favored Rossel for head of administration according to an Yekaterinburg public opinion survey by Viacheslav Zhitenov.[23] The democrats' setback in the Rossel appointment was a sign of their declining influence in Sverdlovsk political life, although, as we observe in another chapter, Sverdlovsk had been unusually fertile ground for anti-establishment mobilization in the early days of Russia's democratic movement activity.[24]

The Sverdlovsk case is illustrative of what happened in many regions and in Moscow. Where parties are developed, the interests of a diversity of social groups are not expressed and the interests of well-placed bureaucrats and the financial-economic groups are promoted. Parties are formed to provide labels for different bureaucrats-turned-politicians that are supported by different businesses and express the interests of these businesses. Gavriil Popov presents an interpretation of such developments with a different cast, observing that democratic activism was a vital force in bringing to power "reform-oriented apparatchiks and *nomenklatura* . . . [and in helping them] to free themselves from the leftovers of ideology, to push aside conservatives, and to start reform."[25]

In retrospect, however, it is clear that the rapid upsurge of democratic activism in the late 1980s and early 1990s ultimately failed to achieve key goals of the movement. That outcome may be best accounted for by two factors. First, pivotal movement figures, both nationally and regionally, did not solidify the democratic trends that were manifest through their actions and policies. This was partially because the movement never became very cohesive and partially because key leaders of the movement were more comfortable with authoritarian than with democratic decision making and chose at critical times to revert to familiar styles and organizational approaches. Additionally, democratic activists did not have a way to get many reformers into key administrative positions. When they did, they often supported reformers who were unsuccessful in their new roles—a number of whom had come from academia, as did Popov in Moscow and Anatoly Sobchak in St. Petersburg.

OPPORTUNISM AND THE VAGUENESS OF PROPERTY AND OWNERSHIP RIGHTS

Nearly a decade after the process began under Gorbachev to transfer state property into private hands, it is still unclear who owns what in many cases or what property and ownership rights de facto owners have. We have documented a broad spectrum of specific cases in which not only is "possession ninety percent of the law," but also possession itself is subject to challenge by better connected, better armed and stronger claimants. This ambiguity has created attractive openings for challenges to early privatization decisions, both among private interests and from government officials who have sought means to restore elements of central control to the production system.

An example of how uncertainty about property rights has led to struggles within enterprises and between enterprises and regional officials can be seen in the management disputes of Serov Metallurgy Works. Serov Metallurgy is a large enterprise in Sverdlovsk whose controlling shares were owned in 1997 by a St. Petersburg financial group, TWAL, Ltd. The board of directors voted to replace the director general in April of that year, but he was unwilling to leave. The director went to court to keep his job, and the local court ruled in his favor in early May. In mid-May, a private security firm that had been employed by TWAL dispatched armed personnel to seize the office of the incumbent director general in order that the newly appointed director could begin his work.

The drama did not end there, however, because the outgoing director was able to enlist local militia to support his attempt to keep his job. At one point the two directors were together in the director's office, engaged in a dispute that lasted through the night, while outside the office there was a standoff between their respective squads of armed reinforcements. The next morning, a group of several hundred company workers had joined the confrontation, and the newly appointed director decided to leave the town, accompanied by bodyguards.

Two weeks later, the oblast court overturned the lower court ruling. This set the stage for the annual stockholders' meeting that began the next day—where, according to a published report, two groups faced off against one another. The St. Petersburg group argued that the old management had diverted a significant amount of production for their own personal gain through a series of "daughter" subsidiary companies that they had created and, in the view of some stockholders, were operating through "half-legal intermediaries." Defenders of the old management replied that the majority stockholders were keeping too much of the company profits for themselves and withholding needed investment capital.[26]

Serov Metallurgy Works was reorganized in the spring 1999 and registered as a worker-owned company. All workers in the enterprise are stockholders, and they own more than 70 percent of the shares. The conflict over ownership and policy continues, however. In October 1999, the director general of the joint stock company organized an armed seizure of the enterprise.[27] It failed and, in March 2000, the worker-elected director general, Anton Bakov, remained in command. His position is shaky. On March 15, 2000, Bakov and the chair of the Serov Metallurgy Works' labor union committee wrote a letter to Russia's Acting President Vladimir Putin, and also the chair of the State Duma and the minister of Internal Affairs complaining that Rossel was trying to replace the current management. The letter continues, "We have already repulsed three armed attempts to seize [the enterprise]. The last of them, on October 5, 1999, included the participation of the militia and OMON of the Sverdlovsk oblast. The redistribution of property in our oblast is underway with open support from Governor E. E. Rossel."[28]

The situation with Serov Metallurgy Works is not an isolated incident. Similar conflicts have been seen at a number of other Sverdlovsk enterprises, including the Kochkonar Smelting Complex—whose turmoil has been the subject of prominent public attention and frequent mass media reports. The struggle for control of Kochkonar Smelting continues, and it illustrates the vulnerability of many privatized firms whose basis for control can be questioned by a variety of interested parties who use privatization irregularities as a basis for their challenges.

It has been commonplace for disputes over property rights to entail charges that privatization procedures were not only questionable but even illegal. For example, in 1996 a Swiss company (Glencore) acquired substantial interest in the Mid-Urals Copper Processing Plant and succeeded in persuading other stockholders to join in implementing major changes in company policy—changes that were opposed by a Moscow company, also stockholders, who took their grievances to court. Glencore responded by arguing that the Moscow group had acquired their stock through illegal privatization procedures.[29]

The Mid-Urals case is indicative of the extent to which "credible commitments"[30] are widely lacking in the economic sphere. There are many others—some involving a high level of violence. Conflict over the control of aluminum is illustrative. Aluminum is a "hot" commodity in Sverdlovsk, and aluminum export is big business. A substantial percentage of aluminum is controlled in Russia by a small number of people who became owners through privatization that was surrounded by allegations of improprieties. There have been charges at both the federal and regional levels that the industry is being run by criminal groups. Charges and countercharges have circulated about criminal involvement in aluminum agreements. Urals Aluminum became a major Sverdlovsk player in this market, and two corporate investors began contending for dominance among Urals Aluminum's stockholders—Unona Trade, a Yekaterinburg firm, and a Russian-American joint venture, Renova-Invest. In April 1996, the director general of Urals Aluminum was killed, and there have been several replacement directors general since that time.[31]

The ongoing struggle for control within Urals Aluminum is connected to a broader conflict among groups that are contending for dominance in the aluminum exporting business. While Aleksei Strakhov was head of administration in Sverdlovsk, a dispute arose over a decision by the oblast property management committee to turn over state-owned aluminum shares to a half-private/half-state company that the committee itself had participated in creating. Rossel objected to this action and promised that if he were elected governor, the property management committee's decision would be reversed. Aluminum was one among many issues involving competing property claims during the campaign—one punctuated by "a whole series of killings and attempts," which ultimately led to a warning from the regional branch of the Department of Internal Affairs to both Rossel and Strakhov of "the possibility of provocation and illegal methods against both candidates and their relatives." Bodyguards were offered to the candidates and also their families as "special safety measures."[32]

THE REASSERTION OF EXECUTIVE POWER

In Sverdlovsk, not only have a number of stockholders in different firms questioned various aspects of privatization, and through that strategy attempted to gain advantage over other stockholders, but the governor has also threatened to renationalize enterprises. Following Rossel's victory over Strakhov in August 1995, Gennady Burbulis's center *Strategiya* charged that Rossel's "coming back into power threatens the oblast with serious problems, because now, unavoidably, will start a new round of property redistribution." Charging that Rossel was tightly connected with trade in nonferrous metals, *Strategiya* analysts stated that "now, Rossel will try to reestablish his former system and `his' firms—and will use in the process all kinds of methods, including force."[33] On the day after Rossel's victory was announced (August 22, 1995), Rossel promised to initiate an investigation of "all the enterprises that were privatized from November 10, 1992 until August 22, 1995." Since winning a third term in office in August 1999, Rossel's activities in this area have intensified.

Land use issues are another example of the broad array of problems that center on property rights. In our study, one business person described the land use problem in Sverdlovsk this way: "When we ask about specific plots of land that we might be able to use, it seems as though here, as in the Klondike, everything has been appropriated but no one knows by whom. What we have to do in such a situation is figure out who has to be bought, to help us." Svetlana Glinkina, director of the Center for East European Studies in Moscow,[34] notes that "the picture of participation of particular groups of the population in privatization is extremely tangled. The vagueness of property relations creates additional openings for the [further] development of a shadow economy in Russia."[35]

Property rights issues provide an open door for executive intervention in enterprise administration. Rossel is just one of a number of regional leaders who has been unhappy with the loss of central control over enterprises that was signified by privatization and who has taken advantage of legal ambiguities to assert control in the economic sphere. Having begun serving his third term as governor in August 1999, Rossel was well positioned to extend executive oversight over a broad range of economic decisions. Soon, two new ministries were added to the oblast government that were intended to coordinate economic activities in metallurgy and natural resources. On January 13, 2000, the Sverdlovsk oblast government issued a decree recommending that, before directors general were removed from their positions in important enterprises, these plans be coordinated with the oblast administration. The decree specified that in cases involving a primary industry in a company town, the governor's approval would be required before a director general could be dismissed.[36]

Governmental involvement in enterprise activities now also includes a provision that oblast ministries and departments review reports that are required from enterprises detailing such dimensions of their operations as the volume of production, salary payments to employees, budgetary decisions, and productivity trends. Additionally, according to the Sverdlovsk deputy minister of economy and labor, German Terent'ev, major enterprises will be required by the oblast government to improve their profitability in the process of achieving their production goals. Where enterprises are unprofitable, managers will be required to improve performance.[37] These developments are clear steps toward reestablishing the type of governmental control over enterprises that characterized the Soviet system.

THE PRESERVATION OF MONOPOLISM

Capital can be used for either competitive or noncompetitive economic activities. In some ways, it tells analysts more about progress toward institutionalizing market arrangements than does the distinction between state and non-state ownership. In Russia, noncompetitive capital has two principal sources: resources that were under the jurisdiction of the former branch ministries in the Soviet Union, which were responsible for different production sectors, and money from noneconomic spheres such as the CPSU, KGB, Komsomol and criminal elements outside the state structure. Those who now control this capital, no matter what its source, pursue advantage for themselves and their organizations or groups in a corporatist context where they are either competing for benefits from the state or working to gain a measure of economic autonomy from the state.

The short-lived Urals Republic has been seen as an example of the latter strategy by a number of analysts and local business leaders.[38] More local autonomy would help local elites gain a larger measure of control over privatization and export-import operations, which are the most profitable spheres of economic activity in the region. Moscow's inability to restrict effectively administrative market activities regionally has made it possible for monopolistic practices at the regional level to flourish.

Although the Urals Republic initiative was unsuccessful, it has had clear political utility for a number of Sverdlovsk elites. This was just one strategy that officials have used, in the view of many, to further corporatist objectives. The most critical factor in facilitating officials' efforts to ensure that they would have authority in the economic sphere through the reforms was the fact that officials controlled key aspects of the privatization process itself from the beginning. Through this authority they were able to establish themselves as vital participants in the activities of privatizing enterprises, beginning, it is often alleged, with deals that were struck in the privatization process—deals that have directly benefited the officials, some have charged, and that often put new owners in the debt of these officials.

Governmental authorities in Sverdlovsk have been able to retain decision making power over a broad spectrum of resources and rights under their administrative control—thus ensuring their active participation in, and their indispensability to, the normal course of business activity. Officials are routinely involved in vital enterprise concerns. They grant licenses for access to valuable natural resources, such as metals and gems. They distribute state money to enterprises for the provision of needed products that will be sold in the region. They decide which enterprises will receive production subsidies and capital investment money from the state, which are available to some firms but are in short supply. Officials decide which businesses will be registered and which will be allowed to lease property (also which property, and for how much). State regulations permit the postponement of tax payments in some cases. Officials decide in which cases this benefit will be made available. It is often alleged that bribe-taking in this process is commonplace.

An illustrative example of how profitable economic activity in Sverdlovsk has often been kept within a circle of "insiders" can be seen in the operations of the Sverlovsk Oblast Trade Committee and the contracts it issues, and money it lends, to private suppliers of consumer goods. The interest rates for these loans are low—often about one-tenth the rates available from commercial banks. A loan from the Oblast Trade Committee, then, is a license to make profit. To obtain a loan, it is important to have connections —to be endorsed by an official who will make the necessary telephone call to the right trade committee representative—a requirement that often involves bribery and an exchange of various favors. Sometimes, the loans are not even used to purchase the consumer goods that were agreed to. The money can instead be deposited in commercial banks for a high rate of return, or used for other purposes. Variations of this process, which in different ways maintain barriers against competitiveness and give extraordinary advantage to insiders, are commonplace across the spectrum of economic relations in Sverdlovsk.[39]

CONCLUSION

We return to the three benchmarks we highlighted in the introduction—factors to facilitate assessment of progress toward democratization at the regional level. First, Is substantial movement evident in the Sverdlovsk region toward identifying and removing the authoritarian elements of the previous regime? Our findings indicate that rather than experiencing a decline in authoritarian tendencies, Sverdlovsk now has a variety of different groups that are striving for unchallenged power in both the economic and political spheres through alliance formation and action that often works more to circumvent and undermine democratic processes than to promote them. The bureaucratic elites who form the core of these groups do not hold exclusive power in their domains, but it is significant that they are now constrained neither by oversight of CPSU structures, as was the case in during the Soviet period, nor by a developed legal system and civil society, as is the case in Western democracies. Increasingly, they have also shaken off oversight at the federal level.

Are institutions being strengthened in the regions that facilitate open expression of complaints and concerns, and that ensure governmental responsiveness? Press freedom is declining, if our measure for that is intimidation of media personal and violence directed against them. On the other hand, it may be significant that in the August 1999 gubernatorial election in Sverdlovsk, second place went to Aleksandr Burkov, the leader of the movement "May" that appeared only the previous April.

That month, a group of activists who announced themselves as "The Movement for the Rights of Working People" seized the office of the head of administration of the city of Karpinsk. They held the mayor captive and stated that they would not leave the office or let the mayor go until salaries were paid of people employed by the state. Payments began to be processed in five days, and by mid-April groups of "May" appeared in thirty-five towns in the Sverdlovsk oblast. At the first conference of the movement in the spring, more than 2,000 people attended. Burkov, an oblast legislative assembly deputy and former chair of the Sverdlovsk Property Management Committee, was unanimously elected leader. His showing in the race for governor surprised nearly all outside political analysts and many others as well.[40] (In the runoff, he received 28 percent of the vote; Rossel got 63 percent.)

The ascendancy of "May" suggests that citizen apathy may not be as widespread as is often believed. (It is worth noting, however, that only 37.7 percent of the voters participated in the second round of the August election, and 41 percent voted in the first round.) Even more importantly, there is evidence that people now see themselves as being freer to express minority political views and to work toward political change than was the case throughout almost all of the Soviet period.

The third benchmark we presented concerns the adaptation of nongovernmental elites. Once a democratic government has been installed at the regional level, do regional elites outside the government change their beliefs and behaviors in ways that are consistent with the objective of consolidating democracy? We find scant evidence that such changes are widespread among Sverdlovsk nongovernmental elites. Rather, many of the most deeply implicated elites in criminality are seeking ways to become government officials themselves, having long been core members of clan structures that are dominated by officials. No trend presents a more pronounced barrier than this one to the consolidation of democracy in regional political structures and institutions.

For defining features of Soviet political and economic relations to be transcended, procedures are required that will pointedly begin reshaping the established institutions of reciprocity and reward in which the socialist culture of the USSR was grounded. As North has noted, in order for formal rules to function effectively, they need to be reinforced by informal norms to legitimate them.[41] North observes that scholars do not yet understand how to create successfully the informal norms that are needed, and he suggests, not without pessimism, that the most promising approach is to create the formal institutions that are needed in the hope that a gradual evolution of appropriate informal norms will follow.[42] One need only recall the 1936 Stalin constitution, however, and numerous other developments of a similar kind, to recognize the limited potential of de jure rules for changing de facto practices.

Ronald Coase and North are surely correct that we have inadequate knowledge about how, as Oliver Williamson phrases the problem, to "get the institutions right,"[43] but some key insights that have emerged from the literature would seem to have applicability to the Sverdlovsk case. Processually, "getting the institutions right" is not a matter of setting policies that are directed toward a predetermined structural arrangement. Ellen Immergut's observation that "the logics of [different] political systems make different sorts of behavior rational[44] is useful here. The point is that, in the matter of Russian institutional reform, internal logics are the most appropriate kinds. In this regard, Williamson recommends that "institutional economists [are] needed to do the archaeology of development and reform."[45] We agree, to a point. In the larger picture, although social institutions "can be transformed by politics,"[46] the creation of social capital is necessarily a decentralized undertaking—one more compatible with the "pattern of consensual gradual reform" of which James Millar writes[47] than of top-down radical change initiatives by elites.

Russia has a formidable challenge in addressing the current task. One might reasonably predict continuing reform failure in Russia, at least in the near term, following Lane's characterization of conditions for successful reform. (See chapter 1 in this volume.) The path-dependent approach would seem to reflect more accurately the Russian situation than the system-transfer approach, and the regional semi-autonomy that has prevailed in post-Soviet Russia shows few signs of strengthening pluralism. This is a stated justification for current efforts to reestablish vertical authority, of course. For this approach to have a chance of succeeding, there would need to be a clear and focused effort from the center to break the current pattern of path dependence. Effective coordination from the center that strengthened the rule of law could provide a concrete basis for the democratizing trend that has until now proven elusive in Russia.

NOTES

Work for this chapter was supported from funds provided by the National Council for Eurasian and East European Research, which, however, is not responsible for the contents or findings of this study. The authors are indebted to participants in the discussions on the "Legacy of State Socialism and the Future of Transformation" (30 March–1 April 2000, King's College, University of Cambridge) for a number of comments that were helpful in revising the chapter.

1. David Lane, "Trajectories of Transformation: Theories, Legacies and Outcomes."

2. Gretchen Casper and Michelle M. Taylor, *Negotiating Democracy: Transitions from Authoritarian Rule* (Pittsburgh: University of Pittsburgh Press, 1996), 2.

3. Casper and Taylor, *Negotiating Democracy*, 10.

4. John Mueller, *Capitalism, Democracy, and Ralph's Pretty Good Grocery* (Princeton: Princeton University Press, 1999), 273n.5. Mueller quotes Philippe Schmitter and Terry Lynn Karl, "What Democracy Is . . . And Is Not," *Journal of Democracy* 2 (Summer 1991), 83. Emphasis in the original. See also Richard Couto and Catherine S. Gutherie, *Making Democracy Work Better: Mediating Structures, Social Capital, and the Democratic Prospect* (Chapel Hill: University of North Carolina Press, 1999).

5. Mueller, *Capitalism, Democracy*, 141.

6. Nancy G. Bermeo, "Democracy and the Lessons of Dictatorship," *Comparative Politics* 24 (1992): 274. See also John Higley and Richard Gunther, eds., *Elites and Democratic Consolidation in Latin America and Southern Europe* (Cambridge: Cambridge University Press, 1992); Jack Knight, *Institutions and Social Conflict* (Cambridge: Cambridge University Press, 1992); and Casper and Taylor, *Negotiating Democracy*.

7. Michael McFaul, "Lessons from Russia's Protracted Transition from Communist Rule," *Political Science Quarterly* 114 (Spring 1999): 104.

8. Casper and Taylor, *Negotiating Democracy*, 13.

9. This development had held promise for impressive growth in social capital, and thus for improved societal efficiency in all spheres. (See Robert Putnam, *Making Democracy Work: Civic Traditions in Modern Italy* [Princeton: Princeton University Press, 1993], 167.) But Yeltsin's decisive turn away from broad democratization, once he took the initiative from Gorbachev and the CPSU leadership, brought an end to much of the optimism that Russia might soon begin shedding the pattern of strong-arm rule that had long characterized Russian society. These events have also had a striking effect on individual political behavior, as people have turned away in large numbers from the civic activity that had mushroomed in Russia beginning in the 1980s.

10. See, for example, "Initsiativa, organizovannost', effektivnost'," *Pravda*, no. 102 (12 April 1985): 1 (speech by M. S. Gorbachev). See also "O sozyve ocherednogo XXVII s"ezda KPSS i zadachakh, sviazannykh s ego podgotovkoi i provedeniem," *Pravda*, no. 114 (24 April 1985): 1 (speech by M. S. Gorbachev).

11. See Vladimir A. Lepekhin, *Lobbizm* (Moscow: Fond "IQ," 1995); and Ekspertnyi institut RSPP, *Lobbizm v Rossii: Etapy bol'shogo puti* (Moscow: Ekspertnyi institut, 1995).

12. See Simon Kordonsky, "Tenevaya ekonomika v tenevom obshchestve: transformatsii administrativnogo rynka," *Predely vlasti* 4 (1994): 102–32.

13. Lynn D. Nelson and Irina Y. Kuzes, "Russian Economic Reform and the Restructuring of Interests," *Demokratizatsiya: The Journal of Post-Soviet Democratization* 6 (Summer 1998): 480–503.

14. Douglass C. North, *Institutions, Institutional Change and Economic Performance* (New York: Cambridge University Press, 1990), 90.

15. North, *Institutions, Institutional Change and Economic Performance*, 96.

16. Putnam, *Making Democracy Work*, 146.

17. Grigory Yavlinsky, et al. *500 days: Transition to the Market*, English translation edited by David Kushner (New York: St Martin's Press, 1991), 128.

18. Yavlinsky, et al., 131.

19. Oliver E. Williamson, *The Mechanisms of Governance* (New York: Oxford University Press, 1996), 97–103; also see Lepekhin, *Lobbizm*, 25–26; and Ekspertnyi institut, *Lobbizm v Rossii*.

20. See Sergei Roshchin, "Metastazy is proshlogo," *Yekaterinburgskaya nedelya* (special edition; 15 August 1995): 2; Viktor Smirnov and Elena Kotel'nikova, "Ural stremitsya vesti sobstvennuyu investitsionnuyu politiku," *Kommersant-daily*, 148 (6 August 1993): 3; and Lidiya Malash, "Yekaterinburg polozhil Moskvu," *Megapolis-express*, no. 48 (8 December 1993): 11.

21. Nelson and Kuzes, "Russian Economic Reform and the Restructuring of Interests."

22. Then the city of Sverdlovsk.

23. Viacheslav B. Zhitenev, "Yekaterinburg na poroge rynochnykh reform" (Yekaterinburg, 1992), 33.

24. Nelson and Kuzes, "Interest Representation in Sverdlovsk," 231.

25. Gavriil Popov, *Avgust devianosto pervogo* (Moscow, 1992), 3–4. Reprinted from *Izvestiya*, no. 189–192 (August 1992).

26. L. Kolbina, "Anton Bakov: `Ia zhdu provokatsyi,'" *Uralsky rabochy*; M. Smyshlyaev, "Serov razocharovalsya v Pitere," *Ural'sky rabochy*; B. Tumofeev, "S parlamentskoy delikatnost'yu," *Ural'sky rabochy*; L. Kolbina, "Bakov s zavoda uekhal," *Ural'sky rabochy*; L. Kolbina, "Rabochaya pauza v bor'be," *Ural'sky rabochy*; M. Smyshlyaev, "Protivostoyanie stanovitsia vooruzhennym," *Ural'sky rabochy*; M. Smyshlyaev "Bor'ba na kovre i pod kovrom," *Ural'sky rabochy*. All of the cited articles were published between April and June 1997. Available at www.ur.etel.ru.

27. Svetlana Dobrynina, "Zakhvat zavoda v Serove," Nezavisimaya Gazeta (6 October 1999). Accessed at http://www.ng.ru/events/1999-10-06/factory.html. URL verified November 12, 1999. It is no longer accessible.

28. Letter to V. V. Putin, G. H. Seleznev and V. B. Rushailo, 15 March 2000. Accessed at http://may.uralmet.com.

29. V. Terletsky, "Fars ili tragediya?" *Ural'sky rabochy* (May 1997). Available at www.ur.etel.ru.

30. Oliver E. Williamson, *The Mechanisms of Governance*, 26–27.

31. L. Shapovalova, "Nakonets-to poladili," *Ural'sky rabochy* (June 1997); "Baykal'sky fondovyi dom" (1 November 1999). Accessed at http://www.bfh.esib.ru/EMTNTS/sual.htm. URL verified November 12, 1999. It is no longer accessible.

32. We have independent information about these developments. See also Natalya Bibneva, "Eksperimental'naya burya," *Moskovskie novosti* 56 (20–27 August 1995): 7.

33. See Elena Tregubova, "'Otets Ural'skoi respubliki' vernul sebe gubernatorskyi post," *Obshchaya gazeta*, no. 157 (22 August 1995): 1.

34. The Center for European Studies is a part of the Institute for International Economic and Political Studies of the Russian Academy of Sciences.

35. Svetlana Glinkina, "Tenevaya ekonomika v sovremennoy Rossii," *Svobodnaya mysl'*, no. 3 (1995): 37. See also Svetlana Glinkina, "K voprosu o kriminalizatsii rossiiskoi ekonomiki, *Politekonom*, no. 1 (1997): 49–51.

36. Svetlana Dobrynina, "Khozyain-Barin: Po etomu printsipu zhivet Sverdlovskaya oblast'," Nezavisimaya Gazeta, no. 2 (25 January 2000). Accessed at http://regions.ng.ru/gubern/2000-01-25/3_hostishost.html. URL verified March 20, 1999.

37. Svetlana Dobrynina, "Khozyain-Barin."

38. Nelson and Kuzes, "Interest Representation in Sverdlovsk," 229.

39. See Nelson and Kuzes, "Interest Representation in Sverdlovsk."

40. Svetlana Dobrynina, "'Tret'ya sila' rvetsya k vlasti," *Nezavisimaya gazeta* (31 August 1999). Accessed at http://www.ng.ru/politics/1999-08-31/3sila.html (URL verified November 12, 1999. It is no longer accessible); and Svetlana Dobrynina, "Narod khochet chuda," *Nezavisimaya gazeta* (1 September 1999). Accessed at http://www.ng.ru/politics/1999-09-01/narod_hochet.html. URL verified March 20, 1999.

41. Douglass C. North, *Institutions, Institutional Change and Economic Performance* (New York: Cambridge University Press, 1990), 40.

42. Peter Stavrakis, Jodi Koehn and Nancy Popson, Notes on "Civil Society, Social Capital, and Development in Eurasia": A Kennan Institute Roundtable on 6 December 1996, "Meeting Report: Kennan Institute for Advanced Russian Studies" 14 (Nos. 11 and 12, 1997).

43. Williamson, *The Mechanisms of Governance*, 324; Ronald Coase, "The Institutional Structure of Production," *American Economic Review* 82 (September 1992): 714; and Douglass North, "Economic Performance through Time," American Economic Review 84 (June 1994): 366.

44. Ellen Immergut, "The Theoretical Core of the New Institutionalism" 26, 1 (March 1998): 12.

45. Williamson, "The Institutions and Governance of Economic Development and Reform," 193.

46. Immergut, "The Theoretical Core of the New Institutionalism," 17.

47. James R. Millar, "From Utopian Socialism to Utopian Capitalism: The Failure of Revolution and Reform in Post-Soviet Russia," *Problems of Postcommunism* (May/June 1995): 14.

6

Institutional and Political Legacies of the Socialist Welfare State

Linda J. Cook

The Soviet welfare state was designed for a low-wage, full-employment, relatively egalitarian socioeconomy in which the state dominated all allocations. The state provided for basic needs and social security through a broad system of universal, employment-linked, categorical, privileged, and special social benefits that extended throughout society. These included: deep and nearly universal subsidies for housing, health care, and education; a broad system of retirement and disability pensions, sickness, maternity, and child benefits; and special privileges for veterans, civil servants, and many other population categories.

Most of the population, including both broad social strata and elites, had some claim to benefits and thus a vested interest in the Soviet-era welfare state. The system was undergirded by nearly full employment, which tied households into the structures of benefit provision. The payments and services provided by the Soviet welfare state were quite poor and inadequate by Western standards. In the relative freedom of the Gorbachev period Soviet academic experts as well as the mass public criticized its quality, organization, and low expenditure levels. It nevertheless provided a measure of social security that was valued by the population.

This inherited welfare state is no longer sustainable for Russia: the decade-long decline in GDP, government spending and the wage bill have gutted the real value of benefits and rendered tax-based social insurance funds insolvent. The structure of the old benefit system is in any case poorly adapted to the welfare needs of the present Russian socioeconomy, which features significant levels of unemployment and high levels of poverty and inequality. Russia's market-oriented reformers and their international advisors have articulated a powerful critique of the inherited welfare state, arguing that its benefits are neither justified, affordable, nor effective in alleviating poverty in the present

Russian context, that they make no sense for the prosperous, provide too little for the needy, are often regressive in their effects on income distribution, and frequently go unpaid, helping no one. These reformers have sought to streamline and rationalize the old welfare state, remaking it in the liberal image.[1] They have proposed the following reforms:

1. eliminate all universal entitlements (subsidies and transfer payments) and replace them with a system of means-tested benefits targeted on the poor and sufficient to alleviate poverty;
2. restrict eligibility, cut payments, and eliminate Soviet-era privileges from all benefit programs;
3. replace state-funding and provision of benefits with private insurance and market-based provision for all but the poor;
4. privatize most social assets and services and move toward full cost recovery for all subsidized services and social goods.

The present chapter argues that the old welfare state has left a legacy of entrenched interests, legal entitlements, institutional practices and attitudes that have proven resistant to such reform efforts. It follows the path-dependent approach set out in David Lane's introductory chapter, showing that embedded institutions, socially based norms, and inherited expectations have substantially shaped the process of Russian social policy reform, and have limited attempts to transfer or transplant Western institutions and policies even when the old system is clearly dysfunctional. It adds to the path-dependent argument the claim that, along with inherited institutions, inherited institutional deficits have also limited reform possibilities and outcomes. And it shows that divisions within the postcommunist elite on the virtues of the socialist welfare state—between reformers in the government seeking to dismantle it and a Communist-dominated Duma majority seeking to preserve—have been a major obstacle to reform.

THE INHERITANCE

The new Russian state inherited a legacy of expectations, attitudes, ways of operating, on the part of both the population and the political establishment, that has helped sustain the old welfare policies. The Russian population emerged from the Soviet period expecting that the state should provide for basic needs—employment, housing, health care, etc. This expectation was complemented by an orientation toward basic provision through much of the political establishment that has often undermined the implementation of welfare cuts. Thus, many Russians have continued to rely on state-provided services even when given incentives to act independently, while officials have often continued to provide services even when recipients fail to make newly mandated payments.

On the other hand, "traditional" conceptions of the needy and deserving from the Soviet period (i.e., single-parent families, the elderly, war veterans) have led officials to continue providing for these groups while ignoring the groups of "new poor" that have emerged in the market economy.

Secondly, Russia's broad-provisioned past is embedded in a complex system of laws and legislation that guarantees hundreds of general and specific benefits to various groups in society. To reform the system legally requires changes in all of these laws, each imposing a cost on some group, and each requiring approval from a legislature that has been hostile to welfare state reform for much of the period under review. By the time neoliberal reformers turned to rationalizing and streamlining the welfare state in the mid-1990s the Communist-led left had gained enough political support to dominate the Duma. Programmatically committed to the inherited system and dependent on the older and poorer sectors of the population for its political support, the Communist Party of the Russian Federation (CPRF) rejected in principle any decrease in welfare entitlements, blocked most reform efforts from 1995–1999, and sought to restore and extend spending according to old patterns.[2] Despite the general weakness of Russian civil society some beneficiary groups, especially veterans and pensioners, also mobilized to lobby, protest, and sue in court to defend established benefits. Municipalities, enterprises, and other organizations pressed for the continuation of benefits that cushioned the impacts of reform on their hard-pressed residents and unpaid workers.

As a consequence, most of the government's efforts at legislative reform of the social sector have failed. A broad-scope effort in 1997 to change the basis of social payments from universalism to means-testing met nearly total rejection from all parties. Piecemeal efforts at reform in various areas have bogged down in legislative bargaining or in bureaucratic conflict within government ministries, where there remains much residual commitment to the old system. In the face of opposition and continued economic decline the government often withdrew its proposals or conceded legislative defeat. Legislative changes that have passed are much more likely to shift responsibilities or supplement existing entitlements with new insurance and savings schemes, than to eliminate benefits. In sum, much of the legislative basis of the old welfare state remains in place.

In addition to this legacy of entrenched interests and entitlements, liberal reformers have confronted a set of "institutional deficits" that impede their efforts. The Soviet state recognized neither poverty nor unemployment, and had no administrative mechanism to cope with either. It provided no guaranteed income or income floor; according to McAuley's classic study, in the Soviet period "public assistance, or minimal financial aid to those who do not fit into one of the benefit categories but are still without means of support, was almost entirely lacking."[3] Secondly, those benefits (pensions, sickness and maternity) funded by wage taxes were paid from a collective pool rather than individual accounts, and direct provision of all types of benefits often took place at or through the workplace. Thus the new Russian state was left with few administrative structures that it could use for means-testing, tracking social security contributions, or distributing benefits independently of employing enterprises.

The following sections of this chapter present case studies of social policy in three areas: housing, pensions, and poverty. Each examines the legacy of the old welfare state in the reform period, focusing on how entrenched interests, legal entitlements, political opposition, and institutional deficits have shaped policy and largely frustrated neoliberal intentions in the first post-Soviet decade.

THE SOCIALIST LEGACY AND THE LIMITS OF HOUSING REFORM

In 1991 most of Russia's housing was owned and heavily subsidized by the state.[4] Though there was some private housing in smaller cities and rural areas and a tiny cooperative sector, 65 percent of the total housing stock and almost 78 percent of urban stock was controlled by either municipalities or state enterprises, divided about equally between the two.[5] Municipalities and enterprises in turn allocated the housing and subsidized its maintenance and operations. Citizens obtained housing from waiting lists. Waits were long and shortages endemic, but once residents got apartments they enjoyed very strong tenancy rights, including lifetime occupancy, rights to inherit and lease, and the near-impossibility of eviction. Payments for housing were nominal: maintenance charges, at a flat rate per square meter, had not been raised since 1928, and while utility charges had increased somewhat, both remained far below real costs. When prices were liberalized in 1992 rents remained frozen, while maintenance and utility costs rose dramatically. The cost of universal housing subsidies skyrocketed, becoming a huge burden for municipal budgets, accounting for some 30 percent of total outlays, and a serious obstacle to enterprise profitability.[6] Housing became the first social policy area slated for comprehensive reform.

The Reform Program

The reform program, proposed by the Russian government with advice from the World Bank and the Washington-based Urban Institute, had four major components:

1. Enterprises were to divest all their housing to municipalities, with residents remaining in place, and the financial burden of maintenance temporarily transferred to the receiving municipality.
2. Municipalities would privatize most housing to residents. Most Russians

could simply apply to privatize their housing for a nominal fee. As a large majority of urban Russians live in multiunit apartment houses, reformers anticipated that after privatization residents would form condominiums to manage and maintain their buildings, and that these would become the dominant form of housing organization. But for a transitional period, as buildings were privatized unit by unit, new owners would normally bear no additional costs except a small property tax. In order to avoid creating financial disincentives to privatization, municipalities would continue to subsidize maintenance and utilities for privatized units at the same level as nonprivatized.

3. Rent Reform: Housing maintenance and utility charges would be raised gradually to achieve full cost recovery from residents. Legislation provided that tenants who fell six months behind in payments could be evicted to dormitory-type housing.[7] This was the linchpin of reform: payments by residents would replace the present, universal subsidies. The government would also try to remove the myriad "privileged" housing subsidies inherited from Soviet days. Costs to residents would rise to about five times their 1992 level over a five-year period, financed by a presumed growth in incomes.

4. A system of targeted housing allowances, for households that had to pay more than 15–20 percent of their income for the "social norm" of housing, would accompany rent reform and replace the existing universal subsidies.

The Russian government developed its housing reform program in 1992, when neither the left nor beneficiaries had yet mobilized on social reform issues.[8] More specific measures were put into place by governmental and presidential decrees in 1993 and 1994. Reformers assumed that most Russians would quickly take private ownership of their housing, as there was virtually no cost and the benefits included rights to sell, lease, use as security for a loan, and will. They saw reform as the first step to creating a middle class that owned real assets, while gradually relieving the state and municipalities of a major, regressive, inherited subsidy burden. In essence, they and their international advisors sought to remake the socialist housing sector in the image of a U.S. market based on private ownership, full cost-recovery rents, means-tested benefits for the poor, and a residual public sector.[9]

These policies did result in the privatization of about one-half of Russia's housing, an incipient housing market in large cities, and a higher but still far from full level of rent recovery.[10] But these changes do not constitute the kinds of deep structural transformations and reallocations of financial responsibility that were intended. Rather, the outcome thus far owes much more to the legacies, both institutional and attitudinal, of the old welfare state.

The Legacy of Interests

As the reform began to create costs and benefits, vested interests and institutions within Russia reacted, selectively supporting and opposing various elements. The post-1995 Duma majority claimed commitment to housing as a "public good" and opposed increases in rent and utility payments. Since some increases had already been mandated, it took measures that shielded parts of the population from the effects. Housing privileges, for veterans, various categories of civil servants and others, usually provided as an exemption from a percentage of charges, were entrenched in Soviet-era legislation. When reform began to push up housing charges, these groups lobbied to protect and extend their privileges and the Duma cooperated, passing the Law on Veterans, which increased the share of families receiving housing privileges, and rejecting government proposals that would have reduced privileges for civil servants.[11] Local governments also reportedly added privileges. It is difficult to judge their cumulative size, but various sources estimate that from 25 percent to as many as 50 percent of Russian households received some privileges, significantly undercutting the key reformist effort to raise rents and provide relief to municipal budgets.[12] Municipalities also resisted reform, sometimes refusing to take over housing divested from enterprises, cutting deals that required enterprises to continue subsidies.

The Legacy of Entitlement

Despite the provisions of reform, a large part of the Russian population, as well as municipal authorities that directly administer the housing sector, continued to treat housing as an entitlement for which public authorities bear responsibility. About half of eligible Russians declined even the virtually free privatization of their apartments, preferring to rely on a legacy of strong tenancy rights thus leaving a large public housing sector (see table 6.1). Most who did privatize failed to form condominiums, leaving management and maintenance of their buildings to the state. Most who cannot pay the newly assessed rents are simply left in their apartments. In at least some municipalities households experiencing wage, pension, or benefit arrears, which have been large-scale and persistent, can delay rent payments without penalty. A 1998 VTsIOM (All-Union Center for the Study of Public Opinion) survey found that most workers with wage arrears have housing debts, and these are apparently tolerated.[13] Most importantly, eviction, which has been legalized as a sanction for nonpayment, is rarely used. While there is anecdotal evidence of evictions from highly desirable housing in major cities, one study concluded, "As to the legal possibility of eviction to dormitory housing for rent arrears of more than six months, local authorities avoid its use in every possible way."[14] Even offi-

Table 6.1.   Municipal Housing Privatization in the Russian Federation, 1992–1999

	1992	*1995*	*1999*
Cumulative municipal housing privatized[a] as percent of total municipal stock	8.2	35.9	45

Sources: T. D. Belkina, *Zhilishchnaya reforma v Rossii: Problemy i perspektivy* (Moscow: TACIS, 1999); Raymond Struyk, *Restructuring Russia's Housing Sector: 1991–1997* (Washington, D.C.: Urban Institute, 1997); German Gref, "Proekt Strategiia Rossiiskoi Federatsii do 2010 goda. Fond "Tsentr Strategicheskikh Razrabotok 2000g, accessed at: www.kommersant.ru/documents/Strat1.ht\.

[a]In 1999 privatized housing, combined with housing that was already private or cooperative, equaled about 60 percent of the entire housing stock.

cially the poor are guaranteed the "social norm" of housing at a set percentage of their income.

Housing Allowances and Institutional Deficits

Beginning in 1994 many Russian cities introduced federally mandated housing allowances for all households that had to spend more than 15–20 percent of their income on housing as rents increased. It was questioned whether a means-tested program would work in Russia—that many households with informal and unrecorded incomes would apply, and authorities would prove unable to assess their eligibility.[15] In fact, most with informal incomes preferred not to risk scrutiny, especially as benefits at this stage were quite modest. The larger problem was finding the truly eligible, and the cost and difficulty of setting up administrative bodies and procedures to accomplish this. Application rates remained well below expectations, with 6–10 percent of households receiving benefits in cities studied and roughly twice as many eligible. The start-up and staffing costs to run a means-testing program in every Russian municipality, even one with sophisticated selective verification methods imported from "best case" Western practice, has to be taken into account here.

In sum, though reform achieved more in the housing sector than elsewhere, residual tenancy rights remained far stronger than market mechanisms in allocating Russia's housing. Even after reform, many residents and local authorities continued to regard housing as a right and not a market commodity. Despite severe decline in GDP, productivity and incomes, most Russians were housed largely as they were before reform, whether or not they could pay. Subsidies by municipalities and enterprises, both open and hidden, continue to make the major contribution to housing maintenance. But the current situation is not sustainable. The financial burden on municipal governments is tremendous, and sources agree that deferred maintenance has reached critical dimensions, that housing has deteriorated and utility networks become degraded, often to dangerous levels. In a critical sense, no matter how ownership and payment are

structured, Russia cannot afford to maintain the housing and utilities infrastructure it has inherited.

THE SOCIALIST LEGACY AND
THE FAILURES OF PENSION REFORM

Russia inherited from the Soviet Union a pension system characterized by broad
coverage of the population and liberal eligibility requirements, combined with
relatively low payment levels. Coverage extended to all civilian state employees,
disabled workers and dependents, with separate provisions for collective farm-
ers, civil servants and the military. Given virtually full employment in the Soviet
economy and the extremely high labor force participation rates for both men and
women, coverage was nearly universal by the end of the Soviet period. Moreover
the retirement age—at 60 for men and 55 for women—was low by the standards
of industrial societies and subject to a great many privileged exceptions, and
"nonworking" periods spent in higher education, military service and maternity
leave to raise a child under 3 years, were counted toward pension eligibility.
Though historically funded from the state budget, the pension system was transferred to a predominantly payroll tax base in 1991, with revenues generated by
a 29 percent wage tax paid almost entirely by employers and accumulated in an
extra-budgetary Pension Fund.[16] In 1992 more than 35 million people, almost
one-fourth of the Russian population, received pensions, making the Pension
Fund the most important social safety net program.[17] Both the liberal rules for
general eligibility and the various privileged exceptions formed a legacy of entitlements that was embedded in Soviet-era legislation and in the assumptions
and expectations of Russia's population.

In the reform period the tax base of this Pay-As-You-Go (PAYG) system has
suffered deep erosion, corporate entities engage in large-scale tax evasion and
have accumulated catastrophic debts to the Pension Fund, large numbers
work in an untaxed second economy, the payer-recipient ratio has worsened
significantly, and the Pension Fund has come to be broadly perceived as non-
transparent and unaccountable. The results have been structural deficits in
the Pension Fund, large-scale arrears in payments to pensioners, pensions paid
at poverty levels and below, and a compression of payment levels that dis-
courages contributions.[18]

Beginning in 1995 the Russian government introduced several initiatives to
reform this system, all taking one of three basic approaches to the problem: (1)
reduce established benefits and/or restrict eligibility to them; (2) create incentives for legal employment and pension contributions so that more money would
flow into the present, state-run, PAYG system; (3) transfer more or less of pension provision from the public/state sphere to individual savings and financial
markets. Reformist governments have proposed various combinations of these

solutions, producing conflicts with the Duma, with mobilized groups of pensioners, and within the government, but failing so far to implement any solutions to these problems. The next sections of this chapter analyze the reasons for these failures, focusing on the role of vested interests, institutional deficits, and the legacies of solidarity and equality that have both limited policy change and determined the allocation of existing resources.

Vested Interests and the Obstacles to Short-Term Reform

First, reform officials sought to change the rules (or parameters) of entitlement to pensions in Russia, in order to provide immediate fiscal relief to the pension system. They targeted the liberal eligibility rules and special benefits, bonuses, and privileges inherited from the Soviet period, proposing changes that, inter alia, would: raise the retirement age; restrict rights to early retirement; cut or eliminate payments to Russia's 7 million "working pensioners"; eliminate privileged pensions for those who worked in dangerous jobs, harsh climates, etc., and suspend long-term service payments. In return, they promised timely payment of pensions and an increase in the minimum sufficient to pull the poorest out of poverty. From the rationalizing perspective of Russian reformers these changes would bring the system closer to fiscal balance and social justice, providing at least short-term relief for the Pension Fund while taking benefits from younger and more able-bodied pensioners and channeling them to the most needy.

Although some have been proposed repeatedly, not one of these measures has passed into law. Both their design and scope contributed to their failure. As we know from other studies of welfare state retrenchment,[19] such immediate and visible benefit cuts are the most difficult politically, and the reformers' broad forays into the entitlements of different subgroups of pensioners spread the damage and eliminated possibilities for divide-and-conquer policy strategies. In any case the political realities of Russia doomed short-term reform proposals that imposed visible costs on pensioners. The Communist-led left-wing majority that dominated the Duma promised to reject any diminution in pensioners' welfare rights, and kept issues of low pension levels and arrears near the top of the political agenda. The lower house also blocked the government's repeated attempts to change the pension contribution formula, refusing to shift even a modest share of the burden from enterprises to employees.[20] In the words of a knowledgeable World Bank official who was deeply involved in Russian pension reform, "good intentions are stranded at the door of the Duma."[21]

The proposed reforms also generated opposition from pensioners' and veterans' organizations, trade unions, and industrial managers. Veterans' organizations, particularly the large Union of Veterans, reportedly lobbied the legislature daily on pension and other issues. Its leadership included many former high-ranking military officers whose links with current leaders contributed to its effectiveness.[22] Pensioners' organizations generally opposed cuts, distrusted the government's pleas of insufficient funds, in some cases convinced that large amounts were mismanaged or stolen.[23] Pensioners also used the press, producing an outcry over proposed benefit cuts that frequently led the government to back down. Trade unions spoke against the reforms. Overall, according to a range of experts, short-term, highly visible pension benefit cuts were simply "politically unacceptable" in the face of the constituencies created by past policy commitments, even though leaving the existing system in place guaranteed pensioners relatively little in the face of declining real pensions, compression and arrears.

Compromise Legislation and Institutional Deficits

The government did manage to generate, and pass through the legislature in 1996–98, several important pieces of pension reform legislation. These avoided the politically unpopular approaches of reducing benefits and restricting eligibility and instead sought to change incentives, shift responsibilities, and expand the possibilities for pension savings, in order to increase the inflow of money and lessen the burden on the general fund. Legislation on personal or individual pension accounts was designed to provide incentives for contributions and longer labor force participation, without requiring later retirement. Legislation on individual coefficients was to bring pension levels more in line with past contributions.[24] While the Duma passed these measures, usually in exchange for substantial side payments, the intended effects of these measures were largely undermined by inherited institutional deficits and continued challenges.

The Russian state could not, in fact, create individual pension accounts because it lacked the capacity to track individual contributions; in the existing system, managements simply contributed (when they did) for the labor collective. In 1995 the Russian government, with World Bank assistance, had just begun to establish a system for individual tracking.[25] It could not bring pension levels in line with past contributions, partly because groups that would lose from the exclusion of "nonworking periods" protested in public and in the courts, to some effect. Faced with claims that people had based their life decisions about work, education and child bearing on the system's provisions, Labor Minister Dmitrieva conceded that it was unfair to change the rules retroactively, and pensioners who so chose were exempted from the new rules on individual coefficients.[26]

The Legacies of Solidarity and Equality

In the spring of 1997 pension reform gained new momentum. A group of "young reformers" was brought into the social ministries of Russia's government and set out to move Russia's main system of pension provision away from public financing and solidaristic (i.e., PAYG) principles toward private, funded (or accumulative) schemes, shifting responsibility from collective/public and state to individual and market. The man placed in charge of pension reform, Minister of Labor and Social Development Mikhail Dmitriev, favored a radical version of reform. Dmitriev, impressed by the Chilean success with raising pensions through market investment and convinced that the Russian system must be divorced from politics, proposed that Russia transfer most age cohorts to individual financing of pensions through funded schemes within several months. All those participating in funded schemes would lose their right to draw a state pension, while the state would aid only the destitute.[27] The nearly total rejection of Dmitriev's proposals by the then-reformist Russian government shows the limits of acceptable reform, and the intense debate surrounding it give evidence of the normative as well as institutional legacies of the old system

Critics of Dmitriev's plan, from among both academic specialists and government, argued that under current conditions it would abandon large numbers of future pensioners to poverty and further exacerbate the deep inequalities and growing stratification in Russian society. Many workers, they argued, could not afford to save for retirement at current wage levels, and would be left without pension security. Women, with lower wages and longer life spans, would see their pensions drop from the present near-equality with men's to less than half. There were also practical objections, and bureaucratic politics and conservatism played a part: Dmitriev's commission bypassed both the Labor Ministry and the Pension Fund, antagonizing their leaders even as his proposals threatened their vested interests in running the present pension system. But there was at base a broad normative consensus against abandoning the redistributive and solidaristic elements of Russia's pension system in the face of current realities, voiced by officials from the Labor Ministry, the Pension Fund, the executive branch, specialists and advisors.[28] According to one participant in the pension reform discussions, "Everyone criticized Dmitriev—the government, the Ministry of Labor. The main criticism was that the accumulative system doesn't protect the poorest . . . and must be softened . . . that the mentality of the Russian people is accustomed to security. Dmitriev was almost alone in his support for the pure accumulative system."[29]

In the event, the reform commission was broadened and a compromised draft produced that combined distributive and accumulative principles (PAYG and funded components) and published as an official government Pension Reform Program in the spring of 1998.[30] The August 1998 crisis brought an end to efforts at systemic reform, throwing the system back an ad hoc financing measures and pushing even average pensions below the subsistence minimum (see table 6.2). The table also illustrates the legacy of egalitarianism in Russian pension policy. Faced with large fiscal deficits, the government made a decision to keep average pensions above the subsistence minimum, even when this required a compression of pension levels that hurt the higher income and encouraged their defection from the pension system. In the wake of the August crisis pension levels in Russia became virtually flat, though all governments have maintained a verbal commitment to differentiation. Pension reform efforts have been revived by the Putin government.

THE SOCIALIST LEGACY AND POVERTY POLICY

The past decade has brought a sharp increase in the incidence and severity of poverty in the Russian Federation. Though the precise figures are disputed, we can reliably estimate that about 11 percent of the Russian population lived in poverty during the last Soviet decade (1980–90), while approximately one-third of the population is currently poor.[31] The overall economic decline, the emergence of unemployment and the reduction and differentiation of incomes are major causes of poverty, but they are not the whole story. The broad array of welfare policies and entitlements that were inherited by the Russian state have "locked in" much social spending to old patterns that provide little to the newly poor. And those programs put into place during the 1990s to deal with growing poverty and unemployment have been both under funded and often poorly administered.

The groups most at risk for poverty in Russia are children and the unemployed and their households. Over the decade poverty has increasingly concentrated in families, especially young, single-parent, and multichild families. Both official and alternate statistics show extremely high rates. According to Goskhomstat, in 1997 over 38 percent, and in 1998 over 45 percent of families with children under 16 were poor; in families with three or more children the numbers rose to 57 percent and 69 percent and in single-parent, mainly female-headed families to almost 63 percent (see table 6.3) The risk of poverty, extreme and/or chronic, increases with each subsequent child; in 1998, 75 percent of the "very poor" consisted of households with either children or children and elderly.[32] The problem is particularly stark because the effects of early deficits on children's development tend to be long-term and irreversible. Russian children have experi-

Table 6.2.   Average and Minimum Pension as Percent of Pensioners' Subsistence Minimum

	1992	1993	1994	1995	1996	1997	1998	1999
Average[a] pension	116.9	138.1	128.6	101	116.0	113	114	70
Minimum[a] pension (est.)		70	75	45				

Sources: For average pensions, 1992-97, *Statisticheskii Biulleten*, No. 3(42), Goskomstat, June 1998, p. 149; for 12/98, *Statisticheskoe obozrenie*, No. 1(28), 1999, Goskomstat, p. 15; minimum pensions are estimated from: *Russian Federation: Toward Medium-Term Viability*, p. 68.
[a]With compensation payments.

enced substantially increased rates of undernourishment, stunted growth, disease, family breakdown and abandonment to institutions and the street.

Unemployment is a major cause of poverty.[33] According to official statistics, almost 54 percent of households with an unemployed member or members was poor in 1997, and over 58 percent in 1998 (see table 6.2). Almost two-thirds of households headed by an unemployed member were poor in the mid-1990s, and almost half of these very poor.[34] There has been a steady increase in the duration of unemployment and in the correlation between unemployment and persistent or stagnant poverty. Moreover, while the overall rate of open recorded unemployment in Russia, about 11 percent, is not especially high by international standards, regional disparities are large and increasing, creating pockets of joblessness and poverty.

While unemployment produces a shock toward poverty, the largest emergent strata of poor in Russia are the "working poor." A new class of poor families with two working adults whose combined earnings are insufficient to provide for one or two dependents, sometimes referred to as the "new poor," comprise about 20 percent of households in poverty. A combination of low wages (the minimum wage in Russia is set at less than 20 percent of the subsistence level), involuntary leaves, enforced short-time work and wage arrears account for the growing incidence of poverty among the employed. The working poor are at a particular disadvantage because they do not fit either old or new categories for benefit eligibility, and they are generally ignored by local social assistance workers.[35] Russian poverty is also significantly feminized; women, as single heads of households, low-paid workers, and elderly, are disproportionately affected.[36] Worst off are the ranks of homeless, vagrants, prisoners, deinstitutionalized and refugees, including Russian immigrants from the Near Abroad.

Soviet Legacies

Poverty in Russia is exacerbated by the distribution of social expenditures. Most of the state's declining welfare resources continue to be allocated to pre-reform subsidy and entitlement programs. As a result, surveys show, most

Table 6.3.   Poverty Rates for Families with Children and Unemployed, Russian Federation

	Percent All Households	*Families with Children to 16 Years*	*Of These: 1–2 Children 3+*	*3+*	*Single Parent*	*Unemployed Member*
1997	25.7	38.3	36.8	57.4	41.5	53.8
1998	30.4	45.1	43.5	69.2	46.5	58.4
1999 (Q3)	41.9	57.8	—	—	62.7	—

Sources: Goskhomstat Rossii 1999, *Rossiiskii Statisticheskii Ezhegod' v Rossii* (Moscow: Ves', 2000).
Note: Data for single-parent households and for 1999 is for families with children under 18 years.

social spending goes to nonpoor households while the poor are disproportionately excluded. A recent Technical Assistance to the Commonwealth of Independent States (TACIS) study, for example, showed that three-fourths of all benefits go to households with incomes above the subsistence level, one-quarter to the poor. By comparison, OECD and some East European countries target as much as 50 percent of benefits to the poor.[37] Targeting in Russia is also less effective than in Latin American economies with large informal sectors. A separate study of locally administered social assistance found that about 13 percent of households received help, with almost no difference between the poor and nonpoor.[38]

Those benefits that do go to poor households, though often constituting a significant portion of their cash incomes, are generally paid at a fraction of the subsistence level, often in arrears, and fail to provide relief from poverty. Unemployment benefits, for example, generally amount to less than 20 percent of the subsistence level. Almost all the truly unemployed who receive these benefits have remained poor, and most of those with benefits as well as secondary employment are also poor.[39] Similarly child benefits (for children under 16 years) have been paid at less than 30 percent of the subsistence level, with months-long delays in some regions and de facto suspension of the benefit in others. Means-testing of child benefits was one of the few reform measures passed by the legislature, but implementation has proven complicated, and so far, changes have not made a significant difference in the welfare of families.[40]

Administrative inadequacies in the delivery of social assistance are also significant. Local social administrations in Russia generally lack the institutional capacity and expertise to run the kinds of means-tested poverty relief programs that have been promoted by Western advisors and international organizations and are developing these capacities slowly and at some expense. Verification of incomes and employment status are complicated in Russia's fluid economy, networks of employment service and social assistance offices are inadequate, and local application of federal rules is varied and often arbitrary. Benefit delivery systems simply fail to reach some of the poor.

A final factor contributing to poverty, though not strictly a legacy, is the decentralized system for financing and payment for social assistance benefits. Though some benefits are federally mandated and the federal government contributes to their financing, regional governments are ultimately responsible. In a country where territorial income differentials are large, the financial resources of local and regional social assistance offices differ greatly. Many of the poorest people live in regions with the greatest inadequacy of funds and the weakest administrative capacities, and suffer most from benefit arrears and nonpayment. According to a recent study: "strongly regionalized systems such as . . . the Russian display the tendency to exclude from access to social assistance households living in wrong regions . . . decentralized financing systemwhere territorial income differences are large . . . lead to large horizontal inequities" in treatment of people at the same income level.[41] Enterprises are also involved in direct provision of social benefits, and lower-income people are more likely to work at enterprises that have large wage and benefit arrears, while lower-skilled employees are more often subject to arrears. Overall, the system suffers from what one analyst has called a "fragmentation in access to benefits."[42]

CONCLUSION

My study of Russian welfare state reform efforts provides strong evidence for a path-dependent approach to transition, demonstrating that embedded institutions, inherited norms and expectations have shaped the transition process. Russian reformers have struggled with quite limited success to restructure the inherited welfare state according to liberal market principles. Most of the state's declining welfare resources have continued to be allocated to preexisting subsidy and benefit programs, which provide little to the "new poor." Political and legislative obstacles have been central, but so have societal orientations and norms. Many Russian households have preferred residual tenancy rights and subsidies to the rights and uncertainties of independent ownership, for example, while local authorities continue to treat housing more as a right than a market commodity. Pensioners resist the application of "insurance principles" to promised benefits, and many in the Russian policy community defend the old solidaristic values against reformist initiatives. Long-established rights and patterns, as well as inherited institutional deficits, have made it difficult to implement the Western-style policies promoted by international advisors and organizations, despite the patent failures of the old system.

The Soviet welfare state legacy has been a liability for transition to a less statist, more market-based system of social benefits in Russia. The significance of this legacy for social welfare, and arguable for democracy, is more ambiguous. On the one hand, benefits are broadly inadequate, poorly targeted, and ineffective at alleviating poverty. On the other hand, in an economy in which one-third of the population lives in poverty, the remnants of the old welfare state have kept people housed whether or not they could pay rent, have provided some level of income for pensioners most of the time, and have sustained at least the erratic distribution of other benefits. When liberal deputies joined the Communists in voting down the proposed reform of the system from universalism to means-testing in 1997, they did so largely from distrust that the state, having withdrawn the old benefits, would in fact provide new ones. In sum, a better welfare policy requires a stronger, more capable state than was in place in Russia during the 1990s.

Welfare states are under pressure everywhere, from demographic changes that worsen the ratios of pensioners to workers, from growing international economic competition, from the high costs of funding cumulative commitments to social programs. The Russian state is affected by all of these pressures, and its present system of social provision is unsustainable. The Putin government has recommitted Russia to a liberalizing reform program that would reduce subsidies, eliminate categorical benefits and privileges, and target spending on the poor.[43] If present trends toward a more cooperative legislature, a more effective state, and a stabilizing economy continue, the prospects for reform will improve. Nevertheless, the legacies of the socialist welfare state have shaped policy over the first postsocialist decade, and will continue to influence the policy process into the future.

NOTES

Support for this research was provided by National Council for Eurasian and East European Research Grant No. 814-1g. Invaluable research assistance was provided by Dr. Elena Vinogradova of Moscow, Russia, and Matthew Crosston, a graduate student in the political science department at Brown University.

1. See Gosta Esping-Anderson, *The Three Worlds of Welfare Capitalism* (Princeton, N.J.: Princeton University Press, 1990). Esping-Anderson's classic study distinguishes three types of welfare-state "regimes," liberal, conservative and social-democratic.

2. See Linda J. Cook and Mitchell Orenstein, "The Return of the Left and Its Impact on the Welfare State in Russia, Poland, and Hungary," in Linda J. Cook, Mitchell A. Orenstein, and Marilyn Rueschemeyer, eds., *Left Parties and Social Policy in Postcommunist Europe* (Boulder, Colo.: Westview, 1999), 47–108.

3. Alastair McAuley, *Economic Welfare in the Soviet Union: Poverty, Living Standards, and Equality* (Madison, Wis.: Univ. of Wisconsin Press, 1979), 297–98.

4. Parts of the housing and pension case studies are adapted from Linda J. Cook, "The Russian Welfare State: Obstacles to Restructuring," *Post-Soviet Affairs*, Vol. 16, No. 4, Oct-Nov 2000.

5. World Bank, *Russia, Housing Reform and Privatization: Strategy and Transition Issues*, Vol. 1, Main Report (Washington, D.C.: World Bank, Aug. 1995), 23.

6. World Bank, *Russian Federation: Toward Medium-Term Viability* (Washington, D.C: World Bank, 1996).

7. Alexander Puzanov and Tatianya Koutakova, "Privatizing Housing and Creating Homeowners' Associations," in Raymond J. Struyk, ed., *Restructuring Russia's Housing Sector* (Washington, D.C.: Urban Institute, 1997).

8. Author's interview (by phone) with Raymond Struyk, Senior Fellow, Urban Institute, Washington, D.C., April 21, 1999.

9. See, for example, the scenario for Russian housing reform in World Bank. *Russia: Housing Reform and Privatization,* Vol. 1: Main Report, No. 14929-RU (Washington, D.C.: World Bank, 1995).

10. According to Tatyana Belkina, an expert on Russian housing reform, in 1998 cost recovery had risen to about 50 percent, while only 2–3 percent of households had arrears of as much as six months; Tatyana Belkina, Department Head, Institute of National Economic Forecasting, Russian Academy of Sciences; interview by Elena Vinogradova, Moscow, Nov. 17, 1998.

11. A. Z. Astapovich, C. A. Afontsev and A. A. Blokhin, "Obzor ekonomicheskoy politiki v rossii za 1997 g." Moscow: Byuro ekonomicheskogo analiza), 1998; "Gosudarstvennaya Duma: Stenograma zasedani," 1997. N. 111(253), I and II; Radio Free Europe/ Radio Liberty Reports (RFE/RL), Sept. 26, 1997. The Duma also initiated measures to reduce the pace of rent increases, extend the period of full cost recovery from five to ten years, and place a ceiling on the rents that could be charged to low-income households.

12. For example, Alexander Puzanov, Project Manager and Board Member, Institute for Urban Economics, Moscow, estimated that half of all Russian households received privileges in 1998; interview with author, Moscow, February 5, 1999.

13. Author's interview with Marina Krassilnikova, Head, Dept. of Living Standards, Russian Center for the Study of Public Opinion (VTsIOM), Moscow, February 3, 1999.

14. See Astapovich, et. al., *Obzor.*

15. Bob Deacon, et. al. *Global Social Policy: International Organizations and the Future of Welfare* (London: Sage Publications, 1997).

16. On the Gorbachev-era pension reforms, see Andrea Chandler, "Democratization, Social Welfare, and Individual Rights in Russia: The Case of Pensions," paper presented at the Third Annual Convention of the Association for the Study of Nationalities Conference, Columbia University, April, 1998; Vladimir Mikhalev, "Social Security in Russia under Economic Transformation," *Europe-Asia Studies,* Vol. 48, No. 1, 1996, 5–25.

17. *Statisticheskii Biulleten'* No. 3(42), Goskomstat, June 1998, 146.

18. On debts to the pension fund and worsening payer-recipient ratios, see: *Statisticheskii Biulleten',* No. 3(42), Goskomstat, June, 1998, 147; *Russian Economic Development,* No. 4, May 1999, 11; Tatyana Maleva, *Sovremennie Problemy Pensionnoi Sfery: Kommentarii Ekonomistov I Demografov* (Moscow: Carnegie Center for International Peace, 1997), 17.

19. See, for example, Paul Pierson, *Dismantling the Welfare State: Reagan, Thatcher, and the Politics of Retrenchmen* (New York: Cambridge University Press, 1994), on constituencies for the benefits of established welfare states and the difficulties of "dismantling" benefit programs.

20. Cook and Orenstien, "Return of the Left," in Cook, et. al., *Left Parties.*

21. Author's interview with Hjalte Sederlof, Program Team Leader, Social and Human Development Programs, Europe and Central Asia Region, World Bank; interview by author, Providence, R.I., April 29, 1999.

22. Author's interview with Alexei Avtonomov, Director of Legal Department, Foundation for the Development of Parliamentarism in Russia, Moscow, February 1, 1999.

23. This was, for example, the view of Valdimir Petrov, Assistant to the President, Russian Pensioners' Party; interview by Elena Vinogradova, Moscow, June 1999.

24. For this legislation see: *Sobraniya Zakonodatelstva Rossiikoi Federatsii,* No. 14, April, 1996, St. 1401; *Vedomosti Federalnogo Sobraniya Rossiiskoi Federatsii,* No. 24, Aug. 21, 1997, St. 115. A third reformist law, on Nonstate Pension Funds, was also passed in the spring of 1998.

25. World Bank, "Russian Federation-Pension Reform Implementation Project," PID Prepared October 15, 1998. (Washington, D.C.: World Bank [Xerox]).

26. Irina Denisova, Maria Gorban and Ksenia Yudaeva, "Social Policy in Russia: Pension Fund and Social Security." *Russian Economic Trends,* 1999, 1, 12–24.

27. T. Maleva (Bureau of Economic Analysis) and O. Syniyavskaya (Carnegie Foundation), n.d. "The Social Sphere" (Xerox).

28. See *Trud*, Aug. 16, 1997; *Foreign Broadcast Information Service (FBIS)*, Sept. 3, Dec. 22, 1997.

29. Author's interview with Marina Baskakova, Senior Researcher, Moscow Center for Gender Studies, Russian Academy of Sciences, Moscow, Feb. 4, 1999.

30. The May 1998 Pension Reform Program proposed for Russia a "national defined contribution (NDC) system. On NDCs see Louise Fox, "Pension Reform in the Postcommunist Transition Economies," in Joan M. Nelson, Charles Tilly, and Lee Walker eds., *Transforming Postcommunist Political Economies* (Washington D.C.: National Academy Press, 1997), 370–84.

31. For Soviet-era poverty estimates, see: Jeanine Braithwaite, "The Old and New Poor in Russia," in Jeni Klugman, ed., *Poverty in Russia: Public Policy and Private Responses* (Washington, D.C.: World Bank, 1997). Current estimates are based on official Russian statistics. The World Bank and some others estimate poverty rates that are well in excess of official statistics, while others argue that the official stats underestimate informal economic activity.

32. World Bank, "Russia's Social Protection Malaise: Key Reform Priorities as a Response to the Present Crisis" (Human Development Sector Unit, Europe and Central Asia Region, draft report, March 19, 1999); *Feminizatsiya bednost' v Rossii* (Moscow: Ves' Mir, 2000).

33. For a more extensive discussion of unemployment, see the chapter by Walter Connor, "Class, Status, Powerlessness: Workers in Postcommunist Russia," this volume.

34. See Marc Foley, "Static and Dynamic Analyses of Poverty in Russia," in Jeni Klugman, ed., *Poverty in Russia: Public Policy and Private Response,* (Washington, D.C.: World Bank, 1997). As with poverty generally, in the early 1990s flows into and out of unemployment were high and there was not a stagnant pool of jobless poor, but the ratio of outflow to jobs declined by the end of 1995.

35. Author's telephone interview with Jeanine Braithwaite, Economist, Poverty Reduction and Economic Management, Europe and Central Asia Unit, World Bank, Jan. 12, 2000.

36. See Feminizatsiya bednost' v Rossii, (Moscow: Ves' Mir, 2000).

37. S. G. Misikhina, "Sotsial'nye posobiya, l'goty I vyplaty be Rossiiskoi Federatsii: Raspredelenie pri gruppam naceleniya s raslichym urovnem dokhoka: problemy I resheniya" (Moscow: TACIS, 1999). According to an ILO study, only about 19 percent of all social transfers in Russia reach families below the subsistence minimum, versus 30–50 percent in most developed countries, including several in Eastern Europe.

38. See Jeanine Braithwaite, "Targeting and the Longer-Term Poor in Russia" (draft, World Bank, February 1999); Jeanine Braithwaite, Christiaan Grootaert and Branko Milanovic, *Poverty and Social Assistance in Transition Countries* (New York: St. Martin's Press, 1999).

39. Commander, 1997.

40. S. G. Misikhina, "Sotsial'nye posobiya, l'goty I vyplaty be Rossiiskoi Federatsii: Raspredelenie pr gruppan naceleniya s raslichym urovnem dokhoka: problemy i resheniya" (Moscow: TACIS, 1999); author's interview with Svetlana Misikhina, Expert, Municipal Economic and Social Reform of Tacis (MERIT), Moscow, June 7, 2000.

41. Branko Milanovic, "The Role of Social Assistance in Addressing Poverty," in Jeanine Braithwaite, Christiaan Grootaert and Branko Milanovic, eds., *Poverty and Social Assistance in Transition Countries* (New York: St. Martin's Press, 1999), 151–56.

42. Guy Standing, "Social Protection in Central and Eastern Europe: A Tale of Slipping Anchors and Torn Safety Nets," in Gosta Esping-Anderson, ed., *Welfare States in Transition: National Adaptations in Global Economies* (London: Sage Publications, 1996), 225–55.

43. For the Putin Reform Program, see German, "Prioritetnye Zadachi Pravitelstva Rossiiskoi Federatsii na 2000–2001 gody po Realizatsii 'Osnovnykh Napravlenii Sotsial'no-Ekonomicheskoi Politiki Pravitel'stva Rossiiskoi Federatsii na Dolgosrochnyiu Perspectivy," accessed at: www.kommersant.ru/documents/high-priority-task.htm; German Gref, "Proekt Strategiia Rossiiskoi Federatsii do 2010 goda. Fond Tsentr Strategicheskikh Razrabotok 2000g," accessed at: www.kommersant.ru/documents/Strat1.htm.

7

Cooperatives and the Legacy of State Socialism

Greg Andrusz

The dominant discourse on "the transition" presents a picture in which the processes of privatization and democratization are being thwarted by institutional legacies and their attendant social relations and cultural practices.[1] The dismantling of the central planning system and public ownership and its displacement by a market-oriented economy and private property were regarded as the sine qua non for the emergence of a dynamic entrepreneurial class and a broader "middle class," which would bolster democracy and sustain a revitalized civil society.

During the first ten years of Russia's apostasy (1986–96), the invading host of Western social scientists were frequently ignorant of the society that they were advising and of the theoretical and policy debates in which these societies were engaged. This meant that they were deprived of the benefits to be gained from taking a longer view of a society's trajectory, which makes it possible to identify patterns in the evolution of its political economy. It also accounts for the naïve belief that *a decade* would be sufficient time to introduce capitalism into Russia. Outsiders working as insiders were even in the face of the evidence triumphalist in their defeat.[2] A dilemma for analysts of the Soviet legacy, even those who are against the application of this therapy, is that they are trapped within the discourse labeled "problems of transition to the market." Thus a key task is to try to construct a new discourse.

This chapter, in its contribution to this task, focuses on a particular property form in two different settings, which emerged during the phase of "mature socialism" and in the transitional period of *restructuring*. Housing cooperatives were relegislated into existence in 1962–64 and cooperatives, more generally in 1986–88. Cooperatives represent *both* legacies of late state socialism *and* alternatives to (state) capitalism. Prior to the demise of the Soviet Union they represented putative, alternative institutional and property forms to state property. Today, they represent legacies and assets of state socialism, which could offer a feasible, though not exclusive, alternative form to capitalism. Cooperatives are best understood as part of a larger movement, which embraces the voluntary or nongovernmental sector and mutualism. In view of their long history they cannot be understood as a static form or idea, nor can they be divorced from the political and socioeconomic environment in which they germinate. As will be discussed, cooperatives in Russia were undermined by both indigenous and exogenous forces.

THE CONTEXT

The underlying assumption of this chapter is that Zaslavskaya's lucid description and analysis of Brezhnev's "mature socialism," submitted to the Central Committee of the Communist Party in 1984 and published as the Novosibirsk Report, was essentially correct. According to her the institutional edifice, which had been erected over the previous half century to run the economy, had served a useful function during the country's "period of extensive economic development" but was now "out of date and a brake on development."[3] It was common knowledge that, in reality, the economy functioned because a large number of actors engaged in unsanctioned, illegal market-like transactions. But, whereas one side believed that existing "administrative means" should be improved to curtail these activities, the other side wanted to harness them, legalize and incorporate them into the economic system. As a measure of its lack of success in suppressing this "sector," by the late 1970s the private sector, according to one estimate, comprised 28–33 percent of household incomes.[4] By the 1980s, then, the internal contradictions were so great that the whole system was on the brink of a *schism* or a *reformation*.

The central dynamic to change came from within the system itself.[5] Exogenous factors, primarily the introduction of a new era of weaponry and strategic defence, also compelled policy analysts to contemplate serious reforms to the system, but these were essentially secondary. The Soviet equivalent of the British Fabian Society (Aganbegyan, Shmelyov, Zaslavskaya) assumed that the blatant truths revealed by the clinical diagnoses that they were offering would be understood and acted upon by the Party whose leadership could introduce and carry through the shifts required. However, the Party elite was divided and other vested economic and political interests opposed change.

Yet, such was the profundity of the systemic crisis that Gorbachev was able to *initiate* a major restructuring of the society. The situation, which faced him when he became General Secretary of the CPSU in 1985, was similar to that faced by Lenin in 1921, who in 1923 committed a *volte-face* on his hitherto stance on cooperatives and made them an integral part of his economic policy.[6]

Sixty-three years later, Gorbachev also turned to cooperatives in order to reverse declining growth rates in production and to counter bureaucratic rigidities throughout the social system.[7]

For perestroika to succeed there would have to be a shift in attitude and behavior amongst all sections of the population. But this was not to be accomplished as it had in the past, by administrative fiat or terror. Instead the media were called upon to play a constructive role in helping the Party in its task, aided by Soviet sociologists who began to abandon the constraints of an ideologically imposed theoretical paradigm on how to study social structure. This enabled them to classify groups in terms of whether they were favorable, indifferent or hostile to the changes being proposed and enacted. Underlying the emerging reality of a deeply divided elite and a socially heterogeneous and increasingly *anomic* population lay a revolutionary class, united by its adherence to a fundamental ideological objective, namely the legitimation of private property.[8] Members of the reforming political elite tried to harness and channel change within the parameters of the system of which they were part and to whose basic beliefs they subscribed. But political will was insufficient.

When glasnost allowed closeted critics of the system to examine the ideology, they found that the system was flawed in part because it neglected the "human factor"; the society contained a defective gene which cultivated passivity and a culture of dependency amongst very broad sections of the population.[9] On the one hand, Gorbachev's introduction of the notion of the "human factor" into political discourse justifies construing the grand changes that began to take place in the 1980s in the Soviet Union as a continuation of the Reformation in Europe, in which the individual, rather than the collective, should be made the agent of account, the subject of a contract and the dynamo of change. The second parallel lies in the fact that Mikhail Gorbachev, like Martin Luther, began by attacking corruption (associated with indulgences [privileges]) within the established church (the Communist Party and the Catholic Church, respectively). Neither man envisaged leaving the church or creating a new religion; they sought to reform the doctrine and practices of their systems by working within them.[10]

On the other hand, the events of the period could be interpreted as representing a *schism* or major rupture in the society's underpinning philosophy and mode of organization, without destroying the system altogether. Light might be shed upon this meta issue by examining the recent history of cooperatives in Russia. From one perspective they were a means to reform and preserve socialism in the USSR. Viewed from another perspective, they stood at the heart of Russia's grand mass apostasy.

THE COOPERATIVE REVIVAL

In its main contours the Soviet economic system of the mid-1980s was the same as the one that had come into being in the 1930s. It allowed three forms of property:

state enterprises (which were state property), state cooperatives, and family household economies (essentially the private household plot of land). The Soviet Union was a society in which people were motivated to act not by market signals but by *a pattern of privileges and punishments*. The aim of perestroika was to expand the second and third forms of property at the expense of the first.

Cooperatives were identified as one of the means for reviving the fortunes of the economy and in 1986 at the XXVII Party Congress, Mr. Gorbachev came out as a champion of cooperatives, stating that they had "far from exhausted their potential."[11] Eighteen months later, the government published a draft Law on Cooperation,[12] which, after a nationwide debate, came into force on 1 July 1988. Complex and sophisticated in its many provisions, it sought to combine a core of socialist beliefs with the flexibility offered by private enterprise to respond to market demand. Opposition to the law emerged immediately, compelling the first major amendments and restrictions on cooperatives to be made in December 1988. Cooperatives became the issue around which supporters and opponents of fundamental reform crystallized. They were indicative of a society in transition towards an expansion in the size and realm of nonstate property.

Public responses to cooperatives revealed that the government had tapped into and released two opposite elemental forces in society: a desire by some to "truck, barter and trade" and thereby become richer; and an equally strong desire by others to enforce the communism of the barrack room. As far as the latter was concerned cooperatives were little more than Trojan Horses of capitalism. The outcome of this antagonism was that the cooperative movement was forced into retreat by a combination of vested political and administrative interests and public opinion; in December 1988 the government issued a decree to "regulate certain types of cooperative activity,"[13] and then in October 1989 the Supreme Soviet amended the Law on Cooperatives.[14]

In 1989, there was little empirical evidence to support the contention that cooperatives were "an essential component in the renewal of socialism and an important condition for its further progress."[15] And to state that it was "justifiable to conclude that the more cooperation that exists, the more socialism,"[16] was more a profession of faith than a statement of fact. Nevertheless, in the brief period of existence, a large number of cooperatives were functioning and many more were registered, even though not in operation.[17] The next stage in the confrontation was for a nascent indigenous capitalist class to wage war on any form of socialistic or collectivist mode of ownership, which included cooperatives. They were aided in this by external agents.

THE CULTURAL AND IDEOLOGICAL ENVIRONMENT

Cooperatives were being introduced into an environment which, under *tsarism*, was culturally not well-disposed towards individual initiative and which, during most of the Soviet period, had been ideologically inimical to entrepreneurial activity. Russian society, as it entered the twentieth century, was rigidly stratified and dominated by a highly autocratic political regime. Like their nineteenth century Westernizing predecessors, a small political elite and a smaller cultural avant garde in 1917 were eager to superimpose on the mass of the population a set of alien ideas, institutions and social relations. The impersonal rules of a Weberian "rational-legal society" were far from being the norm in nineteenth-century Russia. Cultural traditions prevalent in serf and merchant families—most of whose heads could neither read nor write[18]—reinforced the tendency toward short-run profit maximization. However, traditional norms and practices, which emphasized personal contacts and bribery, were in part a functional adaptation to a society dominated by a pervasive and arbitrary bureaucracy,[19] which observed with suspicion any coalition of individuals under whatever guise. For historical and geographical reasons the development of capitalism in Russia only to a limited degree took the classical form of free competition. Moreover, its development was heavily influenced by state intervention and foreign investment.[20]

During the 1930s not only was economic and political power centralized in the hands of the state, but a compact was established between state and society whereby the former sought to insulate its citizens from risk by providing them with the basic necessities of life—housing, health care, education, pensions—and work.[21] It also did much to remove risk from the economy by institutionalizing ways of dissuading individuals from risk-taking behavior. The state was draconian in its treatment of anyone involved in nonstate economic activity, even when, as in the case of teams of itinerant building workers (*shabashniki*), they contributed to economic welfare.[22]

As late as 1986, for most "mainstream" Soviet philosophers and economists cooperatives constituted the single most important obstacle to the country's technical and social progress. Even the Institute of Economics of the USSR Academy of Sciences contended that by 1990 collective farm (cooperative) property would merge with state property.[23] Within one year, the conventional wisdom that still held that social progress could be measured by each further increment of statization was being denounced as formal, abstract reasoning that favored state over cooperative ownership.[24]

It was this cultural and ideological environment that Gorbachev had in mind when he said that "long established ideas, let alone prejudices" would have to be removed before cooperatives could demonstrate their potential. "Unfortunately," he observed, "there is a widespread view that any change in the economic mechanism is practically a retreat from the principles of socialism."[25] Time and again protagonists of the cooperative repeated that, while cooperatives were to be the catalyst to overcoming Manilovism, they could not be "planted" from above. They were correct in their observation and attempts were made to address the problem of how the psychological and institutional obstacles faced by existing and projected cooperatives were to be overcome.

FRIENDS AND ENEMIES

The social relationships that characterized the Soviet system were on the threshold of being transformed. Those who formed a relationship directly with the cooperatives fall into three categories. First, a symbiotic relationship quickly developed between people functioning in the quasi-legal and illegal economy—criminals engaged in bribery, extortion, drugs, protection and robbery—and cooperatives. In fact, the unrestrained criminality of the 1990s is often associated with the appearance of cooperatives in 1987–88, which saw the emergence and then conversion of extortion into a patterned form of protection racket.[26] The reason for its appearance in its present guise is that a large proportion of the assets of the first entrepreneurs derived from the Soviet era shadow economy, who were reluctant to become involved with the state police. At the same time the latter "did not regard cooperatives as legitimate objects to be protected—*not least because of the negative Soviet moral attitudes towards private entrepreneurs*" [my emphasis].[27]

Second, functionaries in the economic system who, besides enjoying a few perquisites deriving from their role in the public economy, were members of different and partially interacting networks. They were often gatekeepers who controlled access to, for example, the right to register as a cooperative and to be "given" premises. They did not themselves want to found or join a cooperative. In one survey of cooperatives aimed at discovering who the extortionists were, almost one-third of the chairmen replied that officials working in local authority departments were the worst offenders; only 7 percent of respondents cited criminal protection racketeers as the principal extortionists.[28] It was not uncommon for gatekeeping officials within the local soviet executive committees to be coopted as members of cooperatives.[29]

A third, similar but different group, consisted of those salaried Party members and functionaries who rejected the notion that all property forms other than state property were by definition legitimate. Local party secretaries were themselves "achievers" and in a good position to be well-informed about inefficient management in their administrative domains. Many such members of the *apparat* sat at the center of a complex web of personal and institutional relationships, which enabled them to be in good touch with public opinion, local needs, demands and feelings. Party members and functionaries who had been watching the waning fortunes of the Party and Gorbachev's shedding of power at home and abroad in Eastern Europe found different ways to adapt their organizational talents to the emerging economic sector. So, although the cooperatives were institutionally weak and vulnerable to harassment by boorish bureaucrats and members of the emerging new order, they had an ally amongst a section of the existing élite, whose members were not necessarily highly educated or articulate but were politically astute. A substantial number founded or became members of cooperatives. Most cooperatives were open to demands from common criminals for protection money and from officials for bribes.[30]

Future studies will probably reveal that cooperatives received little support from foreign organizations. One exception is worth citing. In June 1990, the United Nations Industrial Development Organisation (UNIDO), in conjunction with various USSR government departments, convened in Moscow an "Interregional Symposium on the Role of the Industrial Cooperative Movement in Economic and Industrial Development." The purpose of the symposium was "to provide a forum for the discussion of issues concerning the role of cooperatives." It was anticipated that "modalities and policy guidelines" would emerge on adopting microeconomic methodologies for "engendering decision-making based on market forces, rationalisation and competition." For the conference organizers, cooperatives could function within an orthodox Western economic framework. The task of the symposium was to identify ways in which international economic cooperation could enhance the role of cooperatives in the industrial development process.[31]

From their inception the cooperatives had to endure unconcealed and widespread public hostility, which was an expression, first, of moral outrage—cooperatives were alien to (Soviet) socialism—and, second, of righteous envy at the overt high earnings to be had in cooperatives. The two sentiments were linked by the high prices that cooperatives frequently charged. Underlying these specific resentments towards cooperatives was a more profound fear of change and of insecurity brought by change. Those fearing that change would adversely affect their life chances were drawn from all sections of the population. Uncertainties in the population bred insecurities in the cooperatives, just as they had during NEP. Thus, the prospect of an uncertain and insecure future led cooperatives to a form of behavior that was not in the best interests of the state or society. Instead of investing their profits, they consumed them in the form of wages or bonuses, thereby exacerbating the antagonism already felt towards them.[32]

At first the political question of cooperatives was fought out at the *ideological* level, but as the debate came to focus on specific points in the legislation, it became more *technical*, concentrating on matters such as pricing, rewards and taxation. For instance, cooperatives were dependent on their ability to obtain their material inputs in competition with state enterprises. Invariably, where shortages existed—and these were ubiquitous—the latter received preferential treatment. Thus, the political and legal gains made by cooperatives when they became independent of the state order system were countered by the economic cost of freedom from state tutelage. The priority for supplies that was accorded to state enterprises inevitably generated tensions and conflicts and led both sectors to resort to ever more illegal methods in order to meet their supply needs. In fact, this critical systemic contradiction—how to produce commodities and capital equipment for a nonstate sector when there were insufficient supplies to meet the needs of the state sector itself—could only be overcome by a far more radical transformation of the economic system. Cooperatives were vulnerable in other ways. For instance, a cooperative's credit-worthiness was not necessarily the criterion for granting a bank loan; frequently bank credit was only made available after the payment of "illegal monetary inducements." Over time a negotiated agreement could have been reached over technical questions, but the political stakes were so great that the conflict ultimately transferred from the realms of ideological polemic and technical debate to the battlefield. In the military confrontation and shoot out at the White House in 1993, circumstances and relationships converted the contest for political power into a class struggle "that made it possible for a grotesque mediocrity to play a hero's part"[33] and for him to accept the remedy recommended by Western specialists and governments to treat the sick patient was "shock therapy."

Professional Western economists considered that the fundamental problem faced by the countries of Eastern Europe was that the majority of firms were based on a capital stock and technology that manufactured goods for which demand was limited; the transfer of state assets into private ownership would not, therefore, transform their value.[34] For economists, a robust entrepreneurial sector was of greater importance, but for that to happen legal and administrative obstacles to entrepreneurial activity would have to be removed and an institutional infrastructure conducive to the creation of a viable entrepreneurial sector established. Opinion was divided over whether cooperatives could fulfill this role.

Politicians, however, had a broader agenda than did economists: for them privatization and private property rights were of primary importance. Privatization was the litmus test demonstrating that a country had recanted and returned to civilized behavior, which included "protection of private property, the free flow of trade, capital, investment and repatriation of profits."[35]

In revitalized late capitalist societies, industrial restructuring, management and employee buyouts, and fragmentation strategies are embodied in an organizational form, the small and medium-sized enterprise. The term *SME* is used because of its apparent value-neutrality; it describes a phenomenon with little reference to normative issues such as ownership and work relationships. In contrast, the term *cooperative* is value-loaded. In 1992 the Committee on the Development of Trade at the Economic Commission for Europe (ECE) produced a lengthy document on SMEs, which included examples of successful East–West joint ventures and SME development in Eastern Europe.[36] It only once used the word *cooperatives* and then only in passing. This disregard for cooperatives contributed to the difficulties they faced and helped to ensure that they could not be solved by "political will." Essentially, foreign intervention, principally in the form of aid, provided ideological support for those already wanting to take the fast track to capitalism.

HOUSING COOPERATIVES AND OTHER ALTERNATIVES TO SOVIET HOUSING POLICY

The broad contours of recent housing policy in Russia are sketched out in the chapter by Linda Cook. This section deals with a type of housing tenure, which never realized the potential expected of it by the government, but which is now receiving fresh attention from local and central government.

Housing cooperatives were first established in the Soviet Union in 1924. They were abolished in 1937 and revived in legislation passed in 1962 and 1964. This section focuses solely on the later period. Although the initial deposit on a flat in a cooperative was a relatively high outlay relative to household income, cooperatives were nonetheless quite heavily subsidized. The state, apart from granting low interest credit, provided the infrastructure, which amounted to one-fifth of the cost of erecting residential buildings.[37] In return the state benefited from the fact that the loan was repaid. Moreover, the state did not bear the burden of amortization costs, including capital repairs, which were paid for out of a special fund contributed by the members. Finally, cooperatives were faced with management fees and annual service charges, which covered, inter alia, repairs to lifts and gas installations, for which tenants in state property were not responsible.[38] Therefore, during the loan repayment period, the current outlay of cooperative members was three to five times greater than that paid by tenants in state accommodation.

The comparatively large initial downpayment, together with a high monthly outlay on repayments of capital and interest, were not in themselves a deterrent to individuals wishing to join cooperatives, since the very high propensity to save in the Soviet Union meant that substantial deposits were held in personal saving bank accounts. Thus, the availability of funds for a deposit was not the determining factor of whether or not a person became a cooperative member.[39] However, as statistics published in 1989 revealed, savings were not evenly distributed. The aggregated deposits of the 5 percent of savers with holdings of over 20,000 roubles represented 50 percent of total savings. On the basis of this uneven distribution of "wealth," one leading housing specialist concluded, in support of her case for maintaining a "social guarantee" of accommodation, that "all research demonstrates that most of the population lack savings sufficient to purchase housing."[40]

Despite the fact that the central government regarded the development of housing cooperatives as a means of saving on its housing budget and that more people had the wherewithal to finance housing construction, the underperformance of this sector suggested that local institutional barriers and local informal mechanisms were impeding the implementation of the government's policy on the establishment of house-building cooperatives.[41] Many local authorities were socially and ideologically biased against the tenure on the grounds that it encouraged queue jumping by people who were not well placed on the priority list for new state accommodation. As a result, annual surveys conducted by a central government department (Gosstroi) revealed that local councillors and full-time officials procrastinated in providing the design and cost estimate documentation that cooperatives required,[42] and also failed to meet construction schedules.[43] It was not uncommon to find situations where even when cost estimates had been prepared and the money was available to carry out urgent repair work, the plan to carry them out had not even been included in the five year plan."[44]

Legislation enacted in March 1988, "On Measures to Accelerate the Development of Housing Cooperatives,"[45] attributed poor performance to "a serious underestimation by virtually every major institution of the social and political significance of house building cooperatives." Two main reasons were cited as being responsible for this situation: first, local authorities were adopting a "formal bureaucratic approach towards them," which makes the "allocation of a building site and the furnishing of designs and cost estimates a protracted process"; second, there was a general expectation that the state would provide funds for building.

The preamble to the decree then stated that the new provisions were designed to make housing cooperatives "one of the main directions for expanding housing construction . . . so that by 1995 it will contribute no less than two to three times more than at present to the overall volume of housing construction." In other words, the government intended that this sector would account for 14–20 percent of all new building.[46] By the end of the century, it was envisaged that the proportion of new housing in towns to be built by cooperatives would rise from 8.5 percent in 1986 to 30 percent by the year 2000.[47]

The manner in which this expansion was to take place included a novel element. The law defined two types of cooperative. First, there were the house-building cooperatives created for the purpose of constructing and running dwellings by and for the benefit of the membership. They were also allowed to acquire buildings in need of major capital repairs, renovate and then occupy them. The second type of housing cooperative was not concerned with building at all: it was set up in order to acquire newly erected or renovated housing from enterprises, organizations and the local authorities. Both types of cooperative had much to commend them, in particular their organizational flexibility, which gave them the potential to renovate and modernize the existing stock.

In order to encourage local authorities to adopt a more positive and less obstructive stance towards cooperatives, the decree allowed them to place a 15 percent surcharge on cooperatives located "in the most favorable neighborhoods and places," and to treat it as a budgetary revenue. This policy innovation had a twofold significance. First, it was a fiscal device to strengthen the financial base of local soviets, which increased their autonomy. Second, the payment represented a differential rent and as such was a step towards making rental charges reflect location.

Measures, such as the establishment of specialist banks to grant credits to enterprises and local soviets, were introduced to stimulate the construction of housing and subsequently its sale to housing cooperatives. Enterprises were recommended to offer financial assistance to employees wishing to join either form of cooperative. With the state cutting its direct investment in housing from 70 percent in 1986 to 15 percent by the end of the century, the profits made by enterprises and organizations were intended to become a far more important source of capital for investment in housing. Local authorities were also empowered to make loans or grants to employees working in education, health and other occupational spheres in the so-called non-productive sector from their local budgets to enable them to form or join cooperatives.

The 1990s witnessed astronomical increases in the price of housing, especially in Moscow. The government's sharp cutback on its funding of new construction from the state budget was accompanied by the emergence of real estate agents and the whole gamut of institutions associated with private housing markets. It was at this point that a number of autonomous, grassroot tenant and homeseekers organizations emerged in order to try to meet their accommodation needs. On the periphery of this "social movement" were people who squatted empty blocks of flats and homeless people, who for a few months in 1991 set up a "cardboard city" adjacent to Red Square.

A more orthodox reaction was the creation of housing associations (*zhilishchnye tovarishchstva*), the first of which, "Our House" (*Nash Dom*), was formed in 1991 on the Sol'yanka in the center of Moscow. Established as a shareholding society by the residents in a large old house, its objective was to combine their various resources in order to renovate their homes. They received no assistance from the local authority. Facing opposition from the Moscow city council, *Nash Dom* joined forces with another housing association, *Domstroi*, to form the All-Russian Foundation for Promoting the Elimination of Communal Flats, which brought together roughly 500 housing associations throughout Moscow and in another eleven cities. It then created a Specialist Housing Cheque-Investment Fund (Zhiltovarishch) and a commercial bank (Zhilkredit).

These developments were the direct consequence of the country's rapidly and radically changing housing policies, which generated both considerable anxiety about the future, and enthusiasm among a large number of people who wanted to use their newly granted freedom to organize in order to solve their own housing problems. Housing associations looked forward to taking over the administration of their accommodation and to becoming the real owners. In 1992 representatives from ninety-five housing associations petitioned the mayor of Moscow for assistance. This resulted in a series of decrees, which while removing some of the bureaucratic obstacles hindering the development of housing associations,[48] could not overcome one of the most important of them all, namely, the absence of appropriate financial mechanisms. This led to complex schemes—sometimes ingenious, sometimes hare-brained, sometimes unscrupulously fraudulent—for raising the necessary finance to build low-rise housing estates.

But disillusionment with self-help activities soon set in. Changes in the law empowering people, including knowledge of their legal rights, could not and cannot easily overcome habituation of a strong and large constituency to cheap accommodation, rented from and maintained by the state, a policy that was supported by housing specialists who reaffirmed that the goal of providing "each family with its own home by the year 2000" should be achieved "predominantly by state forms of construction and distribution."[49]

Hostile local officials, combined with a weariness and apathy amongst tenants, helped enthusiasm for housing associations to evaporate. As a result of political developments and changes in the housing system (especially the privatization of publicly owned accommodation), cooperative members began to exercise their rights under the Law on Property[50] to dispose of their flats, either by selling or by bequeathing them.[51]

In conclusion, the March 1988 decree was a valid attempt to build upon a form of tenure that already existed. It provided scope for the gradual transfer of state housing to groups of tenants. But as early as 1990 both this decree and the Law on Cooperatives ratified the following May could be seen as historical, politico-legal landmarks on Russia's route towards large-scale privatization of housing and of its publicly owned assets. It is another sad irony that wide sections of the population should have been so hostile to cooperatives in most spheres of activity, including house building, not knowing, expecting or wanting the privatization that lay just three years ahead.

CRIME AND THE RUSSIAN STATE

The pervasiveness of organized crime and corruption in society offers one of many examples of the specificity of Russian capitalism and culture. The more that is known about crime and social deviance and the interaction between criminals and social control agencies, the less credible becomes the view that the present period of lawlessness may be seen purely as constituting a so-called robber baron phase of capitalism. Nonlegal activity is such an integral part of social life in Russia that analyses of criminality there contribute towards the formulation of an alternative discourse. As a social phenomenon, social networks are hardly unique to Russia. However, there is something "unique" about the manner in which they are involved in institution building in Russia: one needs only consider the way in which individuals transfer their membership from a state security agency to a private security agency.[52] In this instance, the real uniqueness lies less in the fact of the transfer than in the role of the state in legislating for it. This raises the question of how to conceptualize the contemporary Russian state.

Max Weber distinguished six modes (ideal types) of capitalistic orientation towards profit-making, three of which he classified as constituting a politically oriented capitalism, where business is aimed either at making predatory profits through political connections or at making money through force or through a power position guaranteed by political authorities, or at profiting from "unusual transactions with political bodies."[53] Russia's current capitalist phase is encom-

passed within this description and may be readily contrasted to the primary goal
of a modern capitalist firm, which is to make profit and which "allows for a precise assessment of the economic situation before and after each separate deal
and of the exact profit."[54] A significant proportion of the myriad of daily monetary and nonmonetary economic transactions, which take place in Russia's formal and informal economies, do not conform to this desideratum.

Under the soviet system, in order to meet planned targets, managers took risks
for which they were punishable. To protect themselves against this possibility
they entered into or created groups of associates who could trust one another, in
their individual mutual self-interest. Despite the negative economic effects,
which some economists consider result from such an insurance-based-on-trust
system, these malpractices are a common feature of Russian economic behavior
because the value of networks outweighs their high transaction costs.[55] Moreover,
where material inputs and credit are difficult to obtain, people rely on personal
connections.[56] It is therefore easy to agree with the proposition that "if the negative attitude toward official directives and instruments prevails, an institutional
framework that secures a well-functioning market cannot be created."[57] This
raises two questions. First, should it be assumed that a "well-functioning market"
(Weber's modern rational capitalism) is what the Russian state and society are
seeking to achieve? Second, if the postsocialist economy is still largely molded by
all sorts of informal processes and quasi-institutionalized (illegal or nonformal-
ized) procedures, and if law enforcement agencies find it difficult to police the
economic system, would it perhaps be useful to shift into a discourse that does
not look at the society as presenting just so many obstacles in the path of a
posited optimum economic rationality? These questions lead us toward a new
discourse based on the theory of path dependency.[58]

RUSSIA AND THE SOVIET LEGACY

The institutional structure of the Soviet state and economy was logical and in-
ternally consistent within its self-created discourse and legitimating ideology.
In order to understand and explain the Soviet legacy and the modern Russian
state and society, one Russian sociologist has developed a theory that she calls
the "distributional economy" (*razdatochnaya ekonomika*), which, like the market economy, has not been consciously designed but is the outcome of a complex of geographical, social, economic, political and historically contingent
factors.[59] In her theory, virtually everything in Russian society both material
and nonmaterial—land, labor, money, housing, services and food, awards and
appointments (*dolzhnosti*)—are all subject to distribution (*razdacha*)[60] (as opposed to buying and selling).

According to her analysis, Russia's economic history from the ninth to the
twentieth century consists of three long periods. At the end of each there has

been a transitional period during which the society's institutions have been rad-ically transformed and aspects of the market system introduced. By the end of the third period, which extended from the 1930s to the 1990s, the institution of "distribution" embraced virtually the whole sphere of nonindustrial con-sumption: housing, education, health care, preschool facilities, which were pro-vided almost totally free of charge.

The redistribution of resources was governed by a system of norms and regu-lations, which determined how all resources (including labor) were to be allo-cated. This all-embracing system of distribution was complemented by the insti-tution of collection (*sdacha*), whereby wealth and resources are collected (*sdayutsya*) for later distribution. Integral to the institution of collection is the no-tion that any social activity acquires the character of "service labor." Every Soviet Constitution specified that all members of society were obliged to work, that is, become part of the public organization of labor (*sluzhebnaya organizatsiya truda*). The workplace furnished all able-bodied individuals with the basic means for liv-ing: wages, accommodation, child-minding facilities, holidays and health facili-ties, pioneer camps and plots of land. Without work a person could not obtain the necessary registration document (*propiska*); and, without this document it was impossible (legally) to obtain accommodation in towns, receive medical attention or be registered for secondary education. This tightness of control was responsi-ble for activities being defined as "illegal"—the person without a *propiska*, the employer and person renting out accommodation.

The institution of private property came to dominate in both the first and sec-ond transitional periods. Now the third transition has similarly begun as privati-zation transforms the institution of public property into an institution of private property. Accordingly, the Russian economy is now undergoing qualitative change, but rather than being transformed into a market economy, it is being *modernized*, so that by the end of the period it will be in a position to begin to displace or restrict the institution of market trading and private entrepreneur-ship, heralding a new cycle in society's development.

Following Weber, both the earlier period of capitalist development in Russia and the present may be described as "politically motivated capitalism." The country has not created independent firms but dismantled what was a single, in-tegrated economy and replaced it by separate appanage principalities.[61] During these periods of crisis, the state temporarily "withdraws" and lets different social groups and economic subjects take the initiative, ceding its power and authority to regional oligarchs. One thing remains constant: neither privatization nor a weakened central state has abolished the interdependency of political and eco-nomic actors. The two groups are locked in a symbiotic relationship, in which directors of private enterprises maintain close links with senior officials, whom they are habituated to petition for subsidies and privileges.

Bessonova's megadiscourse embraces aspects of both modernization theory and civilization theory, but, ultimately, comes to rest in the bosom of *Eurasian-*

ism, at the heart of which is the notion that has been argued for almost 150 years, namely that Russia has its own unique path of development. The fact that this case remains vibrant, must be cause for thought. If the trajectory of a society's evolution is "path-dependent,"[62] then the theory of the "distributional economy" merits further consideration.

CONCLUSION

The conclusions to be drawn from Weber's reflections on *capitalisms* and the views of anthropologists on *culture*[63] are, first, that a society's culture is extremely durable and it is misguided to seek to impose a hegemonic discourse on it; second, the notion of culture demands that attention should be paid to the whole, and not just to this or that sector of the economy, polity or civil society; third, since profit-making should, as Weber suggests, be seen as an activity oriented to the behavior of others, cognizance has to be taken of the Russian culture and the meaning and value attached to rewards and sanctions; and, fourth, Western prescription writers have to take into account the fact that business in Russia is largely aimed either at making predatory profits through political connections or at making money through force or through a power position guaranteed by political authorities and is centered around rent rather than profit.

The reemergence of cooperatives in the late 1980s was not the result of popular action, but of "the executive of the modern state" acting as a "committee for managing the common affairs of the whole bourgeoisie." The alacrity with which a sizable minority of the population responded to the changed economic and political climate demonstrated the presence among a section of the population of a desire to "truck, barter and trade." This aspiration among some was countered by an urge among others to enforce equality.

The impetus behind cooperatives, therefore, can be interpreted as coming from two different social forces. In both cases, these groups could see the advantages being presented to them by the law, which now allowed them to create cooperatives or derive a profit from them. But in one instance members of these amorphous groups were coalescing into a class in itself, so that taken together they represented an embryonic capitalist class. In the second case the analysis sees the attitudes and behavior of members of the cooperatives and those parasitically associated with them as deeply embedded in a culture of bribery, embezzlement, corruption (false declarations of financial and production plans and of their actual outputs) and cronyism, which was endemic to the Soviet system and integral to its functioning. Cooperatives provided a battleground for different forces to fight and maneuver, the outcome of which was a *sui generis* Russian capitalism.

It is possible that a smaller leap away from statism would have allowed the people and politicians to discover the merits of mutualism. At the very least, state and society could have benefited by hearing from representatives of the mutual societies on the origins, meaning and benefits of mutual associations. This point is underscored by the observation made by Gustafson: "One major reason the fraudsters were so successful was that the equities market was reserved for large players. . . . One possible solution for the future is mutual funds."[64] Gorbachev's comment in 1986 that "cooperatives have far from exhausted their potential"[65] should not be removed from the policy agenda; mutuals could perhaps take up the cooperative baton. Both mutuals and housing cooperatives probably have a future in the Russian (capitalist) state.

NOTES

1. J. Pickles and A. Smith "Introduction: Theorizing Transition and the Political Economy of Transformation," in J. Pickles and A. Smith (eds.) *Theorising Transition: The Political Economy of Postcommunist Transformations* (London: Routledge, 1998).

2. R. Layard and J. Parker, *The Coming Russian Boom; A Guide to New Markets and Politics* (New York: Free Press, 1996).

3. "The Novosibirsk Report," published in *Survey: A Journal of East & West Studies*, vol. 28, no. 1; M. Yanowitch, *A Voice of Reform: Essays by Tat'yana Zaslavskaya*, M. E. Sharpe, London, 1989; T. I. Zaslavskaya, *The Second Socialist Revolution: An Alternative Soviet Strategy* (I. B. Tauris: London, 1990).

4. V. Treml, M. Alekseev, "The Growth of the Second Economy in the Soviet Union and Its Impact on the System," in R. Cambell (ed.), *The Postcommunist Economic Transformation* (Boulder, Colo.: Westview Press, 1994), 21-248. At the time of the crash in August 1998, the second economy accounted for c.40 percent of GDP.

5. The London correspondent of the Paris-based journal, *Kultura* no.132 (1958), J. Mieroszewski, wrote that "communism will not be reformed by sovietologists or any Western party, but only from within, by those who are ideologically committed and belong to the Communist camp." The view that the forces directing change and conditioning new institutional forms emanate from within the system is vital to an understanding of possible future scenarios.

6. V. I. Lenin, *Polnoe sobranie sochenenii*, 5th ed. Politizdat, Moscow (1958–65), vol. 45: 372–3.

7. In his speech to the XXVII Party Congress, the last ever General Secretary of the Communist Party of the Soviet Union pointed to the necessity of "taking a fresh look at some theoretical ideas and concepts. This applies to such major problems as the interaction of the productive forces and the production relations, *socialist ownership* and its economic forms, the co-ordination of centralism with the autonomy of economic organizations and so forth." M. Gorbachev, *Political Report of the CPSU Central Committee to the 27th Party Congress* (Moscow: Novosti Press, 1986), 49.

8. For a critical interpretation of the meaning of "property rights," "ownership" and "privatization," see P. Marcuse, "Privatisation and Its Discontents: Property Rights in Land and Housing in the Transition in Eastern Europe," in G. Andrusz, M. Harloe, I. Szelenyi (eds.), *Cities after Socialism: Urban and Regional Change and Conflict in Post-Socialist Societies* (Oxford: Blackwell, 1996).

9. O. L. Luzhbina, "S kem idem k s'ezdu"? *SPK*, no. 1, (1989): 2.

10. It is worth remembering that the Reformation was a revolution in people's minds that took place over a period of centuries. The revolution in religious doctrine is associated with development of a philosophy of possessive individualism, one of whose key features lies in the work of Hobbes and Locke, for whom the individual essentially is "the proprietor of his own person and capacities, owing nothing to society for them." C. B. MacPherson, *The Political Theory of Possessive Individualism* (Oxford: Oxford University Press, 1964), 3. The doctrine of individual rights, in which the individual has rights against the State and other collectivities, has had few adherents in Russian culture.

11. M. Gorbachev, *Political Report to the XXVII Party Congress of the CPSU Central Committee* (Moscow: Novosti Press, 1986), 51.

12. Zakon SSSR, "O kooperatsii v SSSR," Izd. Izvestiya Sovetov narodnykh deputatov" SSSR, 1988.

13. Postanovlenie Soveta Ministrov SSSR, "O regulirovanie otdel'nykh vidov deyatel'nostei kooperativov v soostvestvii s Zakonom O kooperatsii v SSSR," *SP SSSR* (1989): no. 4, art. 12.

14. *Pravda* (4 October 1989).

15. L. I. Abalkin, "Vozrozhdenie kooperatsii, *Sovetskoe potrebitel'skoe obshchestvo*," no. 2 (1989): 5.

16. Ibid.

17. A. Jones and W. Moskoff, "New Cooperatives in the USSR," *Problems of Communism* (November–December 1989).

18. T. C. Owen, "Entrepreneurship in the Structure of Enterprise in Russia, 1800–1880," in G. Guroff and F. Carstensen (eds), *Entrepreneurship in Imperial Russia and the Soviet Union* (Princeton, N.J.: Princeton University Press, 1983), 61.

19. Ibid., 83. Even in St. Petersburg, the "window on the West," where joint stock companies were more common, the latter "actually perpetuated the old patrimonial pattern of state domination, while the smaller, less technologically advanced share partnerships struggled for an economic livelihood outside the state's control. . . . By 1880 neither had been able to break free of the state's awesome power" (ibid., 74).

20. D. Boffa, *Istoriya Sovetskogo Soyuza* in 2 vols. (Moscow: Mezhdunarodnye Otnosheniya, 1990), vol. I: 16.

21. Michael Ellman lists twelve attributes of the command economy model. See M. Ellman, *The USSR in the 1990s. Struggling out of Stagnation*, The Economist Intelligence Unit, Special Report No. 1152 (London, 1989): 8.

22. See M. A. Shabanova, *Sezonnye sel'skie stroiteli kto oni i kakovy ikh problemy*, Institut ekonomiki I organizatsii promyshlennogo proizvodstva, AN SSSR, Sibirskoe Otdelenie, Novosibirsk (1985).

23. A. S. Tsipko, "Vozmozhnosti i reservy kooperatsii," *Sotsiologicheskie issledovaniya*, no. 2 (1986): 50.

24. For a thorough analysis of the ownership issue, see P. Hanson, *From Stagnation to Catastroiaka: Commentaries on the Soviet Economy, 1983–1991* (Washington, D.C.: Center for Strategic and International Studies, 1992).

25. Gorbachev, op.cit. 50.

26. Vadim Volkov, "Organised Violence, Market Building and State Formation in Postcommunist Russia." Paper given at the European Sociological Association's Annual Conference, Amsterdam (August 1999).

144 *Greg Andrusz*

27. Volkov, 4.
28. See, for instance, *Izvestiya*, 3 February 1990.
29. *Moscow News*, no. 5 (1989).
30. V. Loshak, "Cooperatives under Fire," *Moscow News*, no. 33 (1989): 7.
31. Leading Soviet government officials and senior academics gave papers on: "The Cooperative Movement in the USSR and the Strategy of Perestroika" (L. Abalkin); "Cooperatives and the State: Problems and Prospects" (Y. Tikhonov); "Socialism and Cooperation" (V. Nikilorov). UNIDO consultants spoke on "Soviet Cooperatives: A Force for Major Economic Development"; and "Cooperative Banks in the Soviet Union."
32. Ekonomicheskaya gazeta, 13 (1989).
33. These words of Louis Bonaparte were used by Marx in his essay "The Eighteenth Brumaire of Louis Bonaparte," in K. Marx and F. Engels, *Selected Works*, vol.1, 5th Impression, FLPH (Moscow: 1962): 244.
34. D. Audretsch, "The Role of Small Business in Restructuring Eastern Europe," Paper presented at the Fifth Workshop for Research in Entrepreneurship, Vaxjo, Sweden (28 November 1991): 17–19.
35. The statement was made at a meeting of the CSCE in Bonn in 1990 and cited by W. Hoynck, "Address by the Secretary General," at the seminar "Promoting the Creation of Small and Medium-Sized Enterprises," Bishkek, Kyrgyzstan (23–25 February 1994).
36. UN Economic Commission for Europe, *Small and Medium-Sized Enterprises in the ECE Region*, GE. 92-32210/3294c (November 1992).
37. R. A. Iskenderov, "Edinovremennye i tekushchie zatraty v domakh ZhSK," *Zhilishchnoe stroitel'stvo*, no. 3 (1989): 14.
38. Iskenderov, op. cit. 15.
39. According to the government's official statistical handbook, 29.4 million families (41 percent of all families) saved for the sake of their children. See Goskomstat, *Narodnoe khozyaistvo SSSR v 1988 g.*, 96–7.
40. N. V. Kalinina, "Guaranteeing Housing Reform in the USSR: A Few Suggestions for Reforming the System of Housing Provision," paper prepared for International Conference: Housing Debates – Urban Challenges, Paris (3–6 July 1990): 4.
41. N. Alekseev, *Ekonomicheskii eksperiment. Sotsial'nye aspekty*, "Mysl" (Moscow, 1987): 195–6.
42. D. Pudikov, "Finansirovanie i kreditovanie kooperativnogo i individual'nogo zhilishchnogo stroitel'stva, 'Finansy'" (Moscow, 1980): 63.
43. M. Buzhevich, "Stroitel'nyi kooperativ," *Pravda* (30 September 1985). According to personal informants, construction delays have not been reduced since then.
44. V. Arkhangel'skii, "Kooperativnyi dom," *Sotsialisticheskaya industriya*, 11 (March 1986): 6.
45. *SP SSSR*, 1988, no. 16, art. 43.
46. *Zhilishchnoe i kommunal'noe khozyaistvo*, no. 5 (1989): 6; Goskomstat, *Narodnoe khozyaistvo SSSR za 70 let* (Moscow, 1987): 515–16. In Belarus cooperatives were to contribute 26 percent of new building in the period 1991–95, compared with 11.5 percent in 1981–85.
47. Tsentral'nyi nauchno-issledovatel'skii i proektnyi institut tipovogo i eksperimental'nogo proektirovaniya zhilishcha (TsNIIEP zhilishcha), *General'naya skhema obespecheniya k 2000 godu kazhdoi sovetskoi sem'i otdel'noi kvartiroi ili individual'nym domom*, Goszakaz No. 2-18-0043-88: I. 2) (Moscow, 1988).

48. No. 300 of 9 April 1993; no. 813 of 24 August 1993 and no. 600 of 9 August 1994. Cited in Materialy k vystupleniyu na mezhdunarodnom ekspertnom seminare "Zhilishchnoe dvizhenie i mestnye vlasti" (17–19 May 1995), Prezident-Hotel, Moscow.

49. E. M. Blekh, *Povyshenie effektivnosti ekspluatatsii zhilykh zdanii*, Stroiizdat, (Moscow, 1987): 14.

50. *SZ SSSR*, 1990, "O sobstvennosti," *Izvestiya* (10 March 1990).

51. In November 1994, Luzhkov, the mayor of Moscow, issued a decree "On the Specificities of Registering the Right to Ownership of Accommodation in Housing Cooperatives and House Building Cooperatives." The short decree was concerned with the right to bequeath and inherit a flat in a cooperative dwelling.

52. A key turning point in the legitimation of this peculiarly Russian insurance system came in 1992 when the law sanctioned the legal entry of state security officers into the private market to provide a roof (*krysha*) of protection and enforcement services.

53. Richard Swedberg, "Max Weber's Sociology of Capitalism." Paper given at the 4th European Conference of Sociology, Amsterdam (August 1999): 14, citing G. Roth and C. Wittich (eds.) *Economy and Society: An Outline of Interpretive Sociology*, ed., (Berkley: University of California Press, 1978), chapter 2, section 31: 165. See also R. Swedberg, *Max Weber and the Idea of Economic Sociology* (Princeton: Princeton University Press, 1998), 82ff.

54. Richard Swedberg, "Max Weber's Sociology of Capitalism" (August 1999) op.cit., 24.

55. Stephanie Harter, *From "Third Rome" to "Third Italy"? Economic Networks in Russia*. Research Papers in Russian and East European Studies, No. REES97/1, Center for Russian and East European Studies (University of Birmingham, 1997).

56. In the case of the wood-processing combine in the garrison town of Sertolovo, near St.Petersburg, the director set up a bakery and confectionery within its precincts; he admitted that it was illegal but that he was forced to act in this way in order to pay his debts. More importantly, despite its illegality he had completed all the necessary documentation and had acquired all the official stamps required to do what he was (illegally) doing!

57. Harter, op. cit. 15.

58. R. Putnam, *Making Democracy Work. Civic Traditions in Modern Italy* (Princeton, N.J.: Princeton University Press, 1993). D. Stark, "Path Dependence and Privatisation Strategies in East Central Europe," *Eastern European Politics and Societies*, vol. 6, No. 1 (1992), 17–54; "Recombitant Property in East European Capitalism," *American Journal of Sociology*, vol. 101, no. 4 (1996): 993–1027; G. Grabher and D. Stark, "Organizing Diversity: Evolutionary Theory, Network Analysis and Post-socialism" in J. Pickles and A. Smith, op. cit.

59. Olga E.Bessonova, *Institutsional'naya teoriya khozayaistvennogo razvitiya Rossii*, in T. I. Zaslavskaya, Z. I. Kalugina, V. A. Artemov, T. Yu. Bogomolova, O. E. Bessonova, M. A. Shabanova (eds.) *Sotsial'naya traektoriya reformiruemoi ROSSII* (Issledovaniya Novosibirskoi ekonomiko-sotsiologicheskoi shkoly), Novosibirsk: Nauka, Siberian Enterprise RAS (1999): 245–72; *Instituty razdatochnoi ekonomiki. Retrospektivnyi analiz.* Novosibirsk, 1997; "Razdatochnaya ekonomika kak Russkaya traditsiya," in *Obshchestvennye Nauki*, no. 3 (1994): 37–49.

60. As the basic building block of the system, its (functional) equivalent in the market economy is the "commodity."

61. V. Ushakov, *Nemyslimaya Rossiya. Rossiya kak ideya* (Moscow: Argus, 1995), 416. Cited by Bessonova, 278.

62. In Robert Putman's words, this means "where you get to depends on where you're coming from." R. Putnam, *Making Democracy Work: Civic Traditions in Modern Italy* (Princeton, N.J.: Princeton University Press, 1993), 79.

63. E. Gellner, "The Politics of Anthropology," *Government and Opposition*, vol. 23, no. 3 (Summer 1988): 294.

64. T. Gustafson, *Capitalism Russian-Style* (Cambridge: Cambridge University Press, 1999), 74.

65. M. Gorbachev, *Political Report of the CPSU Central Committee to the 27th Party Congress* (Moscow: Novosti Press, 1986), 51.

8

The Military–Industrial Complex, Technological Change, and the Space Industry

Stefanie Harter

On 23 March 2001, the Russian space station *Mir* stopped after 15 years of reliable service. With a precision unexpected for many outside observers, the remains of the worldwide first space station fell into the Pacific Ocean. The event was of symbolic relevance: no other technological achievement of the former Soviet Union represented the former Communist country so visibly as a superpower whose influence could be felt even in space. And no other event marked the final failure of the Soviet Union's economic development path as painfully as the decision to stop the *Mir* program in favor of the joint international space project, the International Space Station. For almost one decade, *Mir* signified the struggle of a postcommunist cash-strapped country to compete if not economically, but at least technologically with industrialized countries and to preserve its human capital made up of a well-educated, skilled, and technologically versatile workforce, which in Soviet times was, above all, concentrated in the military industrial complex. However, Gagarin's heirs were unable to continue ambitious space projects and had to recognize that Russia no longer could afford to conquer space on its own but had to co-operate with international partners.

Even more, the political-technological elite, which in the early days of perestroika nurtured the vision that the country could transform its economy to a Western-type and wealthy economy by relying on the technological achievements generated in the defense industry, had to acknowledge that this aspiration was unsustainable. Besides being short of money, the late Soviet Union and then Russia displayed a technological backwardness in almost all sectors of the economy that stood in sharp contrast to the Soviet Union's achievements in space technology. The reasons for this unfavorable situation (or its "liabilities") lay, first, with Soviet central planning and, second, the focus on weapon production and large-scale space programs. The central planning system was responsible for organizational fragmentation, functional specialization and organizational isolation of the various components of the research and development (R&D) system. As a consequence, the innovation process in the Soviet Union was inefficient and its performance poor.[1]

Knowledge generated in the various organizations was not systematically exploited in the productive system. The price system provided no incentive for innovation. Technological change was not customer oriented. Production and R&D proved inflexible to adjust to new technological developments, hence, no feedback loops increased efficiency. There was no banking system in place to channel financial means to the most promising technologies. No insurance system cushioned the risks attached to implementing product and process innovation. High costs and a waste of resources were the result of an inefficient production process.

The second reason for the country's technological backwardness was the strong position of the Military–Industrial complex (MIC), which during Soviet times, claimed approximately 70 percent of the budget earmarked for R&D. The sector imposed secrecy requirements, which suffocated exchange of scientific information among the different branches of science and across ministerial boundaries. Organizations like the All-Union Institute for Scientific and Technical Information for the civilian sector and the All-Union Institute for Inter-branch Information for the defense sector had to serve as information channelling agencies.[2] Yet, they could not overcome the structural deficiencies, which were at the roots of a relatively unsuccessful—given favorable material and human endowments of the Soviet economy—innovation and diffusion process. Only sectors that were generously granted material, financial and human resources, and which were exposed to international competition, like the space and missiles industry, could mitigate the effects that insufficient technological change had on economic performance, and in fact produce outstanding high-technology products.

Nevertheless, the unfavorable molding of the innovation system that the Soviet Union bequeathed to Russia, namely inflexible technological networks, the predominance of military and space technologies and high barriers to entry for new entrepreneurs, has certainly contributed to Russia's difficulties in adapting to a market system and to the country's economic decline in the 1990s. Russia's economic deterioration has called forth a wide range of qualitative explanations. The institutional setting was proclaimed to be responsible, inter alia, for the low rates of investment and, hence, for the sluggish technological restructuring of industry. Despite the acknowledgment of institutional deformation, however, it is still unclear what the abandonment of the Soviet National Innovation System (NIS) and the significant cuts in R&D expenditure imply. Above all, two questions remain unanswered.

First, is "unlearning" of militarily oriented scientific knowledge salutary or is the "deskilling" of a considerable part of the working population detrimental to further technological development of the country? In other words, if the MIC has dominated industrial R&D, then the sharp fall in state financing of science and technology must be beneficial, as it rids the country from unwanted knowledge. Similarly, if too many people were employed in militarily oriented R&D, then their outflow into other spheres of economic activity must be healthy for transition. Simultaneously, however, it is erroneous to assume that skills that might be exploited for civilian purposes can be preserved over a decade of continuous decline in production and scientific output and employment. Also, the breaking up of scientific teams is detrimental to technological progress. This ambivalence makes it difficult to assess whether the legacy of the technological base of the MIC is an asset or a liability, and can definitely not be answered unequivocally for all industrial branches and enterprises.

Second, any technological progress builds on previous achievements and insights. A country's technological competence is highly path dependent and more than one technological avenue leads to a nation's wealth.[3] If, however, technological advance is cumulative, what does the discontinuation of the technological innovation effort, as what happened in the Russian Federation, mean for its economy? Organizations, their viability, profitability and survival depend on the institutional structure that has brought them into existence.[4] The complex web of interdependent contracts and other relationships has been constructed on the base of an incentive structure embedded in the institutional/organizational structure of economies.[5] What happens if the nature of the institutional structure is fundamentally altered? While new technologies often are not well accommodated by prevailing institutional structures and therefore require institutional reform, no record exists of what happens when institutional reform takes place before new technologies claim an alteration.

This contribution does not set out to answer these questions in a rigorous way but attempts to provide some ideas of how they could be answered. The following section gives a brief overview over the Russian defense industry in general as it presented itself over the last decade. It sketches economic performance, ownership structures, output and employment structures per industrial sector and provides an explanation of why the defense complex could not live up to the expectations attached to it from a technological perspective. The space industry will then be singled out in the following section. A description of the sector, of its adjustment strategies, and the reasons for its relative success are given. The space industry serves as an example to illustrate the relationship between transition, technological change and economic performance. One reason for choosing this sector is that the space industry is characterized by a close interrelation of basic research, experimental developments, production of space hardware and its exploitation.[6] Aerospace technology reflects directly a nation's science and technology development capability as it synergistically employs the scientific knowledge of almost all disciplines. Another reason for the choice is that the Russian space industry was able to attract foreign direct investment and to become part of an international technology network. The final two sections briefly introduce the concept of national innovation systems and the notion of complexity and its implications for Russia's technological resuscitation.

THE MILITARY–INDUSTRIAL COMPLEX

Under the last Soviet Secretary General, Mikhail Gorbachev, the defense and space industries were still perceived as a source of technological progress, eventually capable of salvaging the entire Soviet economy from decline. From 1992 onwards, however, at the latest, the now changed, and reform-minded new political elite saw the military industrial complex (MIC) as a major obstacle to economic reform. Its poor record of technological spillover effects for civilian goods no longer justified the resources it devoured. Consequently, budget spending on defense declined and the famous nine ministries that had previously managed the sector, were dissolved. Defense spending reductions, declining foreign demand, changes in the decision-making structure on both the federal and the regional levels, and privatization that took place in the wake of the general economic transformation in Russia have left their traces on the internal structure of the defense industrial sector.

Although with a time lag and less intensively than could have been expected, the cuts in the defense budget had a direct impact on the scale of military production and on the R&D sector. In addition, the macroeconomic environment was as unfavorable to the defense industry as it was to all other industrial branches. Reduced civilian demand, high interest rates and thus restricted access to credits, the dominance of barter trade, the state budget deficit and other variables impacted negatively on the sector. The lack of investment resulted in an aging capital stock, which exacerbated the difficulties of the MIC to adjust to the new environment.

The contraction of production has affected the various branches of the defense industry to different degrees. The year 1994 proved for all branches, except the space and missiles industry, the most difficult year. Whereas in 1992 and 1993 state subsidies and interenterprise arrears could buffer the official decline of defense spending and allowed enterprises to continue production, the need for real adjustment became more acute in 1994. In the following year, the armament, communication equipment, radio and aviation industries were hard hit, but the output decline was already less serious. Energy prices proved to be of minor importance to defense enterprises as energy suppliers were not allowed to cut off supply to insolvent clients. This was an implicit subsidization for at least some of the branches. The year 1996 reflected again a significant decline in output, which proved to be especially severe for the electronics industry. Only by late 1999 and then again over the year 2000, did the trend in production reversed.

Table 8.1.   Output and Employment of the Russian Defense Industry, 1991–2000 (1991 = 100)

	1991	1992	1993	1994	1995	1996	1997	1998	1999	2000
Total Output of										
Defense Industry	100	80.4	64.6	39.2	31.2	22.7	19.7	19.2	25.5	32.0
Incl. Military	100	49.5	32.5	19.9	16.6	12.8	9.4	9.9	13.5	17.5
Civilian	100	99.6	85.6	52.6	41.3	29.1	28.7	26.5	34.1	41.0
Employment in										
Defense Industry	100	90.3	79.9	78.2	67.1	58.6	52.7	47.3	44.6	45.1

Source: Julian Cooper (2001), *The Russian Military–Industrial Complex: Current Problems and Future Prospects,* 2.

The decline in output is, again with a time lag and less drastically, reflected in the employment figures of the sector. Russia inherited from the Soviet Union 1,060 military industrial enterprises and 943 R&D and design institutions, which together employed approximately 6.5 million people.[7] Between 1992 and 1995, about 2.5 million workers left the sphere of military production. In the following year, another 368,000 departed and the number of employees reached 2,611,000, in both industry and science. Between August 1996 and August 1997, only 332,000 former defense employees left and employment amounted then to 2,279,000 people. Of those, almost a fourth of the industrial personnel and more than a third of the science personnel was employed by the aviation industry.[8] Thus, the speed of employees leaving the sector has diminished since 1995. By then the majority of those employees with transferable skills has left the military-oriented industry.

The fact that defense workers left the sector is not surprising as monthly wages in the defense sector, were always markedly lower than in the industry as a whole. The only exception was the shipbuilding industry, where orders placed by foreign customers appeared to have compensated for declining Russian orders and therefore allowed for higher wage payments. Only during two years, in 1998 and 1999, did annual average wages in the space and missile branch surpass the shipbuilding industry. One consequence of low wages was that personnel in defense enterprises consisted either of unskilled employees or of pensioners and employees of almost pension age, whereas young, skilled, mobile and flexible employees were far more likely to have left the sector.

In 1996, within the defense complex 2,031 organizations of various juridical status were active. By January 2001, the number of enterprises and organizations has declined to 1,631. (See table 8.2.) A comparison of the total numbers, however, is somewhat misleading as organizations that were previously counted as one entity might have split up and subsequently be counted individually, which increases the figure. An opposite effect occurs when enterprises and research and design institutes that are combined together in a holding or a unitary

Stefanie Harter

state company and then counted as one, or those which are transferred out of realm of the State Committee for Defense Industries and not counted at all.

New forms of property and organization, such as cooperatives and small enterprises emerged as soon as 1989, but the preparations for the privatization of the defense industry started in earnest in 1991. However, the federal law "On enterprises and entrepreneurial activities," which was implemented by decree (No. 445-1) of the Supreme Soviet on 25.12.1990 exclusively reserved the "production of any kind of weapon, ammunition, explosives, pyrotechnical articles, and also the repair of arms" for state enterprises. As a result, many defense enterprises were not allowed to change ownership.

On April 13, 1996 the presidential decree "On measures to implement efficient state control in privatizing enterprises and organizations of the defense complex" listed 480 enterprises and organizations that were not allowed to be privatized. In another 142 enterprises the state either held a golden share or a packet of shares larger than 19 percent of the total value of shares. In addition, even privatized entities continued their cooperation with *Goskomoboronprom*. The aviation industry, the armament producing industry and

Table 8.2. Structure of the Russian Defense Industry, 1 January 2001 (number of enterprises and organizations)

	Fully State Owned	*Joint Stock Company with State Holding*	*Joint Stock Company with No State Holding*	*Total*
Rosaviakosmos	171	124	110	405
Aviation Industry	88	111	101	300
Missile Space Industry	83	13	9	105
RAV Conventional Arms Industry	57	52	24	133
Rosboepripasov Munitions/Special Chemicals	105	19	13	137
Rossudostroenie Shipbuilding Industry	75	52	43	170
RASU	262	223	269	754
Radio industry	120	55	131	306
Communications Equipment Industry	61	45	45	151
Electronics Industry	81	123	93	297
Minpromnauka Industry of Special Purpose	31	—	1	33
Total	701	470	460	1,631

Source: Julian Cooper (2001), *The Russian Military–Industrial Complex: Current Problems and Future Prospects*, 7.

the communication equipment industry were the most actively involved branches in the privatization process. The space industry, by contrast, is until today predominantly state-owed.

Some defense enterprises were in the favorable position of producing military goods that met international demand and could thereby partly compensate for declining domestic state orders. However, the proceeds did not always meet the initial expectations. For one thing, foreign policy factors, like NATO expansion, and the sharp contraction of the world arms market after the Cold War up to 1995 were responsible for diminished exports. Second, the publicity accompanying the conversion program, administrative rearrangements, economic and political instability in the Russian Federation, persisting quality problems, and competition from Western suppliers also discouraged potential customers from entering long-term relationships with Russian weapon producers. Additionally, the long-standing inconsistency of the state and commercial structures, the multitude of intermediaries, organizations, and producers that all competed for the same potential clients damaged Russia's image as a serious arms dealer.

Summarizing all these characteristics, Ksenia Gonchar came to the following conclusion: "At present the worst-case scenario has materialised: Russia's defence-industrial base is autarchic, technologically stagnant, socially depressed and is still organised in the outdated form of a defence complex."[9] Despite a slight recovery since 1999, owed to the ruble devaluation and associated import substitution, some recovery in domestic investment and some modest increase in domestic military procurement, there are no visible signs of a sustainable recovery or conversion. Export products originate in Soviet technological developments and what once was considered the core element of a National Innovation System has sharply lost its reputation with one exception: parts of the space industry.

THE RUSSIAN SPACE SECTOR

Russia has inherited about 80 percent of the space-missile production potential of the Soviet Union. In 1992, about 1,000 enterprises, design institutes, 11 information processing sites on ground, and 3 launching sites belonged to the space-missiles sector.[10] Among the most important companies are the Russian Space Company RKK "Energiya," the Science- and Production Organization Lavochkina, the design bureau "Salyut," which is part of the Krunichev State Research and Production Space Centre and the NPO PM (Applied Mechanics Research and Production Enterprise in Krasnoyarsk-26).[11] Forty percent of the research facilities of the space sector are located in and around Moscow.[12]

The space missile industry, when part of *Goskomoboronprom* (the state committee for defense industry), had in 1996 a total of 205,000 employees (151,000 in industry and 54,000 in science). This number was reduced in 1997 to 189,000 (130,000 in industry and 59,000 in science) people.[13] One has to bear in mind that as early as between 1990 and 1994, the total number of workers in basic enterprises of the space complex decreased by 35 percent, the reduction of specialists turned out to be even higher, namely, 50 percent.[14] The concrete example of the space company "Energiya" illustrates this decline quite well: whereas in the Soviet past about 10,000 workers had worked four shifts, in 1999, only 6,000 workers worked one shift.

The Soviet legacy in the space industry has, above all, three shortcomings. First, it is far too expensive to maintain and badly organized, scattered mainly over three former Soviet republics: Russia, Kazakhstan and Ukraine. The major ground stations were also located in Ukraine, in Central Asia, the Caucasus and even Mongolia. These stations were crucial for control and monitoring purposes; it was here where data processing from the various satellites took place and provided support systems for military communication.[15] In addition, a fleet of support ships, which was equipped with military and academic staff, obtained various national headquarters after the breakup of the USSR. The launching facilities are equally dispersed over the territory, with Tyuratam in Kazakhstan, known as Baikonur, being the most famous cosmodrome. Disputes over the space business started soon after the breakup of the USSR as the Ukraine, Kazakhstan and Moldova feared an increasingly imminent Russian domination. The countries refused to sign further accords on space, which confronted Russia with significant handicaps in its ability to continue the Soviet space program.

The problems included not only launching sites, ground bases, tracking stations and early warning radar systems but also the production and R&D potential.[16] Russia was and still is dependent on subcontractors in other CIS countries. For example, companies in the Ukraine hold "an essential monopoly over technologies critical to electronic intelligence, early-warning and radar ocean reconnaissance satellites."[17] This fact, however, has not deterred Russia from trying to control Ukraine's entry into the commercial launch market.[18] It seems, however, that the need to cooperate finally prevailed, putting the links between the two countries on a more stable footing. A similar pattern emerged with Kazakhstan.

Second, the space industry is characterized by serious technological weaknesses. Soviet space activities were characterized by prowess with the macrostructuring of heavy lift vehicles and manned orbiters but a backwardness in the miniaturization of subsystems.[19] The latter will be decisive for positioning a country in this globalized industry. Third, the high number of organizations, production enterprises and R&D institutes has led to a very low level of cooperation to solve technical, financial and organizational problems. Instead of cooperating domestically, the individual units started to strive to gain a superior position at the expense of other enterprises. Best examples are the attempts to set up different satellite launching facilities.

Given the limited resources the enterprises could attract from state and private investors, the multitude of projects and the lack of consolidation have resulted in reduced production volumes, in decreasing employment figures and in a reduced average wage, which, however, in comparison to other defense branches, was the highest in 1998.[20] Recovering production figures can be observed since 1997.

In addition, the fate of the space station *Mir* vividly illustrates that Russia can no longer live on previous achievements and that it has used up its resources. New funds are needed in order to ensure the maintenance of technological excellence. A reorganization of its production base and, most likely a scaled-down version of its geographically dispersed launching platforms—not least due to their location in countries that are no longer Russian—are needed to streamline the restructuring process. Furthermore, reinvigorated research and development efforts are imperative to ensure continued global interest in the sector.

In the past, nearly all clients of space services were governmental agencies or budget-funded organizations. Like in other countries, the relations between the Russian space sector and other sectors of the economy were nonmarket ones. The prices for space services were set mainly by availability of budget money to the producer and the customer. To some degree this is valid today as well, although commercial application, especially in the sphere of telecommunication, is gaining in importance. Nevertheless, the economic situation of this branch is highly sensitive to the political situation, as well as to the overall economic situation of the country.[21] Both conditions have been unfavorable in the Russian Federation since 1992, and this has translated into sharply reduced budgetary funding of the sector. Since the introduction of reform in 1992 the space sector has, similar to the Russian R&D system as a whole, suffered severe financial cutbacks.[22] In addition to the low levels of finance, the resources are also allocated inefficiently, directed towards nonpromising projects instead of promising ones.[23] An additional problem is the poor funding for science in general, on which the space industry as an integrated industrial branch depends: if science suffers, the space program suffers with it.[24]

Some of the major enterprises of the RKA were relatively successful in accessing extra budgetary funds and sources of finance. Income from commercial orders over the period between 1996–98 amounted to around $1 billion—the same amount that could be secured from the state budget.[25] Also, the organizations of the RKA were able to earn $720 million from foreign contracts in 1997, while the Russian state provided merely $290 million for federal space programs.[26] The cooperation program of the Russian Federation and the United States for sending American astronauts to *Mir* over the period from 1996 to 2000 contributed another $ 400 million to the overall space budget.[27] According to Interfax, the 2000 budget earmarks 3.4 billion rubles ($ 119 million) to the space program, while 1.5 billion rubles in additional budget revenues are to go toward keeping *Mir* in orbit.[28]

Given domestic financial difficulties, the Russian space sector relies to a large extent on international cooperation—a process that started already in the 1970s despite technological, political and economic competition between the United States and the USSR. Although the Soviet space program was guided by secrecy, which at times resulted in outright denial of projects (such as the development of the space shuttle Buran), collaborative international space missions, a focus on commercial activities and the acquisition of advanced Western technologies were emphasized already then.[29] In 1973, Zvezdnyi gorodok, the "Star city" just outside Moscow, was opened to the Americans. In 1975, the Soyuz-Apollo docking raised the hope for future joint projects and first ideas for a joint U.S.-Soviet manned mission emerged at that time. More intensive cooperation was hampered, though, by Soviet military space imperatives on the one side—apparently 75 percent of all Soviet satellites had exclusively military functions[30]—and international relations on the other.

The space sector opened again in the late 1980s for economic, scientific and technological international cooperation.[31] In particular, commercial considerations gained in importance. One reason for this shift in attitude was that space programs have lost both their superior political importance and public support.[32] In the years following 1991, two aspects, namely, financial support during the Soviet era for prestige projects combined with, albeit initially limited, international collaboration proved to be advantageous for the space industry in the years following 1991. Unlike in other branches of the MIC, the technological achievements of Soviet years and international exposure were well suited to position the Russian space industry in the international arena. Besides the cooperation on an organizational level,[33] a number of joint projects between Russian and Western/Japanese companies have since emerged.

International cooperation will be crucial for embedding the Russian space industry into the global market to exchange scientific and technological results. With the fast advancement in communication technologies, space-related activities become a profitable sector and require more than mere technology—complementary assets such as organization, insurance, after-launch-service, training, information processing facilities, secure intellectual property rights and financial services will be critical ingredients for prospering in the market. One example of a successful cooperation can be found in engine production. The Science and Production Organisation (NPO) Energomash, located just outside Moscow, has used the marketing experience of Pratt & Whittney in order to provide American missile carriers with its engines.[34] On a less mundane level, though, international cooperation is needed in order to increase labor productivity and promote investment activity at home.

As Slavo Radosevic has cautioned, technological integration, in particular into a dynamic learning process at the international level, does not automatically accompany foreign direct investment. Although increased productivity as a consequence of foreign direct investment is indisputable, long-term growth prospects based on sustainable technological learning over a longer time span are far more problematic to maintain.[35] This applies in particular to the space launching sector, where foreign firms aim at utilizing Russian technology rather than importing it and at benefiting from the relatively low price of the final Russian product.[36] Furthermore, another motivation for foreign engagement in the sector, it has been argued, is to prevent Russia becoming a major competitor on the international markets, especially in the space-launching market.[37]

Major international projects include the International Space Station (ISS or MKS, the Russian abbreviation), the Sea launch project and satellite launching on a commercial base. Officially, the MKS is replacing the Russian *Mir* in order to focus Russia's sparse finances on one project only, thereby confirming Russian willingness to subordinate its national priorities in space to a U.S.-dominated venture. In practice, however, a range of problems has emerged that are poised to strain NASA/RAKA relations. There is, for example, no scientific plan and working schedule for the Russian segment of the MKS. Due to financial difficulties, the Russian side was also forced to find unorthodox means of payment for working on the MKS. In order to raise $60 million they had to lease about one-third of the segment to NASA for a period of three years.[38] "Morskoi start" (Sea launch) is the other major cooperation project on an international level and includes Russia, the Ukraine, Norway and the United States. The launching platform, from which the booster rocket "Zenit" transports satellites into orbit, has taken up work in March 1999. The project has, besides delineating organizational issues on an international level, also contributed to the reorganization of enterprise links within Russia.

Until the year 2006, the world market volume of launching satellites is expected to amount to a total of $30 billion. The revenue will be shared among the current market leaders, which are the European consortium Arianspace; the International Launch Services, which consists of the U.S. Lockheed Martin and GKNPTs im. Khrunicheva, and Boeing supplying missiles of the Delta series.[39] Russia has always been globally competitive in space launching technology. Between 4 October 1957 and the beginning of 1995, the Soviet Union and later Russia launched about 3,000 booster rockets. At the beginning of transition, in 1993–94, Russia possessed around 60 percent of world capacity for satellite launching, which could, however, not be translated into economic success, as the country held only 3 percent of the world space launch market.[40] During the last decade, Proton-K, the booster rocket that competes with the American Titan-4, the Japanese N-2 and the European Ariane, transported 140 satellites into orbit. It is this potential that makes Russia as a commercial supplier for satellite launches an attractive partner. As the waiting lists for sputniks to be placed into orbit are long, the capability to work at great speed and the availability of boosters definitely are an advantage.[41]

Although Russia can still boast a good reputation and experience, the competition will be fierce in the future and it is not clear whether the Russian positive forecasts to expand its marketshare will come true. The financial collapse of Iridium and the financial difficulties of ICO Global, another satellite-based telecommunication company, cast serious doubts on the economic viability of the branch as a whole.[42] Furthermore, the number of failed satellite launches of Russia and the Ukraine between 1995 and 1999 taken together have doubled in comparison to the launches between 1981–94, despite the fact that the absolute number of launches has fallen.[43] Also, the two crashes of the carriers "Proton" that occurred in July and October 1999 have been put down to human failures due to falling qualifications of the personnel at one of the manufacturing companies. Apparently, the company was at a standstill for at least one year because of lacking orders, and wage arrears have accumulated as well, which negatively influenced workers' motivation.[44] Qualified staff leaves the sector, production cooperation within the CIS is falling, and civilian operators that have replaced military ones proved to be less experienced.[45]

SOVIET AND RUSSIAN NATIONAL INNOVATION SYSTEMS

The experience of the Russian defense sector corroborates the fact that knowledge per se does not automatically lead to the generation and diffusion of technological innovation and hence to economic growth. Rather, nation-specific factors such as the volume and structure of R&D spending, education, labor markets, trade policies, financial systems, industrial structure, competitive climate, public support to industrial innovation, the organization and coordination mechanisms of the science and technology (S&T) system, but also the existence of nonlinear, complex networks play a crucial role. These elements can be subsumed under the concept of NIS. In Stan Metcalfe's words a national innovation system is

> that set of distinct institutions which jointly and individually contribute to the development and diffusion of new technologies and which provides the framework within which governments form and implement policies to influence the innovation process. As such it is a system of interconnected institutions to create, store and transfer the knowledge, skills, artefacts which define new technologies. The element of nationality follows not only from the domain of technology policy but also from elements of shared language and culture which bind the system together, and from the national focus of other policies, laws and regulations which condition the innovative environment.[46]

NIS denotes the larger institutional and cultural system of a country, in which firms, which are the key actors in the implementation and development of new technology, are embedded. NIS includes those "features that draw a divide between what is inside, and what is outside, a particular nation state."[47] Such a definition of a NIS makes clear that assets and liabilities for a move to a technology-based capitalism cannot be disaggregated in social, political and economic factors, but have to be viewed as a unified whole. The transformation of the technological system of the Soviet Union therefore has to take into account the legacies of the past regime but also the permanent changes that occur in society, in the economic structure, in the priorities as laid out by the new government and the way these elements are interrelated.

The main characteristic of the Soviet NIS that Russia inherited in 1992 was—apart from being centrally planned, administered and monitored—the predominance of the MIC and its technological requirements. As a result, Soviet R&D suffered from shortcomings such as a linear understanding of knowledge generation, a high degree of isolation, neglected cooperation between invention and practical application, and hierarchically organized innovation channels.[48]

Deficiencies had been identified from the late 1960s on. By 1971 it was officially acknowledged that an altered institutional environment and better administration were necessary to promote the transition from an uneven pattern of innovation to effective innovation in all sectors. Computerization and long-term planning were put forward to achieve this goal.[49] These instruments were, however, not sufficient to reform the then existing Soviet NIS. The introduction of market forces to improve the performance was opposed not only by the administrative and bureaucratic hierarchy but also by the researchers themselves, whose desire for professional security made them unwilling to radically recast the system.[50] Two decades later, the director of the Yuri Gagarin cosmonaut training center complained that the results brought back by the cosmonauts to earth from their missions were lost like in a big hole. This, he claimed, hinted towards an undirected and purposeless space program lacking continuity and a clearly formulated objective.[51]

Despite the fact that innovative methods of management were introduced and the science and technology infrastructure was improved, the exploitation of R&D results remained the weak point of the Soviet space effort. In 1986, a comparison between Soviet and U.S. capabilities revealed that "the United States is leading in virtually every basic technology that could affect military and space capabilities over the next two decades."[52] As a result of Soviet shortcomings, in microelectronics and computer technologies, both crucial for further development, the Russian Federation today trails not only the United States but also Europe and some Asian countries.

After 1992, financial constraints on the Russian science sector have intensified and the organizational structure of the past could no longer guarantee future working of research organizations. Institutional devices to facilitate the commitment of resources to the innovation process were still missing. A stock market, laws and a legislation to limit the liability of an investor were not in place and could not provide a functioning market for ownership shares. Risks could not be reduced by the fundamental technique of insurance, and obligations between the principals and their agents were not defined. The establishment of new links between research institutes and enterprises proved to be difficult; ill-defined intellectual property rights, and weak contract enforcement mechanisms exacerbated the situation. Although Russia adopted a patent law, the ill-developed court system could not provide effective sanctions for infringement.[53]

These problems have led to a situation where only patchy progress was realized instead of an all-embracing, integrated technological leap forward that would have been necessary to design a coherent Russian NIS. In addition, the Russian R&D sector is characterized by a significant brain-drain as well as dwindling demand for scientific and technological results. The state as the main client has reduced its engagement. Many smaller and less important companies of the branch decayed. Also, smaller research institutes were looking independently for international cooperation partners, rendering the coordination of the sector more difficult. This is an important point if one takes into consideration that "the contribution of technology policy to the objective economic performance of a country depends at least as much on the 'weakest link' in the system which is being strengthened as on the resulting 'best shot'."[54]

One decade after the beginning of the reform process, the most critical points of Russian R&D have remained the same: limited applicability, a lacking cost awareness, an ill-developed banking system, unrealistic assessment of the state of the technological art and one's potential, and insecure intellectual property rights (especially patenting). This is also due to the fact that design institutions and research entities in industry have suffered most from the cut in expenditure of R&D, while the Academy of Science fared relatively better. As a result, basic research has actually increased its share in total R&D.[55] As a consequence, client-orientation and applicability have, on the whole, decreased. A comprehensive approach towards revising the NIS, which does not only focus on R&D funding but includes the promotion of technological networks, the establishment of venture funds, a transparent legal framework and a supporting trade and tariff system for high technology imports is still in its infancy, despite a series of government programs and intentions to improve the situation.

The difficulty in designing an appropriate NIS can also be found on the micro-level. On the one hand, a certain level of stability and security between the various members of the network is needed in order to cooperate in technological and highly complex projects. Trust is needed to compensate contract contingencies. On the other hand, however, if the old ossified links persist—in order to guarantee a minimum level of security—it will be more difficult to implement changes and to reorient Russian research and development processes and routines towards civilian purposes. An exacerbating factor is the resource and power structures that existed within the network: participants are unlikely to give up a situation that still ensures some financial benefit and power. Although this trade-off between stability and transformation applies to the economy as a whole, the innovative sector is particularly affected as the high degree of complexity, long-term commitments and high upfront capital expenditure require a pronounced level of stability in order to yield future results. This, it appears, is also a reason why during transition innovational networks change so slowly and pose problems to delineating suitable institutions for the innovation system.

To conclude, it can be said that the national system of innovation and the accompanying restructuring of enterprises on a larger scale has not sufficiently taken place in the Russian Federation during the first decade of reforms. Industrial and technology policy that might have enabled and stimulated the changes and pressed for a reconfiguration of the policy portfolio were not implemented. A policy that would have "aimed at generating collective learning for cumulativeness in the restructuring process"[56] in order to provide enterprises that lag behind in adjusting mechanisms with an applicable body of knowledge was absent. Thus, the major shortcoming of the Soviet NIS, which was determined by the weakest link, that is, the low ability to provide basic consumption goods at a minimal level of quality, reliability and efficiency,[57] has still not been overcome to a satisfactory degree. A structural coherence of the system capable of coordinating complex processes of technological change, but also facilitating the "transition from each product vintage to the next"[58] has not yet been reached.

THE PROBLEM OF COMPLEXITY

Network flexibility and renewal as well as organizational adaptability are critical when it comes to the acquisition of new core capabilities and complementary assets for enterprises, R&D institutions and state organizations alike.[59] Whereas Western countries can rely on outside sources of technology through formal and informal networks, such as business links, private and state associations, and closer cooperation between universities and enterprises, Soviet technology was predominantly dependent on sources that were embedded in the formal branch structure. Research conducted at institutes of higher education or within the Russian Academy of Science on behalf of the military industry could theoretically fall back on a wider pool of knowledge, but yet again, secrecy requirements very often restricted interdisciplinary scientific exchange and limited knowledge generation and distribution. Cross-sectoral innovations, a common feature of Western technological achievements, were rare in the USSR. Informal and unconventional innovation at the enterprise level was especially directed towards overcoming supply bottlenecks rather than towards adapting production to market demand. Although new product development took place as well, process innovation dominated over product innovation.[60] Science "did precious little pushing," despite the fact that the "dominant conceptualisation of the R&D process was in terms of crude science push."[61]

In addition, the Soviet innovation system has focused to a significant degree on formal research. However, research in market economies has shown that formal research rarely is the core activity in accumulating the knowledge-base for technical change.

> This is because the central feature of technical artefacts is their complexity, reflected in a large number of performance parameters and constraints that cannot be accurately represented or predicted in a simple theory or model, or fully specified in a series of blueprints or operating instructions. Trial, error and experience are therefore central to the improvement of technology.[62]

Innovation in a market economy demands an a priori assessment of the risks, costs and benefits of technological or organizational change, on which a corresponding innovation strategy may be based. Yet, optimizing strategies are only valuable when economic agents can foresee and specify the consequences that are likely to follow from each of them. Yet, all too often—and this applies above all to an economy that transposes its building blocs from one mode of transaction to another—"too many agents [are] doing too many things on too many different time scales" and thereby render foresight horizons complicated.[63] The interaction of many individual decisions produces unexpected outcomes at the aggregate level. Hence, dispersed and heterogeneous economic agents create a self-organizing system, which is, on the one hand, characterized by path dependence while, on the other hand, being inexperienced in establishing adaptive and nonlinear networks that are necessary to cope with the new institutional environment. The difficulty to redesign networks can be observed both on the technical and organizational levels.

Compared to other high technology sectors, the Russian space industry has adjusted with relative success, despite the fact that particularly the space industry—due to compact integration of diverse technologies—relies on a multitude of economic ties and long-lasting economic and technological relationships. These circumstances make it especially vulnerable to systemic economic reorganization, and even more so in the absence of adaptive nonlinear networks. Until the mid-90s, space and defense programs both in the West and in Russia in general fitted with the linear model of innovation, as clear responsibility was needed for each part of the delivery operation.[64] This situation changed, however, when civilian industries in advanced industrialized economies, especially information technologies, became more sophisticated and supplied a considerable part of the required inputs to the defense industry. This fact proves now to be advantageous for Western aerospace enterprises, since the institutional environment had laid the foundation for nonlinear technological development earlier than in Russia.

In addition to that, the American and Soviet space effort showed significant differences, especially in building carrier rocket systems and space apparatuses. The Americans could present qualitatively different systems with technical quantum leaps, whereas the Soviets were characterized by steady further development and modernization of proven systems. The West was also characterized by the tendency to perfectionism, whereas the Russian approach was to deliver solid products based on a pragmatic approach to technological problems.[65] While the Soviet space sector might have to some extent benefited from the linear approach to innovation, other branches, where organizational complexity is even more needed for technological progress and where the successful innovation process does not take place sequentially or hierarchically, have not. They are now badly prepared for adjustment to a changed institutional structure and, due to the interconnectedness of the space sector and other scientific branches, this will also affect the space industry.

Unlike NASA in the United States, no single organization responsible for the space effort has ever been created in the USSR. And, unlike other defense related branches of the Soviet industry, a single "space ministry" has never been established. The Minobshchemash, the Ministry of general machine building, which oversaw the missile production and was part of the nine defense-industry ministries, came closest to a centralizing body. The Communist Party was involved in the management process through the Politburo, which delineated the general direction of the Soviet space program. General executive oversight rested with the Military–Industrial Commission, as the military use of the sector dominated. Due to the technological requirements of the sector, basically all nine ministries in charge of the defense industry were included in the coordination and management of the branch. The Ministry of Defense was also an important player as it was responsible for the launch sites, training centers and many other support programs for both the civilian and military space programs. It was also the principal customer.[66]

The perceived deficiency of a unified administrative body has been tackled in March 1992 with the creation of the Russian Space Agency (*Rossiiskoe kosmicheskoe agentstvo*, RKA). The body was to manage and regulate the space program of the Russian Federation. It issues licenses and formulates government policy for the satellite sector.[67] Already in 1998, by presidential decree the RKA gained the oversight over the space-missile industry.[68] Furthermore, the RKA was supposed to receive more weight with the transfer of 350 aviation enterprises, design bureaux and other branch-related organizations under its supervision. With its extended responsibilities, in March 1999, RKA was renamed Russian Aviation and Space Agency (*Rossiiskoe aviatsionnoe i kosmicheskoe agentstvo*, RAKA). The aviation industry has always played a significant role in the space sector, in particular in producing space-related equipment such as rocket engines. Unfortunately, the RAKA has no legal authority, no adequate administrative apparatus and no staff to fulfill the intended functions. It will probably only be able to solve some secondary technical problems, such as standardization and to tackle some bureaucratic questions.[69]

Another issue, in which all state organizations surely want to be involved, is the control and regulation of financial flows. These stem predominantly from foreign contracts. The RAKA is an agency of executive power and has neither the right to export military products independently nor to get involved in commercial activities.[70] In addition, Rosvooruzhenie, the unitary state enterprise in charge of arms exports, pushed successfully into the market at the end of 1998.[71]

Another company that is highly interested in the launching proceeds and is involved in the sector is the Russian Satellite Communications Company, which is owned by Goskomsvyaz, the State Committee for Communication. It is the former monopolist in the field of satellite communications in Russia and owns some of the Russian commercial satellites. It provides space segment capacity and operates earth stations and satellite network services. This is also the company that represents and manages payment for Russian customers of Eutelsat, Intelsat and Intersputnik and has thus access to considerable financial means: its turnover was more than $50 million in 1996, with subsequent annual growth of 50 to 60 percent.[72]

The multitude of state organizations demonstrates first, that it is difficult to design an institutional structure that provides a level of certainty and predictability for the actors, when the latter themselves exert—from different starting positions, guided by different motives and incentives and acting on different time scales—a considerable impact on the design of the institutions. While the actions might appear rational from one agent's perspective, the aggregate outcome is far from optimal. It is therefore not surprising to observe a Russian space sector that, above all, lives from Soviet achievements but is ill-equipped to promote R&D in the area and transmit knowledge to other branches. Second, it shows that the diversity of interests and the absence of a single managing body allowed for a decentralized approach towards restructuring of the individual enterprises. This has increased competition and has promoted international cooperation.

CONCLUSION

In the introduction, two questions have been asked: first, whether "unlearning" of militarily oriented scientific skills is beneficial for the economy and, second, to what extent the interruption of cumulative technological learning is positively or negatively related to technological progress and the design of a national innovation system in Russia. Both questions relate to the broader scheme of the assets and liabilities of the Soviet system for Russian transformation. As one might have expected, the findings are inconclusive and answers vary for single branches or even enterprises. The space sector, a "best shot" of Soviet science, shows that unconditional "deskilling" that accompanies the sharp output decline of the economy and the concomitant unemployment is detrimental to further technological development. The failure to deliver some satellite launches, but also the technical difficulties experienced over the last years on the space station *Mir* show that it is insufficient to exploit Soviet technological knowledge without investing in new R&D. Furthermore, bad commercial and technological performance will at least in the midterm affect international competitiveness, thereby reducing the chances to access alternative sources of finance, and depriving the sector of being able to conducting future-oriented R&D. Hence, unconditional unlearning of skills is detrimental to technological and economic progress at least in those high technology sectors that experienced preferential treatment under the Communist regime.

However, the branch displayed a considerable absorptive capacity, which denotes a "firm's ability to identify, assimilate, and exploit knowledge from the environment and is itself determined by the nature and amount of the firm's own R&D investment."[73] Above all, the branch was better able to compensate for the lack of state funding by getting involved in the international market by exploiting its originally military knowledge. The development was helped by the upsurge of investment into telecommunication in the last decade. In particular, soft skills were absorbed by international cooperation partners. Hence, the process of cumulative learning was in the case of the space industry not interrupted but modified according to market requirements. The fact that the space industry is dependent on other scientific branches of the industry makes long-term success problematic and requires a coherent national innovation system in order to stay successful.

Also, the diversified organizational structure of the past has both pros and cons. On the one hand, it presents some difficulties for the reorganization of the industry today: too many stakes are involved in a potentially lucrative business. The privatization of some enterprises, the ownership status of sites and enterprises has added to the problems. Furthermore, the costs for reorganization are high as well. Without a clear-cut division of competencies, funding cannot be streamlined and international cooperation is made more difficult. On the other hand, the decentralized structure has allowed the individual companies to set up joint ventures with international partners without the constraining bureaucratic structure of a higher administration. A higher degree of freedom has contributed to a more flexible way of adjustment to the global market and helped to coordinate the sparse budgetary funding in order to maintain the production base and launching sites.

The analysis of the branch shows that the previous institutional structure of the scientific system exerts still influence on today's performance. Yet, without concomitant financial institutions, a competitive environment and a legal environment to support innovation the Russian technological effort of catching up with the major industrialized economies resembles aiming at a moving target while simultaneously standing on swampy ground, without an insurance against backfiring. This will not change unless the correct "interests" of all actors involved in the process of technological change—as has been pointed out in the introductory chapter of this book—are found, articulated and channeled into a direction that supports this trajectory of change.

NOTES

1. Julian Cooper (1982), "Innovation for Innovation in Soviet Industry," *Industrial Innovation in the Soviet Union,* ed. by R. Amann, and J. Cooper (New Haven and London: Yale University Press), 453–513, 455.

2. Stephen Fortescue (1990), *Science Policy in the Soviet Union* (London and New York: Routledge), 87.

3. Daniele Archibugi and Jonathan Michie (1997), "Technological Globalisation and National Systems of Innovation: An Introduction," *Technology, Globalisation and Economic Performance,* ed. by Daniele Archibugi and Jonathan Michie (Cambridge: Cambridge University Press), pp. 1–23, p.11.

4. D. North (1997), "Some Fundamental Puzzles in Economic History/Development," *The Economy as an Evolving Complex System II,* ed. by W. Brian Arthur, Steven N. Durlauf and David A. Lane (Reading, Mass.: Perseus Books), 223–237, 226.

5. D. North (1997), "Some Fundamental Puzzles in Economic History/Development," *The Economy as an Evolving Complex System II,* ed. by W. Brian Arthur, Steven N. Durlauf and David A. Lane (Reading, Mass.: Perseus Books), 223–237, 224.

6. http://www.fas.org/spp/civil/russia/chap_2.htm, accessed 7 March 1999.

7. *Rossiiskaya gazeta,* 14.5.1992.

8. http://server.vpk.ru/www.vpk, 25.10.1997.

9. Ksenia Gonchar (2000), "Russia's Defence Industry at the Turn of the Century," BICC, Brief 17 (November), 21.

10. *Literaturnaya gazeta* (22 January 1992): 12.

11. For a more detailed overview of the enterprises, see http.//iepnt1.itaip.doc.gov/bisnis/isa, accessed 8 March 1999.

12. D. Solopov and D. Osmolovskii (1997), "Kosmagoniya," *Kommersant,* No.43 (25 November): 44–46.

13. http://server.vpk.ru/www.vpk, accessed 25 October 1997.

14. http://www.fas.org/spp/civil/russia/chap_2.htm, accessed 7 March 1999.

15. Mallmann 1989, p. 36.

16. Matthew J. Von Bencke (1997), *The Politics of Space. A History of U.S.-Soviet/Russian Competition and Cooperation in Space* (Boulder: Westview Press), 142–154.

17. Von Bencke 1997, 143.

18. Von Bencke 1997, 146.

19. Neville Brown (1990), *New Strategy through Space* (Leicester: Leicester University Press), 238.

20. http://www.gov.ru/www-vpk/vpk/reports, accessed 7 March 1999.

21. http://www.fas.org/spp/civil/russia/chap_2.htm, accessed 7 March 1999.

22. Stanislav Simanovsky (1998), "Science and Technology in Russia. Problems and Prospects." Bericht des Bundesinstitut für ostwissenschaftliche und internationale Studien (BIOst), No. 18-1998 (Cologne: BIOst), 17.

23. *Nezavisimaya gazeta,* 12.4.2000, electronic version.

24. Von Bencke 1997, 124–7.

25. Walter Schilling (1999), "Rußlands Raumfahrt vor großen Problemen," *Osteuropa,* No. 5, 500–505, 502.

26. BBC, SWB, SU/3120 H/2, 14 April 1998.

27. Schilling 1999, 501.

28. RFE/RL, 13 April 2000.

29. Humble 1988, 116.

30. A fact that does equally apply to the American program, where expenditure for military space activities exceeded the NASA budget by a factor of two.

31. Mallmann 1989, 7–9.

32. *Literaturnaya gazeta* (22 January 1992), 12.

33. In 1992, the Russian Federation became the lawful successor state of the USSR in all aspects of space activities in international relations. Already the Soviet Union was engaged in international organizations and got involved in critical issues such as space law, which is promoted within the frame of the United Nations. The division between airspace and space, direct television, legal issues, rescue operations and disarmament negotiations were examples were the Soviet Union was involved on an international scale. The USSR was also a member of international organizations such as INMARSAT (shipping radio satellite organization), ITU (International Telecommunications Union), WMO (World Meteorological Organization) and COSPAS-SARSAT (Mallmann 1989: 60–1). Today, the Russian Federation is also represented in international committees such as the Forum of space agencies, the CEOS (Committee for Earth Observation Satellites), the International Federation of Astronauts, the COSPAR (Committee on space research), EUTELSAT and others (http://www.rka.ru/koi8-r/coop.html, accessed 22 January 1999).

34. Cf. *Nezavisimaya gazeta*, 13.5.2000; *Vedomosti* (21.3.2000): B4.

35. Slavo Radosevic (1999), "Alliances and Emerging Patterns of Technological Integration and Marginalisation of Central and Eastern Europe within the Global Economy," David Dyker (ed.), *Foreign Direct Investment and Technology Transfer in the Former Soviet Union* (Cheltenham: Edward Elgar), 27–51, 28.

36. Liudmila Bzhilianskaya (1999), "Foreign Direct Investment in the Science-Based Industries of Russia," David Dyker (ed.), *Foreign Direct Investment and Technology Transfer in the Former Soviet Union* (Cheltenham: Edward Elgar), 64–83, 65.

37. Liudmila Bzhilianskaya (1999): 64–83, 77.

38. *Kommersant*, 1 July 1999, 2.

39. *Kommersant*, 12 May 1999, 3.

40. Lyudmila Bzhilianskaya (1997), "The Transformation of Technological Capabilities in Russian Defence Enterprises, with Special Reference to Dual-Use Technology," David Dyker (ed.), *The Technology of Transition* (Budapest et al.: CEU Press), 257–283, 276.

41. Mallmann 1989, 18.

42. For a general overview over the satellite based telecommunication sector, see for example, *Kommersant* (3 November 1999): 8.

43. *Moskovskie novosti*, 9 November 1999, electronic version.

44. *Izvestiya* (6 November 1999): 3; *Ekspert* (1 November 1999): 5.

45. *Moskovskie novosti* (9 November 1999), electronic version.

46. Stan Metcalfe (1997), "Technology Systems and Technology Policy in an Evolutionary Framework," *Technology, Globalisation and Economic Performance*, ed. by Daniele Archibugi and Jonathan Michie (Cambridge: Cambridge University Press), 268–96, 285.

47. Richard Nelson (1997), "Foreword," *Technology, Globalisation and Economic Performance*, ed. by Daniele Archibugi and Jonathan Michie (Cambridge: Cambridge University Press), xv.

48. Stefanie Harter (1998), The Civilianisation of the Russian Economy: A Network Approach, unpublished Ph.D. thesis (CREES, University of Birmingham), chapter 6.

49. Bruce Parott (1985), *Politics and Technology in the Soviet Union* (Cambridge, Mass. and London: MIT Press), 249.

50. Ibid., 299.

51. Wolfgang Mallmann (1989), *Die Weltraumpolitik der Sowjetunion in den 80er Jahren*, Berichte des Bundesinstituts für ostwissenschaftliche und internationale Studien, (Cologne: BIOst), 19.

52. Ronald Humble (1988), *The Soviet Space Programme* (London and New York: Routledge), 18.

53. L. Gokhberg, M. Peck (1997), "The Decline of the Russian R&D Sector and the Prospects of Its Revival," *MOCT-MOST*, No.7, 91–101, 99.

54. Dominique Foray (1998), *The Creation of Industry-Specific Public Goods: New Insights into the Technology Policy Debate*, paper delivered at conference "The Economics of Industrial Structure and Innovation Dynamics," Lisbon, 16–17 October, 2.

55. David Dyker (2000), "The Structural Origins of the Russian Economic Crisis," *Postcommunist Economies*, Vol.12, No.1, 5–24, 13.

56. Morris Teubal (1998), *Enterprise Restructuring and Embeddedness—An Innovation System and Policy Perspective*, paper delivered at "The Economics of Industrial Structure and Innovation Dynamics," Lisbon, 16–17 October, 3.

57. Dominique Foray (1998), *The Creation of Industry-Specific Public Goods: New Insights into the Technology Policy Debate*, paper delivered at conference "The Economics of Industrial Structure and Innovation Dynamics, Lisbon, 16–17 October, 2.

58. Ibid.

59. Robert Rycroft and Don Kash (1999), *The Complexity Challenge. Technological Innovation for the 21st Century* (London and New York: Pinter), 188, 199.

60. K. Poznanski (1987), *Technology, Competition, and the Soviet Bloc in the World Market* (Berkeley: IIS University of California), 155–9.

61. David Dyker (2000), "The Structural Origins of the Russian Economic Crisis," *Postcommunist Economies*, Vol.12, No.1, 5–24, 11.

62. Martin Bell and Keith Pavitt (1997), "Technological Accumulation and Industrial Growth: Contrasts between Developed and Developing Countries," *Technology, Globalisation and Economic Performance*, ed. by Daniele Archibugi and Jonathan Michie (Cambridge: Cambridge University Press), 83–137, 91.

63. David Lane and Robert Maxfield (1997), "Foresight, Complexity, and Strategy," *The Economy as an Evolving Complex System II*, ed. by W. Brian Arthur, Steven N. Durlauf and David A. Lane (Reading, Mass.: Perseus Books), 169–198, 170.

64. Robert Rycroft and Don Kash (1999), *The Complexity Challenge. Technological Innovation for the 21st Century* (London and New York: Pinter), 59.

65. Mallmann 1989, 113.

66. Besides, a number of governmental agencies contributed to the decentralized structure: Glavkosmos (Main Administration for the Creation and Use of Space Technology for the National Economy and Scientific Research), created in 1985, served as an agency for international cooperation. It was also the body that controlled and coordinated Soviet space activities; Intersputnik, the International system for cosmic telecommunication, was created in 1971 and had fourteen socialist member states that financed the agency depending on how much they used it. Interkosmos (Council for International Cooperation in the Studies and Uses of Outer Space), was set up in 1967 to promote international cooperation. Litsensintorg was involved in international commercial deals for the allocation of licenses; Ingostrakh,

the state insurance company insured the payload of foreign states that were sent into orbit; and the Academy of Sciences, finally, was involved with their institute for cosmic research. Cf. Humble (1988), 22–7 and Mallmann (1989), 37, 121–2.

67. http://iepnt1.itaip.doc.gov/bisnis/isa, accessed 8 March 1999.

68. *Rossiiskaya gazeta* (25 May 1999): 1, 2.

69. *Nezavisimaya gazeta* (13 March 1999), electronic version.

70. Therefore, it has set up two joint stock companies: the French-Russian STARSEM (which was allocated the exclusive license to launch middle-range missiles), and the ZAO "Puskovye uslugy" (which claims a monopoly for launching foreign satellites on light missiles). "Puskovye uslugy" has also received the right to launch all foreign satellites on "Kosmos-3M" booster rockets. *Kommersant* (25 February 1999): 2.

71. Vremya MN (6 April 1999): 4. Maybe due to the failure of "Puskovye uslugy" to better develop the global market, but perhaps also due to the fact that "Rosvooruzhenie" threatened to take over the market for launches with light booster rockets, on 24 February 1999 an alliance between RKA and "Rosvooruzhenie" was set up. The two companies concluded an agreement that defines cooperation on the world market for space services, in particular, the launching of satellites. Before, "Puskovye uslugi" presented itself as the monopolist supplier of the Kosmos-3M-launches. The launch of Astrid-2 and Abrixas, as German scientific observatory from Kapustin Yar with the booster rocket Kosmos-3M, produced in Omsk by the PO "Polet" was successfully managed by Rosvooruzhenie. The RKA now conducts the systemic marketing and fulfilment of RF acts in respect to export control and licensing. RKA had effectively no other choice given the financial constraints. In 1998, Russia has earned $880 million and aims at $1bn for 1999. This is not a lot, especially when compared to the United States, where this sum amounts to an annual $50bn. Presumably, the alliance with "Rosvooruzhenie" is aimed at increasing Russia's market share. (*Rossiiskaya gazeta*, 30 April 1999, 3; Ekspert, 1 March 1999, 28. *Nezavisimaya gazeta*, 13 March 1999, electronic version; *Kommersant*, 25 February 1999, 2; *Ekspert*, 1 March 1999, 28.)

72. http://iepnt1.itaip.doc.gov/bisnis/isa, accessed 8 March 1999.

73. Petra Opitz; Thomas Sauer (1999), "Strategic Technology Alliances: A Way to Innovative Enterprises in Russia," *Postcommunist Economies*, Vol. 11, No. 4, 487–501, 488.

III

ADAPTATION OF
SOCIAL GROUPS

9

The Nationalities Question and Soviet Collapse: Weakness in State Socialism or Path-Dependent Breakdown?

Ray Taras

The disintegration of the USSR rekindled the long-standing scholarly debate about the nature of the Soviet system as constructed by Lenin and Stalin. The events of 1991 still bewilder specialists on the USSR. Victor Zaslavsky cannot hold back his astonishment: "The sudden dissolution of the Soviet Union in 1991 was one of the most unusual events in world history; it is probably the only case of a superpower and its empire collapsing in peacetime, and seemingly for largely internal reasons."[1]

A question that follows from this is whether the Soviet Union was simply a new ideological variant of old Russian imperialism or whether it really marked a departure from imperialism to internationalism, as communist party leaders in the Soviet republics had insisted. In order to understand the legacy of Soviet nationalities policy, critically examining whether the USSR was an empire is an essential first step. The second part of this chapter then considers what options (if any) kremlin leaders had to reconfigure the Soviet Union into a viable, responsive political system and how the decisions they took affected subsequent nation-building in former Soviet space.

EMPIRE OR NOT?

Some experts have argued that the USSR was not an empire in the classical sense: "it was the dream of creating a state from an empire that separated Soviet-type imperialism from that practiced by traditional empires."[2] In this view, the USSR represented a sustained effort to overcome both the nationalisms of constituent peoples and the internationalism that Marxist ideologues had superimposed on successive Soviet leaders. By contrast, some

writers have stressed how historical revisionism has cast the USSR as an empire like all others. One study reported how even from those commentators
who during the late 1980s were uneasy about labeling the Soviet Union 'an
empire,' a historical revisionism is now underway in which, in light of the
USSR's collapse along multiethnic lines, the Soviet Union is busily being
reinvented as empire."[3] This is a common understanding in the new independent states. Depicting the USSR as empire performs political functions in
post-Soviet topography: "through the construction of the 'other' as 'empire,'
we can begin to comprehend how the borderland states' interpretations of
their previous and current relations with the Soviet Union help structure the
idea of empire as a continuing and uninterrupted Russian project."[4]

A term employed to capture the relationship between the Soviet center and the
fourteen non-Russian borderland republics is federal colonialism. The Soviet
Union combined features of federalism and colonialism in a distinctive way:
"while sovereignty resided with the center rather than in the ethnorepublics, the
particular nature of the Soviet federation ensured that nation-building took place
at both the ethnorepublic and all-union levels."[5] Moscow did not pursue a consistent, uniform policy of cultural standardization in the ethnorepublics: "one of
the major paradoxes of the Soviet empire was that it provided the social space for
nation-building at the ethnoregional scale"[6] such as through the indigenization
(or *korenizatsiia*) policy providing affirmative action for non-Russian leaders. Zaslavsky supported this view: "From its very inception, Soviet federalism fostered
the policy of preferential treatment of the representatives of local nationalities
within their own territories."[7] To be sure, union republics "were not all treated
uniformly by the center, nor in turn were relations between the ethnorepublics
and the center predicated on similarity."[8] From the perspective of the periphery,
therefore, the Soviet Union might appear imperial but not imperialist.

Official nationality policy proclaimed the goal of constructing a Soviet nation
(*sovietskii narod*), which would allow all nationalities to retain their formal cultural identities while injecting a socialist content and value-system into them.
Whether it was too weakly carried out or too vigorously pursued, creating ethnic
resistance to it, the policy ultimately failed to integrate not only first-order titular
nations like Lithuanians, Georgians and Uzbeks; it also failed with second-order
titular peoples (minorities within the Russian republic itself): Tatars, Chuvash,
and Bashkirs in the Middle Volga region; Chechens, Balkars and Karachai (all de-
ported peoples) in the north Caucuses; Yakuts, Buryats and Tuvans in Siberia.

This cascading nationalism owed much, paradoxically, to an empathetic understanding of national affiliation reflected in state socialist ideology that was at
odds with the idea of a *sovietskii narod*. Valery Tishkov, Russia's foremost specialist on nationalities, described how an "important element of Soviet-style eth-
nonationalism is viewing a nation as a homogeneous body, a kind of collective
individual with common blood and soul, primordial rights, and a single will.
Over the course of many decades, this vision of an ethnonation acquired deep

emotional and political legitimacy."[9] Inevitably, when the Soviet center weakened such "subnations," indoctrinated with Soviet ideology, insisted on being given the status of nations and, shortly after that, of nation-states.

One ancillary feature about the Soviet Union that distinguished it from other empires was the discrediting of the nationalism of the imperial people itself. A resolution adopted by the 1923 Communist Party Congress stated that once Russian nationalism had been eliminated, other nationalisms would lose their raison d'être, on the reasoning that the "Other" would have been removed. This position was reiterated at the Party's 1930 Congress. In the interval, "The Soviet state embarked on a major effort of social engineering aimed at creating the cultural infrastructure of national communities that were at a very early stage of development. New nations were established, given languages, alphabets, cultures and so on, but under the strict control of the communist party."[10] It is true that in 1938 Russian became a compulsory language throughout the Soviet Union and during the war references to Russia's past imperial greatness were a common motif. As Ronald Suny summarized: "The imperial aspects of the Soviet system became clearer in the 1930s as Stalin moved steadily away from the more radical aspects of *korenizatsiia* and gave a much more positive valence to Russian language and culture."[11] But by the 1970s linguistic choice in educational institutions had been reintroduced, and ethnic republics were not unduly harassed if they stuck to the formula of "socialist in form, nationalist in content."

It seems mistaken, therefore, to treat russification as a logical product of state socialism. Viewing the latter as cause, russification as agency, and Russian empire as effect is a misconceived paradigm. Thus Robert Kaiser echoed Suny and lamented how "the postwar focus on Russification in studies of the national question also appears to have been misguided. Most of the Russification in the state occurred during the interwar period."[12]

The Russian reaction to criticism of its supposed nationalism and the faux multiculturalism it wrapped itself in was the emergence of neo-Slavophilism. This was reflected in the works of the village prose writers (*derevenshchiki*) like Valery Rasputin in the 1970s. By the time of perestroika, the works of such quintessentially Russian philosophers as Berdyaev, Florenskii, Losev and Tkachev were being reissued. In politics, the nationalist backlash was personified by Boris Yeltsin beginning with his ostentatious withdrawal from the Soviet Communist Party in July 1990.

In sum, if the USSR really was a Russian empire in disguise and state socialism codified the ordering principles undergirding Russian nationalism, then many of its features irritated traditional Russian nationalists. Roman Szporluk observed how Russians "were used to being the 'leading nation' in the USSR, but they were also an object of manipulation and a victim of political manipulation-their identity made and remade by the party."[13] Under glasnost some nationalists expressed the view that too many non-Russians lived in the multinational USSR. Lands considered historically Russian like the Crimea—indeed, most of

Ukraine—the northern part of Kazakhstan and much of the Caucasus, were seen as having been infiltrated and stolen by other nations. After Soviet disinte-gration, the 25-million strong Russian diaspora stranded outside Russia—termed a "beached diaspora"[14]—felt that it had been demoted to a marginal sta-tus on what were traditional Russian lands. State socialism was the obvious factor to blame when Russians sensed they were no longer treated equitably.

It was inevitable that Russian nationalists began raising the issue of ethnic justice. Why were small or backward Soviet republics receiving more than their fair share of a dwindling pool of resources? They condemned what they saw as the predatory behavior of many non-Russians: "Why do Estonians and Latvians, Armenians and Georgians, enjoy higher standards of living than we do?" Average Russians felt that criminal activity was also disproportionately undertaken by ethnic mafias. The ethnic *kto kovo* question—who was taking advantage of whom—became highly salient. This paradigm differed significantly from the policy formulated by Mikhail Gorbachev. It targeted the authoritarian Soviet structure, not the non-Russian peoples, as responsible for ethnic and other forms of injustice. Important communist organizations backed Gorbachev's re-forms that sought to decentralize power.[15]

An alternative explanatory framework assumes that Soviet federalism had al-ready given non-Russians too much autonomy. Zaslavsky put it this way: "One of the fundamental innovations of federal state formation under Soviet rule was the Stalinist linkage of ethnicity, territory, and political administration." The unin-tended consequence of this was that "The Soviet state erected virtually impen-etrable barriers between the different nationalities."[16] When the Soviet center imploded, nationalist mobilization became nearly ubiquitous throughout Soviet lands. Nationalities were transformed into virtual political parties. And ethnic borders were transformed into state ones. Suny captured the paradox: "a radical socialist elite that proclaimed an internationalist agenda . . . in fact ended up by making nations within its own political body."[17]

These explanatory frameworks share the view that state socialism had mishan-dled the nationalities question. But the system's failings ranged from a purport-edly too benign approach taken to national minorities to a supposed sovietization of the Russians. What is clear is how unconvincing the thesis is that the nation-alist implosion of the USSR was caused by perestroika. Instead the stronger ar-gument is that perestroika's failure was brought on by the nationalities revolution. The nationalisms of Soviet peoples represented a backlash against preperestroika state socialism. Perestroika fell victim to this reaction.

Gorbachev's Options

Unlike his communist counterparts in Eastern Europe when faced with bur-geoning democratic oppositions, Gorbachev never seemed seriously to consider the option of *extrication* from the nationalist Gordian knot that had tied up the

Soviet Union by the late 1980s; on the contrary, he may have tightened it. His resignation speech of 25 December 1991 contained a final plea for the preservation of the union, within which he envisaged the existence of sovereign republics. While such a program had become untenable after the failed August coup, was renegotiated federalism among subjects of the federation still possible in, say, spring 1991? At the least, concluding a transitional *pact* acceptable to central and republic leaders that would manage transition from state socialism while protecting the integrity of the union should have been possible.

This option becomes more compelling given that for a considerable time afterwards in many of the republics there were no drastic changes in the political actors themselves. With the exception of the Baltic states, many communist-era leaders remade themselves into postcommunist ones, notably Kravchuk, Shushkevich, Aliev, Shevardnadze, and the rulers of the five Central Asian republics.

Why had these national elites not expressed secessionist demands earlier on in the Soviet period? The answer is found in Zaslavsky's argument that by promoting the interests of the indigenous elites, "Soviet nationality policy was unusually successful in integrating the groups most receptive to nationalist ideas into the political regime or, at least, in neutralizing their separatist aspirations."[18] These national elites were able to retain many of the *resources* associated with communist rule—especially control over organs of coercion, patronage, and economic overlordship—while appending new ones. These included the political legitimacy they derived from embracing popular notions of the national interest, democratization, and modernization through Westernization.

By contrast, the holdover communist elite that had no republic base faced a particularly sharp decline in its political resources. The institutional transformation of state socialism made new types of resources, like grassroots support, to be salient and older types, like control over the media and cultural reproduction, to decline in importance. Any transitional pact concluded by state actors would have had to be renegotiated and modified several times, given the instability of relevant actors' resources.

Even if Gorbachev had succeeded in eliciting tangible (rather than merely tactical) support for his new union treaty following its approval in the April 1991 referendum (held admittedly in just nine of the fifteen republics), because of the dynamics of shifting resources during the transition phase such a pact would still probably have failed to produce the expected effects and would have quickly collapsed. Gorbachev implicitly recognized that the referendum would still leave everything on the table when he promised to leave the aspiring secessionists with the option to "decide for themselves what they need and what kind of society they want to have."[19] In sum, agreement on a transitional pact in 1991, with Gorbachev serving as the central actor, would still not have guaranteed that the Soviet nationality question would have been successfully resolved.

Apart from actors and resources, we need to consider the role played by political institutions and the structured patterns of interaction they produced. That is because key actors, their resources, and their preferences were deeply structured by the state's "normal" institutional configuration, in this case the 70-year-old state socialist system. Institutions engender sets of expectations about the payoffs and overheads of particular actions, but when they are brought into question so are the benefits and costs.[20]

Institutions derive their power from regularity, that is, the repeated recourse to and use of them by political actors. When this configuration comes under attack during an elite- or popularly grounded bid for regime change and politics become abnormal, the existing formal rules of the game, and even the informal constraints on political behavior, are undermined.[21] The moment the possibility of change of a particular rule is mooted, the institution represented by that rule is weakened. This is most dramatically illustrated by the fate of the Soviet Union itself: once the terms and rules of the union were put into question, the USSR itself was seriously crippled. Another important example is the fate of the Soviet parliament, which by 1990, in the words of Valery Tishkov, "de facto acquired the expression of an assembly of nations."[22] We can add that when the probability of a rule change becomes high and even inevitable, then the political game that it underpins is cast in doubt. For political actors will no longer predicate their actions on the basis of the disintegrating rules. Gorbachev's error was to do just that.

Transition begins with the appearance of uncertainty, itself engendered by failing rules. In the Soviet case, the CPSU Congress (meeting in July 1990 for, it turned out, the last time), its Central Committee, its Politburo and, finally, its General Secretary were delegitimized as sources of authority. Constraints on republic leaders, such as consulting with the Kremlin before deciding policy, disappeared when Yeltsin called for a complete rewriting of rules governing center-republic relations and urged the subjects of the federation to take as many powers as they could swallow. The result was that no institutions were left to structure transition. Politics became progressively more uncertain, together with their rules and, of course, their outcomes.

It is difficult to agree, therefore, with the proposition put forward by Robert Daniels: "In the aftermath of the failed coup and the eradication of the institutions associated with Communist dictatorship, Russia and the other ex-Soviet republics completed the transition back through time to the democratic hopes and political pluralism of 1917."[23] So long as rules and the institutions they generate remain uncertain, political transition continues. A tabula rasa, not a 1917 political landscape, was the outcome following the collapse of institutions. Daniels again underestimated the dynamic and unpredictable nature of institutions under transition in asserting that "Yeltsin's broad-mindedness about the minorities reflected the extra year of political maturation and the democratization of the electoral rules that had taken place between the election of the Union government in March 1989 and the election of the Russian government in

March 1990."[24] Rules were under constant negotiation in this period. The most that can be said is that Yeltsin was quicker to recognize the vacuum within which new rules and constraints were being formulated than Gorbachev, who clung to the legitimacy of obsolete rules.

For the next decade, postcommunist rulers in possession of new resources attempted to write new rules and construct new constraints (wars in Chechnya are the most ruthless example of this). A decade after Soviet disintegration, many rules and constraints were still either ineffective or elusive. No better example of the failures of rule-making for post-Soviet nations can be advanced than the pitiful fate of the Commonwealth of Independent States (CIS). But even bilateral relations between Russia and its two Slavic neighbors, Ukraine and Belarus, remained in a state of flux in 2001 and it was unclear how they would evolve.

In sum, both Gorbachev's perestroika, which envisaged a modernized alternative model of state socialism that would be both democratized and decentralized, and Yeltsin's decommunized model, which sought to push democratic and devolutionary trends further, failed to institute new rules for conduct among post-Soviet nations (even if succeeding in writing rules—sometimes flawed—for other arenas, such as elections and privatization). The election in 2000 of a strong president, Vladimir Putin, may be conceptualized as a mandate for more effective and binding rule-making.

The Legacy of an Unconsummated Nationalities Pact

The consequences of a failed or, sensu stricto, unconsummated pact about Soviet nations provided a systemic legacy that imprinted itself past the point of the pact's stillbirth and beyond the borders of the USSR. The Soviet Union and, with it, state socialism, were destroyed, the bipolar world ended, globalization was left unfettered to structure the international political economy while, paradoxically, in former Soviet space state sovereignty was preferred to regional integration. In inquiring about the causes and legacy of Soviet collapse, it is important to consider what their consequences have been for theories of political change.

There are at least four robust explanatory frameworks we can examine. One, the study of nationalism, is particularly appropriate for this chapter and is considered in the next section. By contrast a second, the institutionalist approach, is rarely employed to explain the nationalist overrunning of the USSR and of state socialism. I focus on this framework in this section. The interest group framework (encompassing elite theories) and class-based analysis are the two other approaches. The case for studying interest groups is weak when we recognize how undeveloped aggregated interests and even civil society were in the late Soviet period. In turn class analysis is usually associated with advocates of the resurrection of state socialism. While not necessarily to be disregarded for that reason, a class approach is usually dismissive of the primacy of national identity and national mobilization, which is the *explanandum* of this chapter.

For institutionalists, political actors interact within an institutional structure and that fact is itself significant to outcomes. Particularly at a time of crisis, transition, and change, outcomes are not reducible to actors' immediate preferences. Marjorie Castle has elaborated on this logic: any interaction between political actors demands rules of the game, and even if they may be uncertain, rapidly changing, and/or one time only (as during perestroika), in some form they determine the nature of the game and the method of play. The transition period is not, therefore, directly structured by institutions or by established expectations created through repeated games. Nonetheless it remains a process structured by a series of one-time-only games.[25]

Why, we may ask, were such single-play games allowed to lead to consequences unfavorable for Gorbachev and the most powerful actors in the Kremlin? The answer lies in the sequencing and timing of the games. Each game results in a redistribution of power. Thus, permitting political pluralism after decades of one-party rule changed the nature of the game as well as the weight and distribution of political resources. The patronage embedded in the nomenklatura system, which shaped the hierarchical relationship obtaining between higher and regional elites, became obsolete. In these circumstances, an even quasi-competitive election, or indeed any election that produced a political arena for discrediting incumbent forces, changed the game decisively. As Juan Linz and Alfred Stepan underscored, "elections can create agendas, can create actors, can reconstruct identities, help legitimate and delegitimate claims to obedience, and create power."[26]

Under conditions of what can be termed electoral populism, new political possibilities arise. The emergence of a new political opportunity structure favoring out-groups, more precisely, the most outsider of the inside group, like Yeltsin's entourage, takes on crucial significance. A turning point in the rise of new actors (even if they often are the old officials) playing in new arenas was the conclusion of an informal alliance of nomenklatura members with ethnic entrepreneurs.

Positioning and sequencing become urgent political imperatives. For being the first to embark on new constitutional and electoral procedures is likely to determine which political actors with what relative strengths become dominant. Linz and Stepan highlighted the decisive nature of, surprisingly, regional elections held in Soviet republics in 1990. The authors focused on Georgia, Moldova and Ukraine but subsequent Russian elections proved to be even more momentous. Republic elites' positioning themselves as rule-setters resulted in advantageous sequencing: they held general elections that preceded implementation of Gorbachev's top-down reform program.

For Linz and Stepan, getting a head start through republic elections produced five compounding, state-disintegrating dynamics: (1) the Gorbachev administration's legitimacy was damaged vis-à-vis nationalist forces in the republics; (2) the elections preempted the emergence of any union-wide political organization that could serve as a counterweight to the republic forces; (3) political identities "be-came more narrow, compounding, exclusive, and unsupportive of participation in a potentially all-union democratic entity;"[27] (4) the elections could be inter-preted as a mandate for the republic leaders to stifle dissenting voices—such as those still adhering to a state socialist perspective—within their core national groups; and, (5) the weakening of the center that ensued produced a domino ef-fect, including on the national economy, and therefore "The cataclysmic politi-cal collapse of any central or coordinating authority preceded and created the economic crisis, not vice-versa."[28]

The institutionalist perspective holds that with repeated plays actors learn what the implication of a given resource in a political game will be.[29] In a new or changing game, however, they must guess, and some leaders arrive at more educated guesses than others. In Gorbachev's case, he repeatedly guessed wrongly in the conditions of uncertainty prevailing in the second half of the 1980s. He sided with democrats too early in the game, as at the January 1987 Central Committee plenum advocating democratization. Then he tacked with Leninists when they no longer had wind in their sails, as during the March 1990 Congress of People's Deputies session at which he was chosen to head a strong presidency. He consistently was wrong on the nationalities question: Paul Goble characterized it as Gorbachev's "running against the republics" after 1985.[30] The inconsequential, anti-climactic September 1989 Central Committee plenum on nationalities and the irrelevant March 1991 referendum on fine-tuning the union treaty were good illustrations of this.

In the final years of the USSR, the substitution of successive single-play games for stable institutions and the lesser determinacy of structural factors al-lowed for a greater role to be played by the contingent choices of individual lead-ers. As Castle set forth, "Because of the increased opportunity for significant strategic choices to be found in the improvisation and play of the single-play games of transition the role for contingent choice in such periods would be larger than usual, while the range of available choices would still be limited by structural constraints."[31] This analysis has particular applicability to the range of policy choice on nationalities available to Gorbachev. Furthermore, it alerts us to the fact that the contingent choices about institutional arrangements that he made under uncertainty affected both the nature of transition and its outcome.

The arrangements implicit to the proposed "pact" Gorbachev advanced were based on many mistaken guesses and had the effect of distributing advantages and disadvantages in an unintended way. He gravely crippled the hitherto dominant actor, the CPSU elite, and he promoted new players to prominence, the nationalist republic elites. In trying to avoid confrontation, his decision to seek compromise with nationalist republic leaders or, worse, to ignore them al-together resulted in his losing control over the transition, which, ultimately, produced a fatal outcome for him. His exclusion or relegation of certain actors at various points in time, above all Yeltsin but also Sakharov, represented a misguided choice under contingency. Castle underscored the implications of this: if an excluded actor, relatively insignificant at the time of pacting, later attains the capacity to disrupt the political game, the viability of the pact itself comes into question. This seems even more salient to a situation where a pact is only proposed. The emergence of new political actors showing little or no interest in pacting is an indication of the rise of spoilers. Gorbachev's inability to improvise a central policy on nationalities allowed new actors to engage in sovereignty games and thus take on the role of spoilers.

A key issue for transitions theorists is the extent to which the incumbent elite controls the process of change. In the Soviet case most scholars are agreed that transition was engineered top down. In addition, since a pact was not reached with mass actors, transition was carried out through imposition. However, the communist elite fragmented in the course of the transition game, in particular between a minority preferring a renewed communist federation and a growing majority favoring republic sovereignty.

For Terry Karl and Philippe Schmitter, the most likely candidates for consolidated democracies are those transitions implemented by pacts where elites dominate but pursue negotiation and compromise.[32] Burton, Gunther and Higley emphasize that "the key to the consolidation of new democratic regimes lies in the transformation of political elites from disunity to consensual unity via elite settlements or elite convergences."[33] In the Soviet case, there was neither a pact nor a unified elite, which flawed the democratization process from the outset. The nature of transition has had an enduring impact on the nature of the political systems that have evolved in the post-Soviet states (though this may be less true of the Baltic states). Elements of the transition rules were encoded in the proto-institutions of the emerging states and some remain influential. The legacy of an unconsummated nationalities pact is discernible even today, therefore, in the political systems functioning in the new independent states.

THE LEGACY OF STATE SOCIALISM AND NATIONALITIES STUDIES

If institutionalism captures the dynamics of political improvisation and experimentation, nationalities' studies explain how ethnic mobilization can destabilize a political system. Focusing on Russians' mobilization is especially illuminating. Is their identity still linked to possession of empire, one being constructed on the ashes of the preceding Soviet one? Was the Russian imperial idea truly banished with the demise of state socialism?

From the perspective of Moscow, the answer is conclusively no. But from the periphery, among Chechens and many of their neighbors, the answer is just as clearly yes. For a dominant nation's rule can be a minority nation's subjugation and, conversely, one nation's subjugation may be another nation's empire. The issue might best be framed as whether Russia can ever extricate itself from empire. As Alexandr Solzhenitsyn framed the question, "Should we be struggling for warm seas far away, or ensuring that warmth rather than enmity flows between citizens?"[34]

Empires may be ruled over using military force but they can also be controlled employing soft power such as economic resources. Russia of the 1990s used the two strategies in combination to keep the near abroad just that. Whether this leads to the conclusion that Yeltsin's Russia behaved imperiously towards its national minorities and its far-flung regions is debatable. To be sure, when important differences about important issues arise Moscow has imposed its own preference. For example, ethnic Russians supported the draft of a new Russian Federation constitution in the December 1993 referendum (60 percent of voters in the Federation's nonethnic regions voted for approval) but only a minority (48 percent) in the ethnic republics did. The constitution was, of course, adopted.

The charge of Russian colonialism inevitably surfaces. In the view of some specialists, state socialism was an instrument "enabling Russia to resist successfully that liquidation of colonialism carried out elsewhere in the world."[35] We can ask whether Yeltsin-style "democracy" could conceivably be an instrument of Russia's transition from Soviet republic to empire. It is telling, after all, that since its independence at the end of 1991 the Russian Federation has been viewed as a renewed threat to both the newly independent states neighboring it and to the "submerged" nations, or national minorities, within Russia.

Longtime Sovietologist Helene Carrere d'Encausse rose to the defense of the new Russia. She contended that "The idea of the cost of the empire led to the slogan 'Russia out of the empire,' which became very popular in the early 1990s. . . . In the new Russia, the Russian mind is no longer an imperial mind; on the contrary, the Russian population is largely, if not unanimously, convinced that the progress of the nation and the progress of the empire would be difficult to reconcile."[36] Leon Aron credited Yeltsin with this makeover: "Yeltsin is the first Russian leader who has not expanded, or at least strengthened, the domestic empire. . . . Yeltsin has reversed a 400-year old political tradition in which the Russian national idea was identical with the Russian imperial idea."[37]

But how others view Russia is also crucial. Mark Beissinger pointed to "the widespread perception throughout the region that, in spite of the collapse of the Soviet Union, the empire lives on."[38] Further, "perceptions of empire, a longing for empire, and a discourse of empire remain characteristic features of post-Soviet politics."[39] As a result, "In the fractious realm of Russian domestic politics, one clear consensus among groups of all persuasions is that Russia should remain one of the world's 'Great Powers.'"[40] Szporluk asserted, then, that "just as in the case of the tsarist empire and the Soviet Union, modern Russia cannot behave simply as though it is the nation-state of the Russians. Whether that makes it imperialist is another question."[41]

If Russia's imperial status has diminished, its imperial identity may persist because of the strengthening of the Western "Other" and of its refusal to grant Russia recognition as a great power. What recognition was extended was of Russia's marginal status as NATO enlarged, Serbia was attacked, the G-7 kept Yeltsin on the outside, and the IMF compiled a school-like report card on Russia's economic behavior. The West's perceived humiliating treatment of Russia has caused imperial identity not to recede, evidenced in the widespread support for Putin's restorationist agenda.

Ilya Prizel summarized the debate about the collapse of state socialism: "Some feel that Russia will not be able to retain its truncated integrity without at least a partial resurrection of the empire, while others believe that the demise of the empire has had a liberating effect on Russia that will allow it to become a normal nation pursuing its own national interest rather than imperial demands."[42] In his view the first approach was more influential: "the ideal of Russia as a superior civilization and a transcendent empire with a universal mission has remained. Indeed, a Russian national identity without this vision has yet to emerge. Were the Russians to establish such a concept of national identity, it would allow Russia to make peace with itself and the international system."[43] This is a pious wish, and it is far from certain that a thoroughly "deimperialized" Russia would usher in an era of peace for Russians or their neighbors.

The crisis of Russian identity needs to be contextualized. It is interconnected with the more general postcommunist crisis of statehood. As Judy Batt has written, many issues bearing on nationalities, like the status of minorities, are "inseparable from the fundamental questions that the majority nation itself has to resolve concerning its own identity, its relation to the state, and the state's place in Europe and the wider international order."[44] Especially given a weak state and weak central authority, Russian identity is in a profound existential crisis.

In the 1990s a variety of discourses on Russian identity appeared. In the words of postmodernist writer Svetlana Boym, "There is still, in present-day Russia, a great urge to find a single, all-embracing narrative—national, religious, historic, political, or aesthetic—to recover the single dramatic plot with devils and angels, black and white swans, hangmen and victims, that would explain Russia's Past, Present, and Future."[45] The undertaking has been taken up by political leaders but is also of concern to historians, philosophers and writers.

The political discourse promoted by the Yeltsin administration was statist and accepted that the Russian homeland was now the Russian Federation and nothing beyond it. However, two empire-restoring, irredentist discourses emerged, one from the political right, the other from the left. The first highlighted the need for reuniting historic Russian lands settled centuries ago by Russians, principally, Ukraine, Belarus, northern Kazakhstan and the Narva region of Estonia. The second invoked the goal of a reconstituted Soviet fatherland (*sovetskaia rodina*): "As the motherland of socialism, Russia is the advanced point of exemplarity. A major theme in this discourse is that of Russia's national greatness, which coexists uneasily with the theme of international brotherhood."[46] From this perspective, it is the mission of the Russian people to bind together other peoples in a common destiny. Finally, a discourse of identity developed that accepted both the idea of a Russian nation subsuming its diaspora, and the Russian Federation as the natural Russian homeland (*otechestvo*). Thus, by offering extraterritorial citizenship to all those who have a connection—ethnic or historic—to the Russian homeland, Russia has attempted to redefine the nation while at the same time acknowledging the inviolability of the borderland states' sovereign spaces. . . . The regime has therefore attempted to create a Russian nation without restoring the homeland-empire."[47]

These various discourses of identity are grounded in differing visions of borders and borderlands. One Russian imperial identity proposed in place of the Soviet one has been Eurasianism. Philosopher Lev Gumilev stressed its ethnographic character: "Eurasia is not merely a huge continent, it contains in its center a super ethnos bearing the same name."[48] Eurasia is part of a tripod that includes the Muslim world to the south and Germano-Latin world to the west. The Eurasian idea asserts that "If Russia is to preserve its cultural heritage, it must maintain a culturally non-threatening union with the Turkic people or face a cultural annihilation inflicted by the West. . . . Since, according to many statists, Russians cannot exist as Russians outside a Russian state, making a multinational Russian state across Eurasia is vital to the survival of Russians as a people."[49]

Andrei Tsygankov called attention to a bewildering political characteristic of Eurasianism: "Unlike Western realists who emphasize nation-states as key players of international politics, Eurasianists argue in favor of empires as the key units of action."[50] They express the belief that a Eurasian Russia must be at least the size of the USSR and perhaps even greater. Eurasianism contains two currents. "Modernizers offer the restoration of the Soviet Union under the name of the Eurasian empire to maintain geopolitical balances and international stability."[51] By contrast, in order to contain U.S. imperialism—the main threat to Russia, Europe, and Asia—"Expansionists advocate a further imperial expansion of Russia beyond the borders of the former Soviet Union."[52]

In either case, Eurasianists and neocommunists share a common cause and seem natural partners in a political coalition. Novelist-turned-political-activist Alexander Prokhanov was a key figure in the effort to forge a unified opposition to Yeltsin, working closely with communist party head Gennadiy Zyuganov to establish a "patriotic" front based loosely on Eurasian ideas. In Prokhanov's newspaper *Den* (renamed *Zavtra* in 1993), Alexander Dugin established himself as the leading theoretician of neo-Eurasianism.[53] His vision of world history was of perpetual conflict between "the order of Eurasianists" and "the order of Eurasianists." Thus, "The Germans and Russians have embodied the Indo-European ideal of rooted, spiritual, Aryan Eurasianism in more recent history; the Jews, British, and Americans, the rootless, materialistic, commercial Atlanticist idea."[54] For Dugin, with both Islam and a spiritually revived Europe as allies, "Russia's long-term task is to unite the anti-Atlanticist, antimondialist forces of Eurasia in a new imperial alliance. . . . Dugin's envisioned continental imperial alliance will span the Eurasian landmass from Dublin to Vladivostok, with Moscow ('the third Rome') serving as the continental capital."[55]

Such versions of Eurasianism fly in the face of admonitions for Russia to avoid the mistakes of the past. They also fly in the face of much of Russian public opinion. The general cultural orientation of Russians is towards Europe.[56] A stigma is attached, especially by the better-educated, to the "Asiatic" element of Russia's makeup. Solzhenitsyn cited other reasons for rejecting a Eurasian-based Russian nationalism. Russia had to "free itself of great-power thinking and imperial delusions. . . . The time has come for an uncompromising choice between an empire . . . and the spiritual and physical salvation of our own people."[57]

Before Putin's assumption of power, one popular proposal to address the problem of centrifugalism within the Federation was to promote a "Russia of regions." The risks associated with devolution of power to regions would be worth taking if Russian identity was strengthened. Danish semiotician Ulf Hedetoft advanced a model of partial convergence between national identity and regional cultures in which the latter "identify with the nation, but in the sense that they see themselves as the best, highest, most particular manifestations of national identity, thus partly appropriating this identity for themselves, whilst (in most cases) still recognizing the rightful belongingness of other regions to the national sphere."[58] The weakness of the Russian center would, under this model, be compensated for by regionalism as a vessel of the national. Putin's crackdown on the power of regional governors since 2000 has made this model a moot issue.

CONCLUSION

Writing about what used to comprise Soviet space, one scholar concluded: "It remains to be seen whether these postcommunist regimes will be able to transform the bases of their legitimacy from nationalist to democratic principles."[59] Because for centuries Russia's identity was defined by the possession of empire, opting for democratic principles and assuming a postimperial identity seem, on the surface, to be crosscutting.

A new identity for Russia based on a liberal policy and a democratic form is plausible, if not probable. A more viable and likely alternative may be a form of social democracy. The adoption of a mixed economy and of a social democratic system, "offers the ex-Soviet republics the chance—perhaps thrown away already in some of the former satellites—to construct with minimal resistance . . . a new model of democratic and pluralist socialism."[60] A social democratic identity would embrace the legacy of the postrevolutionary experience and would also accept the legacy of the nationalist revivals that destroyed the USSR.

Let us link the issue of nationalisms and identities to the main question addressed in this book. Is what we have now in Russia and ex-Soviet republics the result of a *system transfer* whereby defective state socialism was replaced by the implantation of "correct" institutions (like polyarchy, free market and a new federal union)? Or is *system collapse* the way to conceptualize how nations and identities appear as they now do in post-Soviet space (see chart 1.2)? From the discussion in this chapter it is obvious that in most of the Soviet republics national mobilization underscored rupture, radical regime change, and therefore system collapse. We can next ask whether the previous structures, such as Soviet federalism and Soviet multiculturalism, were assets for the new regimes? For the majority of the new independent states the answer is no: Soviet structures for national development were liabilities and fetters that impeded the flourishing of national cultures. In the case of Russia, too, Soviet structures prevented the emergence of a distinct ethnic Russian national identity and corresponding arena. However, when we consider the effect of system collapse on *rossiiskii* identity, understood here simply as the norms and values underpinning a Russian imperium, then the Soviet system had been an asset, as many Russians still affirm in opinion polls. Unfortunately for Gorbachev, this logic held little sway in the pivotal years of 1990-91.

NOTES

1. Victor Zaslavsky, "The Soviet Union," in Karen Barkey and Mark von Hagen (eds.), *After Empire: Multiethnic Societies and Nation-Building: The Soviet Union and the Russian, Ottoman, and Habsburg Empires.* (Boulder, Colo., Westview Press, 1997), 73.

2. Mark B. Beissinger, "Elites and Ethnic Identities in Soviet and Post-Soviet Politics," in Alexander J. Motyl (ed.), *The Post-Soviet Nations: Perspectives on the Demise of the USSR.* (New York, Columbia University Press, 1992), 162.

3. Graham Smith, Vivien Law, Andrew Wilson, Annette Bohr, and Edward Allworth, *Nation-building in the Post-Soviet Borderlands: The Politics of National Identities.* (Cambridge, Cambridge University Press, 1998), 3.

4. Smith et al., *Nation-Building in the Post-Soviet Borderlands*, 9.

5. Smith et al., *Nation-Building in the Post-Soviet Borderlands*, 4.

6. Smith et al., *Nation-Building in the Post-Soviet Borderlands*, 5-6.

7. Victor Zaslavsky, "Nationalism and Democratic Transition in Postcommunist Societies," *Daedalus*, 121, no. 2 (Spring 1992), 101.

8. Smith et al, *Nation-building in the Post-Soviet Borderlands*, 7.

9. Valery Tishkov, *Ethnicity, Nationalism and Conflict in and after the Soviet Union: The Mind Aflame.* (London, Sage, 1997), 233.

10. George Schopflin, "The Communist Experience and Nationhood," in Andre Gerrits and Nanci Adler (eds.), *Vampires Unstaked: National Images, Stereotypes and Myths in East Central Europe.* (Amsterdam, Royal Netherlands Academy of Arts and Sciences, 1995), 192.

11. Ronald G. Suny, "The Russian Empire," in Barkey and von Hagen, *After Empire*, 152.

12. Robert J. Kaiser, *The Geography of Nationalism in Russia and the USSR*. (Princeton, N.J., Princeton University Press, 1994), 393.

13. Roman Szporluk, "Introduction: Statehood and Nation Building in Post-Soviet Space," in Szporluk (ed.), *National Identity and Ethnicity in Russia and the New States of Eurasia*. (Armonk, N.Y., M. E. Sharpe, 1994), 6.

14. David D. Laitin, *Identity in Formation: The Russian-Speaking Populations in the Near Abroad*. (Ithaca, N.Y., Cornell University Press), 1998, 29.

15. They included two journals of the prestigious Writers' Union of the Russian republic, *Nash Sovremennik* and *Moskva*, as well as the Komsomol (Young Communist) newspaper *Molodaya Gvardiya*.

16. Zaslavsky, "Nationalism and Democratic Transition," 99, 105. For a similar argument, see also Gregory Gleason, *Federalism and Nationalism: The Struggle for Republican Rights in the USSR*. (Boulder, Colo., Westview Press, 1990), 135.

17. Suny, "The Russian Empire," 153.

18. Zaslavsky, "Nationalism and Democratic Transition," 103.

19. Mikhail S. Gorbachev, "Interview," *Der Spiegel* (25 March 1991): 175.

20. Adam Przeworski, *Democracy and the Market*. (Cambridge, Cambridge University Press, 1991). An excellent analysis of the logic of transitions theory can be found in Marjorie Castle, "A Successfully Failed Pact? The Polish Political Transition of 1989." Doctoral dissertation, Stanford University, Department of Political Science, 1993, chapter 1.

21. Douglass C. North, *Institutions, Institutional Change, and Economic Performance*. (Cambridge, Cambridge University Press, 1991), 91.

22. Valery Tishkov, "Ob ideye natsiyi," *Obshchestvennye nauki*, no. 4 (1990): 95.

23. Robert V. Daniels, *The End of the Communist Revolution*. (London, Routledge, 1993), 53.

24. Daniels, *The End of the Communist Revolution*, 126-127.

25. Castle, "A Successfully Failed Pact?"

26. Juan J. Linz and Alfred Stepan, "Political Identities and Electoral Sequences: Spain, the Soviet Union, and Yugoslavia," *Daedalus*, 121, no. 2 (Spring 1992): 133.

27. Linz and Stepan, "Political Identities and Electoral Sequences," 134-135.

28. Linz and Stepan, "Political Identities and Electoral Sequences," 135.

29. See Terry Lynn Karl, "The Limit of Democratization in Latin America," *Comparative Politics*, 23, no. 1 (October 1990).

30. Paul Goble, "Gorbachev and the Soviet Nationality Problem," in Maurice Friedburg and H. Isham (eds.), *Soviet Society Under Gorbachev*. (Armonk, N.Y., M. E. Sharpe), 1987.

31. Castle, "A Successfully Failed Pact?" chapter 1. This balanced approach thus addresses the critique offered by Ken Jowitt about transitology ignoring the Leninist legacy. See his "Weber, Trotsky, and Holmes on the Study of Leninist Regimes," *Journal of International Affairs*, 45 (Summer 1991).

32. Terry Lynn Karl and Philippe C. Schmitter, "Modes of Transition in Latin America, Southern and Eastern Europe," *International Social Science Journal*, 128 (May 1991): 269-284.

33. Michael G. Burton, Richard Gunther and John Higley, "Introduction: Elite Transformations and Democratic Regimes," in Higley and Gunther (eds.), *Elites and Democratic Consolidation in Latin America and Southern Europe*. (Cambridge, Cambridge University Press), 35, 131.

34. Gertjan Dijkink, *National Identity and Geopolitical Visions: Maps of Pride and Pain.* (London, Routledge, 1996), 101.

35. Walter Kolarz, "Colonialism: Theory and Practice," in George Gretton (ed.), *Communism and Colonialism: Essays by Walter Kolarz.* (London, Macmillan, 1964), 23.

36. Helene Carrere d'Encausse, *The Nationality Question in the Soviet Union and Russia.* (Oslo, Norway, Scandinavian University Press, 1995), 54.

37. Leon Aron, "The Emergent Priorities of Russian Foreign Policy," in Aron and Kenneth Jensen (eds.), *The Emergence of Russian Foreign Policy.* (Herndon, Va., U.S. Institute of Peace, 1994), 19.

38. Mark R. Beissinger, "The Persisting Ambiguity of Empire," in *Post-Soviet Affairs*, II, no. 2, 1995, 149. See also William Odom and Robert Dujarric, *Commonwealth or Empire? Russia, Central Asia and the Transcaucasus.* (Indianapolis, Ind.: Hudson Institute, 1995) and, Uri Ra'anan and Kate Martin, *Russia: A Return to Imperialism?* (New York: St. Martin's Press, 1995).

39. Beissinger, "The Persisting Ambiguity of Empire," 163.

40. O'Prey, "Keeping the Peace in the Borderlands of Russia," in William J. Durch (ed.), *UN Peacekeeping, American Policy, and the Uncivil Wars of the 1990s.* (New York, St. Martin's Press, 1996), 411.

41. Quoted by Paul Flenley, "From Soviet to Russian Identity: The Origins of Contemporary Russian Nationalism and National Identity," in Brian Jenkins and Spyros A. Sofos (eds.), *Nation and Identity in Contemporary Europe.* (London, Routledge, 1996), 245.

42. Ilya Prizel, *National Identity and Foreign Policy: Nationalism and Leadership in Poland, Russia, and Ukraine.* (Cambridge, Cambridge University Press, 1998), 10.

43. Prizel, *National Identity and Foreign Policy*, 155.

44. Judy Batt, "The Politics of Minority Rights in Postcommunist Europe," in Finn Laursen and Soren Riishoj (eds.), *The EU and Central Europe: Status and Prospects.* (Esbjerg, Denmark, South Jutland University Press, 1996), 48.

45. Svetlana Boym, *Common Places: Mythologies of Everyday Life in Russia.* (Cambridge, Mass., Harvard University Press, 1994), 228.

46. Smith et al., *Nation-Building in the Post-Soviet Borderlands*, 11.

47. Smith et al., *Nation-Building in the Post-Soviet Borderlands*, 13.

48. Lev N. Gumilev, *Ot rusi k rossii: ocherki etnicheskoi istorii.* (Moscow, Ekoproc, 1992), 297. Quoted by Prizel, *National Identity and Foreign Policy*, 230.

49. Prizel, *National Identity and Foreign Policy*, 230.

50. Andrei Tsygankov, "Hard-line Eurasianism and Russia's Contending Geopolitical Perspectives," *East European Quarterly*, XXXII, no. 3 (Fall 1998): 318.

51. Tsygankov, "Hard-line Eurasianism," 322.

52. Tsygankov, "Hard-line Eurasianism," 323. For all the differences between modernizers and expansionists, see table 1, 330.

53. Aleksandr Dugin, *Konservativnaya revolutsia.* (Moscow, AKIRN, 1994).

54. Quoted in Wayne Allensworth, *The Russian Question: Nationalism, Modernization, and Postcommunist Russia.* (Lanham, Md., Rowman and Littlefield, 1998), 250.

55. Quoted in Allensworth, *The Russian Question*, 250-251.

56. See David Kerr, "The New Eurasianism: The Rise of Geopolitics in Russia's Foreign Policy," *Europe-Asia Studies*, 47, no. 8 (December 1995), 977-988.

57. Alexander Solzhenitsyn, *Rebuilding Russia*. (New York: Farrar, Straus, and Giroux, 1991), 10.

58. Ulf Hedetoft, *Signs of Nations: Studies in the Political Semiotics of Self and Other in Contemporary European Nationalism*. (Aldershot, Dartmouth, 1995), 160.

59. Steven L. Burg, "Nationalism Redux: Through the Glass of the Postcommunist States Darkly," *Current History*, 92 (April 1993), 163.

60. Daniels, *The End of the Communist Revolution*, 190.

10

Class, Status, Powerlessness: Workers in Postcommunist Russia

Walter D. Connor

This chapter looks at the experience of workers—once the rhetorical "leading class" of Soviet poster art, now Russia's postcommunist proletariat. It examines the institutional legacy of the Soviet system, especially the economic aspects relevant to labor; how Gorbachev faced them in an attempt to reform them in perestroika; how Russia's post-Soviet leaders assessed, rejected, or coped with them, as elements of a failed system, and how the post-1991 experience of workers illuminates a major component of Russian society.

The legacy Gorbachev confronted was a living one; economic institutions and practices working badly in many cases, but still viewed as reformable: hence, the restructuring of "socialism." Gorbachev would attempt to deal with different features of the economic system as discrete problems to be addressed separately. Ultimately, of course, he would fail in this project, for a complex of reasons that went beyond the adequacy/inadequacy of specific economic measures. (In the later crisis of the end of the Soviet system, Yeltsin and his team would face a legacy radically altered, a complex of institutions in disarray, deemed to have failed and gone beyond the possibility of restructuring—a very different situation.)

In economic policy as in other areas, Gorbachev took some time to show his hand. The mix of measures that emerged, after early talk of "acceleration" and an upgraded machine-tool sector, was not particularly subtle or inspired, but did reflect a certain realism. Reallocation of labor, more employment flexibility, enhanced discipline, more differentiated material incentives for a changing working class, attempts to modify managerial behavior, and to "involve" workers in new mechanisms of "participation" on the shop floor—were the major components of his vision of successful perestroika. Each would involve response to Soviet-model legacies. (As the sociologist Tatiana Zaslavskaya had observed since late in the Brezhnev years, slowly cumulating social change in the post-terror years since 1953 had seen the emergence of a "new worker"— in no sense a rebel (for a realistic docility born of generations of repression was *also* part of the "legacy")—but one on whom the old methods of mobilization and control did not work as they once had on ex-peasants.[1])

A prime element of the legacy was too *many* workers, too many in material production, that sole producer of "real" value, especially in its more backward branches. The objective then was *reallocation*—reducing the numbers of the traditional, largely factory-bound working class, shifting current and future workers toward jobs in more newer, developing branches.

This was to be accomplished with the minimum of disturbance to the *second* element of the legacy—100 percent job security, zero unemployment. Not firings or forced early retirement, but nonreplacement of natural vacancies would accomplish the contraction. All reasonable enough, but the suggestion by a labor economist in January 1986 that in a more efficient economy "one could do the work of seven," and that to meet reasonable productivity and growth targets, the contraction in manufacturing should amount to 13–19 million jobs by 2000, generated massive controversy despite assurance from official sources that no "unemployment" was in the offing. The "normal" flexibility of other economies where people looked for jobs, rather than vice versa, was now being touted to a people unfamiliar with it, to whom full employment meant "full," to whom job security meant tenure. The government, constrained, would suffer heavy "public relations" consequences in this without getting much reallocation at all, or showing the political resolve to push hard against this important element of the legacy.[2]

A *third* legacy—the "right not to work hard" when jobs were so plentiful and secure, a workforce as often as not seen as "slack," "lazy"—was a familiar one. Andropov had tired to enhance labor discipline in 1983 mainly via crackdowns on drunkenness and absenteeism during the workday—with indifferent results in his short time at the helm. Gorbachev, while no friend of absenteeism, and near-teetotal in his views on Russia's complex historical relationship with alcohol, went directly to the assembly line. The discipline he proposed would be monetary. Most workers were paid according to quantitative norm fulfillment: base pay, plus bonuses for 100 percent or more "according to plan," the bonuses typically amounting to some 40 percent of the base. Critical in the process was a toothless quality-control system, wherein end-of-production-line inspectors (whose own bonuses depended on "plan fulfillment" by those whose work was being checked!) examined output for defects. Needless to say, few items— judged by technical specifications established by the Gosstandart bureaucracy, rather than consumers/users—went into the reject bin.

Gorbachev's solution was a new system of "state acceptance" (*gospriemka*), introduced into some 1,500 mainly large industrial enterprises in 1987. It took the inspectors out from under factory administration, giving them new bosses, and a mandate to show neither fear nor favor to workers or management. Rejection of only a small proportion of total output (since the bonus-earning aim was to "overproduce" only to the tune of 101–102 percent or so) could leave a shop or whole enterprise below "plan" and thus bonusless, with 99 percent of the plan target fulfilled—significant cuts in a pay packet that—bonuses included—was seen as an entitlement. Thus did things develop in many plants, to general frustration. Simulation of fulfillment now assumed new forms—back-channel access to Gosstandart itself was employed to get specifications lowered to a level plants could meet. But "quality" of product is, typically, assured by proper design at the outset, not oversight on the assembly line, and affirmed by a satisfied user. The Soviet economy, and Gorbachev's reform, still lacked any sovereign consumer (save the military). Both design and execution thus suffered and *gospriemka*, never explicitly abandoned, faded away.[3]

A *fourth* legacy was that of state-fixed and controlled retail prices. Gorbachev, from the outset, likely understood some of the irrationalities; for example, the standard bread loaf, selling seemingly forever at the same low retail price that by the mid-1980s amounted to less than half the procurement price of the grain that went into it. Bread, at least was available: but utility-grade stewing beef, "on offer" at the same price since the mid-1960s, could not be found in the state stores. On the whole, the Soviet public did not, could not, make the linkage between fixed prices and shortages. Price "reform," then, was a logical but controversial element in Gorbachev's general plan, delayed—even as in the black market real prices soared—until April 2, 1991, and then imposed administratively by the state rather than by decontrol. Public reactions ran from confused anger to localized rioting, but it was too little and too late a move to affect the real consumer economy in any major way.

The *fifth* legacy was a rough egalitarianism in wages/salaries, which, enhanced by an economy of shortage and "standard" state direct-provisioning of much housing and services, made for a rather flat economic landscape, and little even of the principle of socialist (as opposed to communist) material motivation: "from each according to his abilities, to each according to his work."

Gorbachev's line of attack involved increased—but more importantly *differentiated*—incentives via the pay packet, and the repetition of the familiar denunciations of wage-leveling (*uravnilovka*), voiced by his predecessors, but whose policies had done little to eliminate. The not overly frequent upward wage adjustments, typically branch/ministry-wide, generally worked by "bumping up" the base rate for the lowest skilled and least senior, and adjusting everyone above in proportion, tended to compress the wage scales. The new approach, announced in 1986, specified increases favoring the (somewhat) better paid with higher percentage increases in recognition of skills and qualifications: 20–25 percent for production workers, but 30–35 percent for engineering-technical personnel, and 40–45 percent for "leading categories of specialists." It was thus a matter of legitimating higher "returns" to education and formal training than the system had typically provided; an intent underlined by 30 percent increases authorized for the educated but underpaid in education, medicine and other "helping" areas in which compensation fell below average blue-collar pay. Within manual ranks the need for greater returns to (manual) skill was underlined by a specification that the top four ranks—but not the lowest two—on the typical six-level skill- "normed scale" (*tarifnaya setka*) for jobs in a particular industry would be eligible for extra bonuses for high-quality output—again, a move toward greater differentiation and a hint to the lowest skilled to upgrade or suffer consequences.

But unlike the past, the state would not simply hand the rubles for such raises to the enterprises. Now, the plant itself would have to find the wherewithal. Though the directives were rather general, the notion was that plants would either (1) improve and upgrade their products and charge more for them (to the same state customers, presumably) thus financing the raises, and/or (2) find ways to cut redundant jobs/employees while retaining roughly the same wage fund, spreading it more thickly over the few and favored.[4]

These notions were rooted in Gorbachev's assumption that a *sixth* legacy—the dependency of plant managers on ministerial directions from above, their behavior as production engineers rather than producers for a diversity of buyers and users—could, and would, be changed. He assumed that managers would soon exercise more autonomy, behave more "economically" (to say "entrepreneurially" would be to stretch the ideas of the mid-late 1980s), all based on the new game rules of the Law on the State Enterprise, enacted across much of the economy in 1988. The assumption was unwarranted. Confusion and inconsistency, the competing logics of new institutions not yet fully in place, vs. an old planned economy made for managers both disoriented and *still* subordinated to branch ministries, whose own rationale was no longer clear. Managers were reluctant to shed workers, especially since they still faced prime responsibility for finding jobs for those they let go. Managers would not behave "as if" they were in something like a market economy, with choices among suppliers, order books to fill, rivals to fight for "market share," because they were not. They could, and would, use their new autonomy to raise prices on products, claiming "improvements" in quality and design that were far from evident (amounting to a new label or "Mark II" nameplate), and behave like the monopolists many were, correctly predicting that their (state-sector) customers would not rebel, thus trying to provide some of the raises authorized, and benefit both their workers and themselves.

The *final* legacy was a pattern of authority relations in the plant that combined a significant amount of informal worker "control" over the production process with a good deal of managerial "divide and rule" capacity in the exercise of control over nonwage benefits like housing, internal distribution of scarce goods, etc. The "mix" varied greatly. It is not really evident that Gorbachev ever had a handle on any of this, or where he thought a balance should be struck.

True, the Law on the State Enterprise provided both for a new, seemingly large, worker role in *electing* managerial personnel right up to the director level, and for "councils of the labor collective." These would, in the short time they had to work, fall short of changing anything really substantive.[5] Any thoughts of other ways to enhance workers' clout (like scrapping the old system of state "trade unions") went unexpressed. Yet the radically changed overall political context by the summer of 1989 would be a critical facilitating factor in the massive wave of coal field strikes that swept the country at that time. They would show that state trade union structures were unable to prevent labor conflict from reaching critical points, or to bestir themselves at such a point to "take charge" and lead their members in any organized way.

The state enterprise law's provisions for the elections of managerial cadres and institutionalized worker participation in management, were overtaken by events, and changes in thinking. It was only in the terminal crisis of the economy—from summer 1990 on—that the possibility of large-scale state divestment, de-etatization, *privatization*, really arose, as it dawned on the "players" that socialism as they understood it could not be saved. Control would likely, in the future, come with ownership. Owners would decide on managers, not workers. Managers working for owners would command the work process, not workers organized in "councils." And if somehow workers became partial owners as well, it would be only as owners that they would exercise whatever power was theirs. Even then, Gorbachev was not able to choose, in the fall of 1990, between the unrealistic gradualism of the "government" plan offered by the finance minister Pavlov and the blitz privatization laid out in the Shatalin-Yavlinskii "500 days" plan. Time ran out—on Gorbachev, on the Soviet state, on the Soviet economy.

AFTER GORBACHEV: RUSSIA'S RULERS CONFRONT THE SOVIET LEGACY

The fall of the USSR did not mean the disappearance of Soviet institutions and practices in the economy. The "plan" for the new Russian economy was formulated quickly, and under pressure, even as the USSR itself was coming apart in November-December 1991. The plan had been formulated quickly, in the context of economic collapse and political turmoil—in it, no particular attention was given to workers, or any other large socio-occupational category for that matter. The logic of rapid marketization, of shock therapy, should of course favor those who could learn the new rules rapidly, or who from foreign experience knew them already, as well as those whose skills/talents "fit" a market economy. For most workers, for most citizens, this was not good news: overnumerous, ill-deployed, many in production units starved of investment, with little idea of what was coming.

Thus, in dealing with the fourth legacy—state-controlled prices, often subsidized—the government, freeing most of them, still kept a fair number under some control, fearful that there would be no "supply side response" on certain classes of goods. In 1992, the government still owned virtually all the factories, but it did not control them, could not issue binding orders to management or workers, any more than had Gorbachev's government in its twilight. The "command economy" was gone. The state could, and did, print money and issue credits to cover the interplant debt obligations and wage bills generated by those factories: the "budget constraints" were soft indeed. Part of the relative calm in the face of economic pressure was attributable to an employment security remarkable in the situation: Yeltsin and Gaidar, in effect, did not try to confront the second legacy—that of job security and (near) 100 percent employment of the labor force. Output was contracting sharply, especially in branches wherein one found much of the core Russian working class, yet there was, early on, very little shedding of labor. If there was some usefulness in this legacy for Gaidar's reformers, it was that having a job, having that "link" to the factory where so much of life was organized (and where certain nonwage goods and services/benefits were obtained) eased the pains of falling real wages and economic deprivation for many, lowering the chances of much-feared "social explosion."

Certainly no direct state action was taken to encourage trimming labor forces in the pursuit of efficiency. Here, neoliberalism remained rhetoric. When later, unemployment would come, it would be "market" forces rather than the state that would drive it (and peculiar elements of the relation between Russian workers, their wages and the plant would still moderate the level of unemployment). Maintaining a relatively high level of unemployment in the face of a brutal economic contraction was less a matter of what the government did, than what it did not do. In addition to the moderation just noted, it had not decontrolled wholesale energy prices to anywhere near world levels—no Russian plants, typically wasteful in any case, could have paid them. The legacy of full employment may have been too politically useful for Gaidar and his associates to tamper with, but behind Russia's "good" employment numbers loomed a much bleaker economic picture.

Three of the other legacies—the hypertrophic material production sector with its too-many workers, the slack work discipline in many plants, the (low-)wage egalitarianism of sector and branch pay scales—were targets, one can assume, that Yeltsin's economic team sought to address via changes in the "ground rules" of the economy and, ultimately, privatization. In 1992, conceiving of privatization "generally" (they could do little else, since aside from the blanket authorization of private trade, and the co-ops inherited from the later Gorbachev era, there had been no real privatization, and future procedures were not yet clear), Gaidar and his team must have seen it as the near-automatic solution to these "legacy" problems.

Similarly, a regime of private ownership driving management appropriately, would impose an enhanced discipline on the shop floor. This would flow both from owners' positive interest in bottom-line profit, and from a negative—an absence of any incentives to hoard excess labor, such as the old Soviet system had generated. Private ownership's logic would, finally, dictate paying a premium for scarce skills in the production of goods and services for which effective demand existed, but offering none for efforts and skills that did not. The disciplinary effects on the unskilled might be harsh, but this was part of the logic of going beyond perestroika all the way to the market. "Returns" to skill should thus increase markedly, the rather flat/compressed scale of wage differentiation of the Soviet period be left behind.

Nothing, of course, would quite work out so automatically. There *would* be incentives to hoard labor, reasons to keep a value-subtraction process flowing, things that would contribute to the conservation of aspects of the Soviet legacy, for reasons different than those that had given rise to them in the first place.

It was not, obviously a first-order concern of Gaidar to intervene directly to alter authority relations in plants. Changes in ownership and organization were, in time, supposed to produce "normal" effects. Whether managers (and now, owners) would have the kind of power over workers they had enjoyed when so much of worker compensation came in housing and other services. The ability (or not) to turn one's wages into desirable goods in a plant's internal "distributor" would depend on how rapidly housing stock could be privatized (in most cases, by giving all or most of the equity to sitting tenants), and how much more goods and services "marketed" in the normal way. (Certainly, this Soviet legacy of managerial ability to withhold or bestow nonwage benevolence was not something the reformers wanted to see preserved, but in many regions, and in many branches of the economy, decoupling the supplying of goods and services from the factory would not come quickly, nor would it be welcome for workers who had no alternative recourse.)

A measure of informal worker control over the production process (virtually universal in any collective labor process under formal command from "above") was a legacy more or less likely to be preserved as managers/owners found that they could not, or could, extend their sphere of control at workers' expense. Again, in their considerations of what they had inherited, reformers must have thought about the prospects of developing some formal, rule-regulated worker control, via "work rules" arrived at in negotiations between labor unions and management. Here, in the possibility of operating in the way that was "normal" in the market economies of Western Europe, was a massive prospective change from the Soviet legacy.

But here, in the early (1992–93) period, there were many complications as well. The formerly "official" trade union organization, the FNPR, was warring with smaller upstart "free" trade unions, and now with a government that was still, however unwillingly, the owner/manager of virtually all large-scale industrial capital and plant. Thus, in any European-style soft-corporatist scheme for regulation labor relations, the state "sat" both on its own side of the table as "the government," and in most of the seats on the employers' side, target as government not only of the FNPR unions on the third side but of its "own" subsidy/rent-seeking managers on the employers' side. The actual Russian trilateral commission launched at the beginning of shock therapy was thus in fact structurally premature, with state sector employment still so predominant, and labor unions still unused to "classic" modes of representing worker economic interests.

Worker control has in most cases been a casualty of things more primal than getting the choreography of labor-management relations "right." The contraction of Russian GDP until 1999–2000, ongoing and severe for so long, rendered a great deal of ostensibly employed labor actually redundant, and thus quite weak in the claims it could advance on management. But management, as it turns out, has exercised its powers in peculiar ways that, while exploitative, do not follow the patterns of the more successful East European market transitions.

It is time, then, to turn to some data on the results of the Yeltsin government's encounter with the legacies of the Soviet command economy, to numbers that indicate something of how workers have been affected by a mix of legacies abandoned and those willy-nilly preserved to one extent or another.

WORKERS IN A CHANGING ECONOMY

Teasing the specifics of the working-class experience out of state statistical data, separating the classic workers—manual operatives in manufacturing, construction, transport and a few other sectors—from the many other suffering categories in the Russian population is not easy.[6] Even surveys offering individual-level data, including occupation, that thus allow multivariate analysis, often seem to focus their attention elsewhere. We limit ourselves here to a discussion of a few indicators, mindful that a broad definition of "workers," given how large they bulked in the old Soviet labor force, means that, virtually by definition, they must fall near the average on many indicators.

From the "overfull" employment of the Soviet period, Russia since 1991 has seen a significant decline in the number employed. The demography of an aging population, coupled with relatively low retirement ages (though many pensioners in the past continued to work) has a good deal to do with this. In more recent years, the slow but real onset of unemployment, and a drop in labor force participation not only by the old but by those aged 16–20 contribute to the outcome.[7] Data trace the winnowing of the numbers of the employed. Russia's (the RSFSR's through 1991) employed numbered 73 million in 1980, increased to 75 million plus 1985 to 1990, fell below 74 million in 1991, and by 1998 had contracted to 63.6 million. Echoes of the 1998 collapse of the ruble, which by pricing imports beyond the reach of so many also encouraged an expansion of domestic production in some sectors, then led to a slight upturn in employment to 64.4 million in the second quarter of 1999, and has continued since.[8]

This contraction in the employed population has been "moderate" when contrasted to the decline in Russian GDP, industrial output and some other indicators. Certainly, there has been a good deal of involuntary exit—from a job, from the labor force; by retirements that mix voluntary and involuntary elements; by shifts to undocumented status for some who work "off the books" (though the size of this population, according to most social surveys, is not large, and would not if included in statistics dispel the picture of poverty familiar to observers of today's Russia).[9] Workers have suffered from all of this. Though their sufferings have not been unique, certainly, it is "traditional" sectors of the economy, those material-production branches where one finds workers, that have contracted, rather than new sectors like "financial services and banking," where one does not look for them.

Unemployment—involuntary joblessness or substantial underemployment in a job position recorded as being filled—was slow (in comparison to Eastern Europe) to become a major phenomenon, but in more recent years has built to significant levels. The 1992–2000 numbers, on unemployment by adjusted ILO definitions, and the much smaller numbers registered with Russia's state employment service (FES), tell the story succinctly (table 10.1).

Variations in the data gathering techniques, differing mixes of survey data vs. projections from earlier basepoints sometimes limit strict comparability between years in unemployment statistics like these.[10] Still, the 1999–2000 figures likely show the uneven working through of "positive" side effects of the 1998 crisis: as the ruble collapse made imports too expensive, domestic production increased, and with it, employment. (Just as employment grew marginally in 1999, so the [ILO] unemployment rate calculated in a new data series [which lists 1997 and 1998 rates, respectively, as 10.8 and 11.9 percent] rose to 13.9 percent in the first quarter of 1999, but then fell to 12.6 in the second.)[11]

These are grim figures. Though not out of line with unemployment rates in some affluent European states, they are recorded against the backdrop of a poor Russian economy. Neither the FES money benefits nor its marginal job-finding services motivate anything like a majority of the unemployed to turn to it for help. Unemployment assistance and insurance funding in Russia in 1997 amounted to 0.24 percent of GDP, compared to 1.67 percent and 2.16 percent in Poland and Hungary, respectively—countries with a much higher per capita GDP than Russia. As a percentage of the average wage, average unemployment payments in Russia are much lower than in East Central Europe.[12]

Table 10.1.   Unemployed, Russian Federation, 1992–1998 (as percent of labor force)

	1992	1993	1994	1995	1996	1997	1998	1999	2000
ILO definition	4.8	5.3	7.4	8.8	9.7	11.0	12.4	11.7	9.4
FES-registered	0.8	1.0	3.1	4.4	5.1	4.3	4.4	2.9	2.3

Sources: Russian Economic Trends, no. 4, 1997, 81 (1992); no. 1, 1998, 28 (1993); no. 3, 2000, 87 (1994-2000); year 2000 figures are second-quarter.

Thus, the market forces Gorbachev toyed with, the ones Yeltsin's economic advisors sought to set loose, have done some of the expected work—the legacy of full employment is no more. Yet to reiterate, given the scale of the economic contraction, these are moderate rates of joblessness. Much is explained here by the prevalence of wage arrears—delay or failure in paying workers and employees. If inequalities in wage levels are much greater now, Russian workers on the whole are still quite cheap to begin with. Wage bills as a share of factory expenses tend to be low—and if workers need not be paid to be "retained," they are all the more likely to appear as employed. Unpaid, Russian workers do not necessarily quit. A mix of the old legacy and new elements—dependence of workers on plant-connected noncash benefits, opportunities to use plant facilities/tools on their own, even sometimes payment in kind in lieu of wages, all go some way toward explaining workers "commitments" to plants at which they may do very little work, and from which they may have seen no cash wages in some time. The limits on geographic mobility and housing exchange—legal/administrative legacies of the old USSR—make broad searches for new jobs infeasible for most. The lack of any real benefit to be gained from FES registration means no real "pull" factors motivating workers to leave their jobs. Management in many cases has little to no incentive to dismiss such workers, while the necessity of making certain severance payments to formally dismissed workers is a disincentive. Unlike East Central Europe, where arrears are essentially unknown, Russian "workers have traded real wages for relative employment stability."[13]

It is not just manual workers who suffer from the arrears problem. Persistent and large-scale,[14] it spreads across many population groups.[15] Teachers and medical personnel in the "budget" sector have been major victims, as well as workers. There are regional differences, and—not surprisingly—relatively greater incidence of arrears in older branches like manufacturing construction and energy, as opposed to finance, "trade and distribution," and the like—the latter less blue-collar sectors. Combined effects of region and branch are neatly summarized by the authors of a 1999 study that employs sophisticated analytic techniques on a data base of more than 17,000 households.

> we estimate that an unskilled, male worker aged 35 to 44 living in the Volga region and working in a manufacturing enterprise of over 1000 workers for more than 10 years has an arrears probability of 95 percent. In contrast, a 25-year old woman graduate working in a finance company that employs less than 10 workers in the metropolitan area (sic) has a 5 percent chance of suffering wage arrears.[16]

Thus, the arrears problem is such that some categories seem near-immune from the risk (another, 1998 study found that "most of those who are not now owed money for wages have *never* experienced significant non-payment of wages" (emphasis added),[17] while some others, especially but by no means only those situated in the classic one-industry city, or sotsgorod, beloved of yesterday's Soviet planners, have little chance that if one household member goes un-paid, another may get a full pay packet the same month: "in remote company towns, the non-payment of one tends to mean the non-payment of all."[18]

Thus, while pay levels in industry and construction—loci of so many work-ers—in the late 1990s, as in the Soviet period, were well above those in educa-tion, health and science (but below new categories like "finance"), we need to remember that those statistics indicate wages due—and that workers, as well as the white-collar sufferers in the mass helping professions, have been more likely to experience arrears—while those in "finance" do not. Until the very late 1990s, the experience of arrears linked fairly tightly to that classic manifestation of job discontent—strikes. Teachers and health personnel proved on the whole to be more strike prone than workers (perhaps because government was their pay-master, and might have been seen as susceptible to embarrassment in a way reg-ular employers were not). Pay, surely, is a preventative: a total of 6,372 strikes in the first quarter of 1999, involving 170,000 people for 1.19 million man-days lost, fell to 249 strikes in the second quarter, involving only 14,000 people for a total 36,000 day loss—in that quarter, both government and enterprises "paid up" substantially on arrears, looking toward Duma elections at the end of the year. (That quarter's arrears level was the same as spring 1996—just prior to that year's presidential election!) Overall, arrears are still significant, but declined somewhat into the first half of 2000. Reductions by mid-2000 were much more marked in the budget sector, however—reflecting Putin's "tough" approach to things, and the clout he can exercise most readily over the government sector. Other than protesting arrears, strike activity has little rationale: workers are not in a position to "win" anything by withholding labor that is cheap to free (and sometimes "virtual" in any case). Indeed, in 2000, the bottom fell out of strike activity: 770 strikes were reported over the first three quarters, compared to 6,839 in the same period of 1999, involving only 29,000 participants, vs. 196,000 in 1999.[19]

Workers are a very diverse population in a complicated situation. The old fa-vored extractive/energy-related industries—though now gas more than coal—have increased their relative advantage in pay over other branches like metal fab-rication and machine building, which have been "hurting."[20] Wage differentials have grown generally between sectors and branches, much wider than in Soviet times, the "winners" generally so only versus other workers who have "lost." Large-scale sample surveys collecting individual-level data vary in detailed find-ings, but some basics seem well-established. Though "returns to education" were small in the Soviet system (i.e., more years of education did not translate readily into more earnings), and thus workers were not per se economically dis-advantaged by moderate schooling levels, on the whole returns to education are not systematically greater today. Nor does (manual) skill seem to command any automatic premium in the new Russian economy compared to lack of such qual-ification (though some data on wage levels in the earlier transition years seemed to show skilled urban manuals retaining a good deal of their Soviet-era advantages vs. routine nonmanuals and nonsupervisory specialist personnel. The new inequality does not, therefore, necessarily follow according to the new principles of differentiation as reformers though it would.[21]

Workers on the whole have been economic "losers"—along with the vast majority of Russians— when contrasted to proprietors (owners, independents) and managers. (All "classes," all socio-occupational categories have lost vs. these *novi homines* who possess both power and money in a Russia where the latter now can buy anything.) "Managers," as the authors of one large sample survey-based study conclude, "exploit their organizational resources to get rich at the expense of their workers."[22] (Yet not all managers do, or can, to the same degree. One study indicates that the largest source of overall wage inequality is not branch or region related, but rooted in the "differential ability of employers to pay." In a given branch, in a given region, some plants can and do pay, others do not—the core conditions are "firm-specific" and hence elude any categorical pattern.[23]

Add to all this, finally, the continuing massive dependence of so many on the plant, and one taps into another element of the legacy with which post-Communist Russia has yet to part. It is, in particular, an area of worker disadvantage (except in those rare cases where a plant may both pay relatively regularly, and by effective economic as opposed to—or perhaps combined with—bureaucratic effort, maintain a range of services for "its people").[24] This sort of dependence remains radically "out of synch" with the market principles that supposedly animate policy, since on the whole workers are not paid enough (or often enough, or both) to buy what they need. For many, cash wages fall far short of the level they need reach if they are to finance the major share of their material living standard. Thus, a mixed picture emerges of how aspects of the Soviet legacy have fared versus the fact of the Russian state's withdrawal from some of its old functions relevant to working class existence.

The legacy, after all, as well as its human bearers, were products of extraordinary times and conditions. The USSR molded "its own" working class, not inherited and converted one from some previous institutional structure that might, post-1991, be *re*-converted. It had concentrated the workers in largish factories, when smaller might have been more adaptable. It built "company towns"—sotsgoroda—rather than the multifunction urban agglomerations market economies produce. It deployed significant numbers of workers, free and convict, permanently to places (Vorkuta, Noril'sk) where no other type of system would have sent them.

CONCLUSION

Both geographically and institutionally, it was bound to be a long journey back, from the Vorkutas and Noril'sks, from the more persistent legacies of the Soviet system, and so it has proven for post-Communist Russia. It has not actually been a matter of a journey "back" to a time before those legacies were laid down. Tsarist Russia, the USSR's predecessor, though it was changing rapidly in its last decades, never assembled the full institutional inventory necessary for a real market economy—and the Soviet period destroyed what *had* been developed.

Poles, Czechs, Hungarians, others in East Central Europe and the Baltics, have been able to travel "back" and find usable legacies in pasts that are less remote, legacies that connect more readily with market economies and market societies in the present and the future. They have been luckier.

Russia and its workers have, then, little usable pre-Soviet past to reconnect with, to learn from. As to elements of the overall Soviet-period legacy, it seems clear that Gaidar and the rest of Yeltsin's economic team were, a decade ago, ready "in concept" to break with all of them. But they found themselves in some cases incapable, and in some others unwilling, to close the door completely on what they had inherited. For the workers, this has meant an environment altered in many ways, still familiar in some others, and premiums both on "luck" and on the ability to adapt.

The old ironclad job security is, of course, gone, and workers are consequently less "secure" than in the days gone by. Yet—very much in contrast to the East European experience—unemployment experience as such has been slow to arrive and, given the contraction of GDP over the years since 1991, is still relatively low. Arrears, furloughs, short-time "explain" a good deal of this, but it is still the case that Russia's workers have had in many respects less employment disruption to adapt to than have Eastern Europe's. The durable link with the plant also reflects a persistent dependency of workers on things the plant may provide, outside of wages—housing, services, even the opportunity to use facilities for work on one's own account. Most of these are legacies of the past, and persist because workers, like most other Russians, do not earn enough to buy all that they require.

The old subsidized/controlled prices are gone, and workers suffer along with a majority of Russians—although so many of those prices were "qualified" by shortages of the items that it is probably workers in factories formerly "favored" by the state and thus well-supplied with those items who have, comparatively, suffered more. The old rough egalitarianism in salaries and wages is gone as well, but there groups other than workers who have probably felt the effects of this change more severely.

Finally, a new weighting of GDP components toward services and away from manufacturing means that the worker has lost his place at the center of the economy that he held in Soviet times. In a profound sense, the classic worker does not revolve around a blue-collar center as it once did. This displacement, now and even more so in the future, is the central fact of change, amidst many varieties of persistence noted here and the most important break with the Soviet legacy.

NOTES

1. See Zaslavskaya's writings in the 1980s, gathered in *A Voice of Reform* (Armonk, N.Y.: M.E. Sharpe, Inc., 1989) and *The Second Socialist Revolution: An Alternative Soviet Strategy* (Bloomington: Indiana University Press, 1990).

2. See Walter D. Connor, *The Accidental Proletariat: Workers, Politics, and Crisis in Gorbachev's Russia* (Princeton, N.J.: Princeton University Press, 1991), 187–192, on the suggestions, the reactions, and the limited attempts to implement this manpower vision as policy; see also Linda J. Cook, *The Soviet Social Contract and Why It Failed: Welfare Policy and Workers' Politics from Brezhnev to Yeltsin* (Cambridge, Mass.: Harvard University Press, 1993), 94 ff.

3. See Connor, op. cit., 145–147, and Cook, op. cit., 101, on *gospriemka*.

4. See Connor, op cit., 144–145, and Cook, op. cit., 100, on the differentiated pay raise authorization. Provisions.

5. See Connor, op cit., 193–194, and Cook, op. cit., 101–102, on the Law on the State Enterprise.

6. Some of the problems in tracing workers among the other socio-occupational categories are discussed by the present author in "Observations on the Status of Russia's Workers," *Post-Soviet Geography and Economics*, 38, 9 (1997), 550–557; "Five Years without a Plan: Workers in Russia's Economic Revolution," in A. Jasinska-Kania, M. L Kohn and K. M. Slomczynski, eds., *Power and Social Structure* (Warsaw: Wydawnictwa Uniwersytetu Warszawskiego, 1999), 212–224.

7. Simon Clarke, "Poverty in Russia," *Problems of Economic Transition* 42, 5 (September 1999), 26.

8. *Russian Economic Trends* (*RET*), no. 2 (1994): no.1 (1998), 28; no. 3 (1999): 93.

9. See Clarke, "Poverty," op. cit., 28–29.

10. See, for example, the differences between the statistical series in the table and the varying ones in *Russian Economic Trends*, no. 3 (1999), 93 (table 21) covering the same years.

11. *RET*, no. 3 (1999): 93.

12. Irina Denisova, "Social Policy in Russia: Employment Fund," *RET*, no. 1 (1999): 6, 9–11.

13. See Simon Commander and Ruslan Yemtsov, "Russian Unemployment: Its Magnitude, Characteristics and Regional Dimensions," in J. Klugman, ed., *Poverty in Russia: Public Policy and Private Responses* (Washington, D.C.: World Bank, 1997), 134.

14. See Nadezhda Ivanova and Charles Wyplosz, "Arrears: The Tide That Is Drowning Russia," *RET*, no. 1 (1999): 24–35.

15. Hartmut Lehmann et al., "Grime and Punishment: Job Insecurity and Wage Arrears in the Russian Federation" *Journal of Comparative Economics*, 27 (1999): 604.

16. Ibid., 608.

17. Simon Clarke, *New Forms of Employment and Household Survival Strategies in Russia* (Coventry and Moscow: ISITO/CCLS, 1999): 115.

18. Ibid., 116.

19. See *RET*, no. 3 (1999), 46, 95, and no. 3 (2000): 88–89; see also Walter D. Connor, "New World of Work: Employment, Unemployment, and Adaptation," in Mark G. Field and Judyth L. Twigg, eds., *Russia's Torn Safety Nets: Health and Social Welfare during the Transition* (New York: St. Martin's Press, 2000), 191–212.

20. See Bertram Silverman and Murray Yanowitch, *New Rich, New Poor, New Russia: Winners and Losers on the Russian Road to Capitalism* (Armonk, N.Y.: M. E. Sharpe, 1997), 86–90 and sources cited therein.

21. Ibid., 92, table 5.5.

22. See Theodore Gerber and Michael Hout, "More Shock than Therapy: Market Transition, Employment and Income in Russia, 1991–1995," *American Journal of Sociology*, 104, 1 (July, 1998): 5, 28–33 (quote, 33).

23. Simon Clarke, *The Formation of a Labour Market in Russia* (Cheltenham, U.K.: Edward Elgar, 1999), 39, 267.

24. For background, see Simon Commander and Mark Schankerman, "Enterprise Restructuring and Social Benefits," *Economics of Transition*, 5, 1 (1997): 1–24, and Maxim Boycko and Andrei Shleifer, "Russian Restructuring and Social Benefits," in Anders Aslund, ed., *Russian Economic Reform at Risk* (London and New York: Pinter, 1995), 99–118.

11

The Changing Position of Women: Trafficking, Crime, and Corruption

Louise I. Shelley

At the end of the Soviet period, the female population was well educated and nearly fully employed. Socialist ideology proclaimed the equality of women and Russian women achieved very high levels of education and labor force participation.[1] Women were not viewed as sexual objects; in fact many were involved in the most unfeminine activities: building bridges, paving roads, casting iron and constructing railroads.[2] Although the socialist ideology of equality for women existed as propaganda rather than an institutionalized reality, tremendous resources were invested in the education of women and significant state funds were spent to guarantee child care for working mothers. An elaborate system of after-school enrichment and summer programs were provided for children at minimal cost.[3] While women's professional positions were generally in lower status and lower paid occupations like teaching, the medical profession and nursing, these occupations had a recognized and established position within society and a guaranteed income.

The social benefits provided by the Soviet system, including subsidized child care, summer programs and many cultural and athletic programs for children made it possible for women to work and support families. Despite the fact that health standards in child care were rather poor and children were not provided top quality care, women were nevertheless able to become an integral part of the Soviet economy. The high divorce rates and the difficulties in the consumer sphere gave women a double burden of work and household responsibilities. Excluded from positions within the Party bureaucracy by an absence of time and the patriarchal power relations of society,[4] women were a presence in the workforce rather than in the political process. Sustaining this legacy of full employment and investment in education for women was difficult in the economic

crisis of post-Soviet society, particularly when huge amounts of national resources and state budgetary resources were transferred overseas.

ECONOMIC TRANSITION

The economic transition from a socialist to a market economy was made with
very little attention to the social dislocations it would cause. The primary focus
of the transition was to ensure the impossibility of the return to communism
rather than to provide an equitable distribution of property to the citizenry. The
male-dominated power relations of the Soviet period affected the property distribution of the post-Soviet period. In the socialist period, when men only controlled rather than owned property, women had a chance at social and economic
benefits. But the power balance between men and women became even more
skewed in the postsocialist period when the redistribution of property occurred
only to those who had enjoyed power prior to the collapse.

The feminization of poverty was a consequence of an economic transition conducted without consideration as to the impact of policies on women and children.
The design of the privatization process was inherently disadvantageous to
women. The financial crisis of the post-Soviet states led to the collapse of the social safety net attached to many enterprises, a problem exacerbated by Western
policy advisors who advocated that Russian enterprises be stripped of their social
welfare functions in the name of economic efficiency. The child care, summer
camps and other programs that benefited women were dropped. This was often
not a prelude to more efficient enterprises, as Western advisors hoped, but instead allowed even more assets to be stripped from enterprises by management.

Women were at a disadvantage at all stages of the redistribution of state
property—vouchers, auctions, small business privatization and that of larger
businesses. Women had little chance of acquiring any valuable assets from the
state because privatization in Russia was structured to give managers a disproportionate share of former state property. Therefore, the Soviet legacy of male
management was translated into the post-Soviet property distribution. Very few
women in the post-Soviet period acquired more than an insignificant share of
the enterprises in which they had worked.

Factories were privatized to employees but in this aspect of privatization, women
had another real disadvantage in acquiring the wealth of the former Soviet states.
Many women factory workers were employed in feminized industries such as tex-
tiles, food production and processing, which were not competitive in a more open
economy. In the years following the collapse of the USSR, these industries were destroyed by cheap textile imports from China and Italy. Russia in the 1990s became
almost entirely dependent on imported food. Therefore, women disproportionately
acquired stakes in industries without value, whereas men were more likely to acquire shares in extractive resource industries, which were more profitable.

Voucher privatization delivered nothing of value to women. The voucher privatization was intended to give Soviet citizens a share of the privatized state, but it proved a total farce. The vouchers, when issued, had a total value of about $10, and the stock funds in which citizens could invest these vouchers were unregulated and riddled with fraud.[5] Auction privatizations also left women at a disadvantage. Women were often physically barred from many auctions of state property by the enforcers of organized crime.

The rise of organized crime and the pervasive corruption significantly affected women's ability to obtain property. The brute force of organized crime was often exercised to deprive women of their property rights. Women employed in the service industries could not acquire stakes in their businesses because restaurants, cafes and small stores were likely acquisition targets of organized crime, against which no one could compete in obtaining property. Post–Soviet organized crime represented the most patriarchal elements of Soviet society. It combined the *blatnoi* world, the professional criminals of Russia, with members of the *nomenklatura*, former military (particularly Afghan war veterans), KGB, and police.[6] Therefore, the corrupt and criminal networks operated without hindrance because they had merged with the state structures.

Oligarchs hired the privatized coercive forces of the state to deprive women of their property.[7] Illustrative of this is the case of the privatization of a typography plant in central Moscow acquired illegally by one of the oligarchs. The employees, mostly women, had found the finance to purchase the plant, which under the rules of privatization they had the first option to buy. But the oligarch defended his illegal purchase by hiring the alpha troops and aiming tanks at protesting female employees. This abuse of power was shown on television to no avail. The women went to court to exercise their property rights. The court found in their favor but there was no means to obtain an enforceable judgment. The criminalization of the banking sector had multiple negative effects on women's lives. Many women lost their life savings in unregulated banking institutions, leaving them without any financial security. Banks did not function as lending institutions or sources of loans for legitimate entrepreneurs but were often merely vehicles to launder money out of the country. Women who could have been successful entrepreneurs of small businesses, if given access to capital, were often forced to take loans from organized crime.[8] Some of these women became entrepreneurs engaged in small-scale entrepreneurship such as operators of kiosks, travel agencies and shuttle traders. In many cases, successful businesses launched by women, with or without the financing of organized crime, were expropriated by the criminals using extortion and force. Women were less able than their male associates to retain protection services to safeguard their financial interests.

The corrupted privatization process left the state without the resources it needed to function effectively. Valuable properties were transferred to insiders for relatively small sums, depriving the state of much needed revenues.

Compounding the problem was the export of capital on a massive scale and money laundering from all the former Soviet states, which left the successor states starved for capital. The state could not afford to pay wages, and those most affected were women employed in the state sector as teachers, doctors, nurses and factory employees.

Thus the flawed design of privatization, the collapse of state institutions, the rise of organized crime and the proliferation of corruption combined to ensure that women had few economic alternatives in the 1990s. Women were left with limited opportunities to function in the legitimate economy, a situation that served the traffickers who thrived on the vulnerability of women. Many of the women affected were too old to be subjected to trafficking but their impoverishment left no way for them to support their daughters and grandchildren. The sense that women are responsible for their extended families and are pillars of society, a legacy of the Soviet era, made many women seek any available work abroad in the absence of legitimate opportunities at home.

POST-SOVIET PROSTITUTION AND TRAFFICKING

During most of the Soviet period, very little overt prostitution existed. Socialist ideology proclaimed the end of prostitution and the criminal code did not acknowledge its existence. By the final decades of the Soviet period, thousands of women were prostitutes, monitored by the police and often forced to collaborate with the secret police. A full range of prostitution existed, from women who served the Party elite and the emergent business community to the lowest level who frequented railroad stations. Yet prostitution did not become a mass phenomenon until the Gorbachev years. In the perestoika period, reminiscent of the NEP period of the 1920s, many young women became prostitutes catering to the new business class and the foreigners who came to Russia. In surveys of high school and vocational schools, many indicated prostitution as a favored career choice, a response that reflected the benefits of foreign currency and the lure of the business world.[9]

The final years of the Soviet Union marked not only the end but the rejection of socialist ideology. The "emancipation from the desexualization of life under communism" meant that for many there was a glorification of the erotic and the idealization of the prostitute as an individual breaking barriers.[10] This accounted for some of the attraction to prostitution. Since the late 1980s there has been an enormous rise in prostitution within Russia. Because of the latency of the phenomenon, there are little data on the scope of the problem. But data from the Russian Far East reveal the phenomenal growth in the late 1990s. In the Khabarovsk region, in 1997 there were 550 brothels while in 1999 there were 1,000. This represents the presence of thousands of women in just one region of Russia.

Different strata of women are drawn into prostitution, not only the poorest and the abused. Many of them are also women who are more enterprising and seek this activity as an alternative to their limited economic horizons. In one notable case, an educated Vladivostok woman, trafficked to Macao, returned home only to be killed by her boy friend, a distinguished Hong Kong lawyer, who came to Vladivostok to buy her out of prostitution.[11] Many of the women involved are the risk takers who see a chance to achieve more outside of Russia than their presently dead end lives provide.

Yet many come from impoverished regions with limited economic alternatives. Some were single mothers with no means of providing for their children in communities where work for women is low paid or almost nonexistent. For example, in the Russian Far East, women's unemployment stands at 73 percent.[12] Particular targets for the traffickers were not only women from the Russian Far East but also from poverty stricken parts of the Urals and Siberia as well as Ukraine and Moldova.[13] Interviews with women from the Far East reveals that many had high school educations but went into prostitution because of their limited prospects and their boredom with the impoverished lives of their communities.

A significant group of young female prostitutes come from the lowest tier of post-Soviet society. These are the homeless, children of alcoholic and abusive parents and the hundreds of thousands of abandoned and orphaned children and youth confined to childrens' homes who are all natural sources for the traffickers. The homes where children live for years in abusive conditions give the residents little preparation for life after the institutions. The decline in expenditures on these homes have left the hundreds of thousands of residents in egregious conditions.

Another likely target for the traffickers are women subjected to domestic violence and spousal abuse. Violence against women has a very long history in Russian society, but the collapse of the USSR and the accompanying economic crisis in many families has contributed to a rise in domestic and sexual violence, a problem that is not addressed by the totally inadequate social and law enforcement resources.[14]

The way in which women agree to prostitution varies. Trafficked women sometimes already worked as prostitutes in brothels, whereas others are recruited solely to be sent abroad. A portion of the women have been coerced or duped into the sex trade. A second group received some information on what they would do at their intended destination but lacked a full picture. For example, they may have been told that they would strip for clients or work in bars but they were not informed that they were also expected to perform sexual services. Many signed phony contracts expecting to be paid high wages that never were provided. Instead, the women were made to work off a significant debt and had no alternative because their passports were confiscated at the time of arrival at their destination. Another group agreed to go with traffickers but were not aware that they would be subjected to significant physical abuse by those who trafficked them or by those to whom they would "be sold."[15]

Trafficking and Organized Crime

The trafficking of women from the former Soviet Union began on a large scale after the breakup of the Soviet Union. In the last decade, estimates indicate that as many as 175,000 women may have been trafficked from the former USSR and Eastern Europe. No region of the former USSR has been immune from the problem. Even in relatively more affluent regions, such as the Baltics, there have been numerous women trafficked for prostitution as a recent trafficking case prosecuted in Chicago revealed.[16] Most are trafficked to Western Europe, particularly Germany, Italy and the Netherlands.[17] The exact numbers cannot be calculated because there are no measurable data from the source countries and few host countries have attempted to assess the pervasiveness of the phenomenon. The trafficking of women is not entirely for sexual exploitation, however, this is only one component of the problem. Many women are also placed into slavery-like conditions of domestic servitude, forced labor or sweatshop labor.

Trafficking in women is organized by both larger and smaller organized crime groups. Groups from the former Soviet states often work with their colleagues in Eastern Europe to traffic women.[18] Groups in the Russian Far East work with Japanese and Korean organized crime to transport women to China, Japan, Korea, Thailand and other destinations of the Pacific Rim. These ties are particularly important for Russian organized crime as Japanese groups have years of experience in this area. Groups in the Caucasus work with traffickers in Turkey to move women to brothels in Turkey, Cyprus and elsewhere in the Middle East. Women from Kazakhstan are trafficked to Bahrain, where the Moslem links of the traffickers provide women for this free trade zone.[19]

In the Asian region, the largest number of women are trafficked to China, followed in frequency by South Korea and Japan. The latter two are less frequent because of the higher costs of transport and also the costs of obtaining entry documents for the women. Among those working under registered businesses the figures are different. According to the internal affairs department of the Khabarovsk region last year, there were twenty-seven firms specializing in finding foreign employment in show business. In six months in 2000, 407 people left under these show business firms. Among these 240 went to South Korea, 160 to Japan and 5 to China.[20] But many more women went to China under different terms because border crossings are easier between Russia and China than other Asian countries.

Regardless of the purpose, the mechanisms by which women are trafficked from the former socialist countries are quite similar. All trafficking involves the "recruitment, transport, harboring, transfer, sale or receipt of persons within national or across international borders, through the use of fraud, coercion, force or kidnapping, for the purposes of placing persons in situations of slavery-like conditions . . ."[21] The key elements of the trafficking include deception, coercion, debt bondage and/or a combination of these factors.[22]

The trafficking organizations that control this activity range from small scale operations, which traffic a limited number of women each year to significant criminal organizations, which use trafficking in women as a major revenue source of their criminal activity.[23] Some of the trafficking organizations operate through travel agencies that form groups and obtain tourist visas for these women in conjunction with legitimate tourist groups. Survey research done on the visa lines outside the German embassy in Moscow in the late 1990s revealed this method of trafficking women. For some of these groups, such as those operating in Israel, trafficking in women is a means of laundering money because cash from illicit activity is moved through bars and other businesses where the women operate. Women are also sold to pay off debts held by the traffickers.

The prices commanded by the women differ by the region to which they are trafficked. In the Netherlands, women can be sold to brothel owners for as much as $15,000. In Turkey, there is a higher price for Slavic women than those from the Caucasus. The latter may be sold for a few thousand dollars, a small sum compared to the investment made in the development of this human capital. This reflects the women as commodities rather than as women as potential contributors to an economy. The amounts commanded in Asia appear to be less because the women are not permanently there but go for shorter periods.

Traffickers in women to Belgium, Netherlands and Germany have used violence against competitors and trafficked women to gain a foothold in the lucrative prostitution markets of Western Europe.[24] Ukraine may be the largest source of women trafficked from the former USSR. Dutch researchers suggest that approximately one-third of the women illegally engaged in prostitution in the Netherlands are from Ukraine and that the countries of the former USSR have overtaken all other countries in providing the preponderance of women engaged in unauthorized prostitution in the Netherlands.[25] The problem is not unique to the Netherlands but the patterns their researchers have identified are common throughout Western Europe.

The very brutal treatment of the trafficked women became so evident in Belgium and the Netherlands that parliamentary hearings and investigations in the mid-1990s were instigated by Dutch and Belgian women, deeply disturbed by the mistreatment of women prostitutes in their countries, a problem that many thought had been solved by the greater tolerance of the phenomenon. The situation of trafficked women in China may even be worse. Research conducted among these women revealed that they had been treated inhumanely, had been inadequately fed and housed and had received no or almost no compensation for their work of providing sexual services.[26]

The international links of the traffickers is a very central element of the equation. The ability to threaten the women under their control and to threaten retaliation against family members in the Soviet successor states makes the women particularly vulnerable. In one case in New York, a Russian woman rescued from forced prostitution in New York by a Wall Street executive found that not only her life was at risk but also that of her parents at home in St. Petersburg, where her father was a former high-ranking military official.[27] The same techniques used to threaten prostitutes are also used against hockey stars from the former USSR to force them to pay protection money. These athletes are threatened in the United States and Canada and are made aware that their families at home will be subjects of retaliation if they refuse to comply.

The women in positions of sexual servitude, however, enjoy less protection than the hockey players or other high wage earners living abroad. In most cases, the women are working in their new countries illegally. Therefore, they are in a state of dual illegality. Obtaining asylum for trafficking victims is extremely difficult in many countries of continental Europe and England.[28] In the United States, new legislation has made it easier for trafficking victims to stay, but the visa process is still quite difficult. In most European countries, with the possible exception of Belgium, the situation is analogous. In many European countries, the women can stay during the trial of the traffickers if they are witnesses. In the Netherlands, they receive $500 when leaving the country. Therefore, there is little possibility for the women to exit the life they have entered, and the best they can hope for is eventual deportation without money and the possible retaliation of traffickers when they return home.

The political-criminal nexus, which is a legacy of the Soviet period, is also an important component of the durability of the trafficking phenomenon because it "protects the criminals and their political collaborators, and denies ordinary justice to the citizenry."[29] Illustrative of this phenomenon is the immigration case of one beautiful women kidnapped by an organized crime boss in a Western Ukrainian city. When she refused the overtures of the crime boss, she was provided as an offering to the mayor of the city, the chief of the procuracy and the head of the police.[30] The contact that the crime boss had with these officials and his ability to offer them a beautiful woman reveals that women become an integral part of the close relationship between the criminals and the politicians. This ensures protection not only from trafficking prosecutions but also crackdowns on other forms of criminal activity. The predominance of this political-criminal nexus on both the local and regional levels is an important and distinctive element of the political structure in much of the former USSR. It also explains why so little has been done to combat the trafficking networks.

Post-Soviet trafficking in women is sharply differentiated from that committed by Chinese organized crime groups, the other major crime network that traffics in human beings.[31] In many Asian countries, uneducated girls are sold into prostitution by poor families who cannot afford to feed their children or see this as a financial solution to familial difficulties. Chinese traffickers control the recruitment of individuals and then the same or related groups run the brothels to which the women are transported. In the post-Soviet case, women are more often sold into prostitution to brothel owners and pimps of different nationalities. While post-Soviet groups do control the sex trade in Israel[32] and, to a smaller extent, run some sex services in the United States and Europe, the women are traded as a commodity like drugs and arms. They are not used as a continual source of financial profit as is the case in the people-smuggling trade out of China or the prostitution rings procuring women for the brothels of India or Thailand.

Unlike Chinese organized crime, which views trafficking as a means of generating capital for development at home or to finance the future human smuggling of family members, trafficking from the former Soviet Union is different. Chinese trafficking activity mirrors the Chinese legitimate economy just as post-Soviet trafficking mirrors the legitimate economies of the successor states. In the Chinese case, careful financial records are kept of trafficking transactions and control is maintained over the trafficked women to ensure maximum profits. The profits from the Asian trade in young girls and women are sometimes invested in the community and fund housing, small restaurants and some illegal business.

Trafficking becomes a source of development capital in Asia, whereas in the former USSR trafficking in women drains human capital and returns no financial resources to the community. Rather, the trade in Russian women resembles other aspects of Russian organized crime: it seeks short-term profits and has a raider mentality towards its own resources, whether they be natural or human. In the former Soviet states, the human resource of women is plundered like the precious metals, oil and gas of the former Soviet Union. While the Chinese trafficking trade facilitates the growth of both the Chinese legitimate and illicit economies, the post-Soviet trade mirrors the overall downward development of the post-Soviet economies. In the former Soviet states the trade in women drains the countries and limits their potential for future economic growth and sustainable development. Women may be commodities in both situations but the economic and demographic outcomes for the countries is very different.

Law Enforcement Response

Local Russian/New Independent States (NIS) law enforcement agencies and prosecutors tend not to prioritize the prevention and prosecution of human trafficking. They often view the women who are trafficked as deserving of their fate or motivated by financial necessity and thus tend not to be interested in investigating or prosecuting crimes involving sexual trafficking and prostitution. Research conducted among law enforcement in the Russian Far East on female trafficking revealed that the lack of response can be explained by multiple factors. Analysis of uncompleted investigations in the records of the MVD suggested that there might be pressure on investigators not to complete trafficking investigations that they had begun. Other members of law enforcement suggested that with all the problems facing Russia, investigation of trafficking cases was a low priority.[33]

The ability of law enforcement personnel to act against the phenomenon is further undermined by their lack of knowledge and training in combating organized crime. Because human trafficking crimes are a relatively new phenomenon in Russia and the NIS, law enforcement officials and prosecutors are inadequately trained to prevent trafficking or to investigate and prosecute traffickers. Law enforcers from the NIS are still largely being educated with a curriculum from the Soviet period, in which organized crime is not even addressed. Many law enforcement personnel are therefore not even aware that organized trafficking of women and children exists and is a major profit-making activity for organized crime groups in their countries. Moreover, they do not realize that the large profits from trafficking are used to fund other forms of organized crime activities, and that many traffickers simultaneously traffick in arms and drugs. At the close of a week-long training program in early 2001 on trafficking in human beings at the International Law Enforcement Academy (ILEA) in Budapest, one of the participants explained at the close: "Until I was in this seminar, human trafficking would be my sixth priority, but now that I understand the diverse ramifications it rises to the top."[34]

Illustrative of the low priority given to the trafficking component of a crime case is the prosecution of Tarzan, a Russian organized crime figure, who owned Porky's Strip Joint in Miami where he attempted to sell Russian submarines from the Baltic fleet to members of the Cali cartel. Tarzan was prosecuted and convicted on several counts but was not prosecuted for his trade in women for his club.[35] The same can be said for Semyon Mogilevich, who has been implicated in the YBM stock fraud and other serious organized crime activity. Many Western law enforcers acknowledge that the capital for Mogilevich's diversified illicit activity originated in the trade in women. But at this time, human trafficking is not a focus of Western law enforcement investigations of his activities.[36]

Within the former Soviet Union, those interested in addressing the trafficking problem are often helpless because of its international dimensions. Without the knowledge of those with whom to communicate abroad and the financial resources to facilitate the communications, even the best intentioned law enforcers cannot pursue investigations. Duma hearings in Russia in 1997 revealed that Interpol was receiving numerous inquiries from foreign law enforcement about women trafficked from the former USSR but was not capable of acting on the inquiries received.[37] There was no mechanism to transfer or obtain information from the home regions of trafficked women. Western law enforcement officials were, therefore, frustrated in their efforts to break trafficking rings because they obtained no assistance from the Russian side.

The Role of Corruption

The failure of NIS law enforcers to address the problem is a result of many other factors as well. According to survey research conducted in Russia by MiraMed, a nongovernment organization (NGO) working to combat trafficking, many citizens mistrust law enforcement personnel, believing law enforcers are highly corrupt. In fact, corruption within NIS law enforcement contributes in numerous ways to the trafficking in women. Passport services under the control of the Ministry of Interior issue phony passports to facilitate trafficking. For example, false documents are issued on the Jewish origins of the women, facilitating trafficking to Israel, where under the law of return they can immediately obtain Israeli citizenship. Payoffs are made at the border to bribe border guards to look the other way. Payoffs are made to local police to gain their tolerance of brothels in their communities or to individuals recruiting women for prostitution. The infiltration of Interpol and its information channels by organized crime groups means that efforts to attack the international links of the crime groups may also be undermined by corruption within Russian law enforcement.

The Organized Crime Study Center in Irkutsk, in cooperation with our Washington office of Transnational Crime and Corruption Center (TraCCC), surveyed former government officials and enforcement personnel in a specialized labor camp on the mechanisms of corruption. This research revealed that 90 percent of surveyed law enforcement officials passed bribes up the command chain. Therefore, the higher levels of law enforcement are profiting from the payments made at the local level, and it is thus in their interest to take payments to tolerate such behavior.[38]

These findings are very similar to those reached in the investigation of trafficking of women in Thailand. Law enforcement personnel there were deeply implicated in the trade in women and also received very significant payoffs from brothel owners, which were then passed up the chain of command within the police organization. The low salaries of the law enforcers and the institutionalized corruption made it impossible to fight the trafficking in women because the police were key components of the trade.[39] Because a more significant percentage of the Russian trade in women is overseas rather than serving domestic markets and foreign tourists as in Thailand, the financial dimensions and the corruption components are somewhat different. But in both countries the domestic capacity to address the problem is prevented by the complicity of law enforcement.

In the NIS, the involvement of present and former KGB and FSB personnel is a central element of the corruption and the durability of the criminal organizations trafficking in women. American law enforcement personnel working in the U.S. Embassy in Moscow have their phones tapped by the FSB. In one wiretapped conversation, for example, a reference was made to a provincial Russian *matryoshka* exporter to the United States. Unknown to the Americans, "matryoshka" not only refers to the traditional nested dolls but is the slang word for trafficked women. FSB personnel soon appeared at the "matryoska" exporter and demanded to know about his export business in women. Their investigation was not motivated by a desire to curtail the phenomenon but by an interest in extracting their share of his profits. To their great surprise, the man in question was selling only nested dolls and was very puzzled by their visit. Such stories, as well as cases under investigation in the United States, reveal the very heavy implication of former security personnel in the trafficking of women. This is a unique element of post-Soviet trafficking in women, which entails not only the corruption of law enforcement but the heavy involvement of the former security operatives with their international ties and experience in money laundering.

The Soviet case also involves a new twist because it shows how the new technological capacity of post-Soviet organized crime benefits its operations in many ways. The FSB enjoys a comparative advantage in the post-Soviet period because it enjoys special access to the telecommunications networks. The FSB ability to monitor telephone conversations and e-mail that enter the country allows its personnel to place themselves in an ideal position to be aware of trafficking and to profit from its continued existence. The FSB mandate to investigate organized crime in drugs and arms allows it access to many of the multi-faceted large criminal organizations that also trade in women. Therefore, security personnel have an unparalleled advantage in using new technology to promote the oldest trade—prostitution.

Despite these problems, the failure to address the trafficking issue cannot be placed solely in the hands of NIS and Eastern European law enforcement.[40] Law enforcement in general except in a few distinct cities in Europe, is not particularly motivated to address the problem of trafficking in women. Those that do try to address it have faced insurmountable difficulties. Many of the women refuse to cooperate with authorities because there are few or no protections for these woman and they face deportation and threats against their families if they assist foreign law enforcement. Often the law enforcement authorities do not even know the women's country of origin because the organized crime groups have deprived the women of their passports. Many Western law enforcement personnel have encountered serious corruption among their Eastern European colleagues. This corruption jeopardizes the lives of these women and often precludes successful investigations.

Complicity and corruption of law enforcement, passport services and consular divisions are also not confined to the countries of the former Soviet Union or Eastern Europe. Investigators at the U.S. State Department found that a Czech working in the visa division of the U.S. embassy in Prague was issuing visas for Czech traffickers to bring women to the United States. Although this is the only completed embassy investigation, it is not a unique circumstance. Canadian officials are presently investigating corruption in its overseas visa offices, and accusations have been made against the consular divisions of several Western European countries to which many women are trafficked.

CONCLUSION

Investment in female education can result in societal benefits and alternatives for women only if they live in a non-Hobbesian state where brute force is not the major determinant of one's fate. The suppressed organized crime of the Soviet era emerged in full force on a global scale in the 1990s assuming power in a weakened and compromised state that had no power to combat the phenomenon or control its members. Under these conditions, the educated but impoverished women of the post-Soviet period were vulnerable targets of the well-developed criminal organizations and enjoyed no possibility of protection. Russia at the end of the twentieth century was part of a global economy and possessed powerful and internationally connected criminal organizations. Consequently, the trade in women became an international phenomenon unlike the domestic phenomenon which existed in the postrevolutionary period.

The situation of women worsened in the post-Soviet period not only because there was a feminization of poverty but also because the worst features of the Soviet period were perpetuated and institutionalized in the post-Soviet societies. There was a collapse of communism but it was not replaced by institutions that respected law, citizens' rights or the rule of law. The Soviet legacy of corrupt institutions of social control, a male-dominated power and managerial structure, and a criminalized economy prevailed after the collapse of the USSR. The violence of the Afghan war veterans was transformed into the enforcement arm of the organized crime networks. The overseas connections of the security apparatus and their access to telecommunications facilitated their central role in the trafficking networks. Men, once the managers of Soviet enterprises, were now the owners, no longer restrained by the protective workers' legislation of the Soviet period.

In contrast, the most beneficial features of the Soviet period such as broad access to education and employment for women and social services were dropped almost immediately. The enforcement mechanisms of the Soviet period were no longer operable. Women could no longer ensure the collection of child support through the courts and state institutions. In the face of this enormous reversal in the status and possibilities for women, women retained their sense of responsibility to support their families. In this difficult transition, women had never been less financially equipped to provide for their extended families. Middle-aged women could not support young women in their teens and twenties. Young women, many of them already single mothers, felt a strong responsibility to support both children and parents. Under these conditions women were vulnerable to the financial offers of traffickers.

Economic policies to ensure that Communism was irreversible were promoted with total disregard for the needs of women. Western advisors seeking to make Soviet enterprises more efficient and profitable urged that enterprises abandon the nurseries and social benefits they provided their women employees.[41] The loss of the enterprise social safety net without its replacement by the state or civil society led to great personal hardship for women and the children they supported.

Due to corruption and poorly conceived privatization policies, women received a very small share of the state's former resources. The weak courts and the absence of enforcement mechanisms meant that women could not successfully contest illegal privatizations that deprived them of their property rights. No provision was made to ensure women access to capital. The domination of capital markets by criminal organizations and crony capitalists left no opportunities for women to engage in small scale business. Those who did faced extortion and intimidation by organized crime. This situation proved doubly advantageous to the crime networks because they placed women in an economically precarious position. Women were left without property, employment or the possibilities to initiate businesses. In many cases, the only "thing" of value that women had left was their bodies. In a market economy, their bodies were turned into commodities on a global scale satisfying an international demand for attractive Slavic women.

Trafficking in women is an enormous waste of human capital and state potential to develop the next generation. It reverses all the achievements of socialism, which provided women access to education and security in the labor force. It removes or psychologically scars a critical sector of the population as potential mothers. Moreover, it moves hundreds of thousands of women away from the legitimate economy into the darkest elements of the shadow economy. Trafficked women face a life of abuse, violence and sometimes early death. It is even more of a tragedy because the former Soviet states did not learn from their history. Twice in one century, both after the revolution of 1917 and the collapse of the USSR in 1991, women have suffered the same fate following social and economic revolutions. The patriarchal nature of Russian society has prevailed to the detriment of women. Women have become commodities on a mass scale, destroying the women's futures and contributing to the demographic crises of many post-Soviet states.

NOTES

1. David Lane, *Soviet Economy and Society* (New York: New York University Press, 1985), 224–226.

2. H. M. Shishkin, *Sotsial'no-ekonomicheskie problemy zhenskogo truda* (Moscow: Ekonomika, 1980), 50.

3. Anthony Jones, "The Educational Legacy of the Soviet Period," in *Education and Society in the New Russia* ed. Anthony Jones (Armonk, N.Y.: M. E. Sharpe, 1994), 3–22.

4. Tatyana Mamonova, *Women's Glasnost vs. Naglost: Stopping Russian Backlash* (Westport, Conn.: Bergin and Garvey, 1994), 161.

5. Louise I. Shelley, "Privatization and Crime: The Post-Soviet Experience," *Journal of Contemporary Criminal Justice* Vol. 11, No. 4 (December 1995): 244–256.

6. Louise Shelley, "Post-Soviet Organized Crime," *Demokratizatsiya* Vol. II, No. 3 (Summer 1994): 341–358.

7. "Women's Rights under Privatization in Bulgaria, Poland, Russia and Ukraine," Women, Law and Development Institute (Washington, D.C., 1999).

8. Illustrative of an alternative is that in an EBRD-Chevron program to promote entrepreneurship in western Kazakhstan, 80 percent of those obtaining loans for small businesses are women and 98 percent are able to repay their loans on time.

9. "Eva ischet Adama s valiutoi," *Sovetskaia militsiia* no.1, 1990, p. 38; Andrea Stevenson Sanjian, "Prostitution, the Press and Agenda-Building in the Soviet Policy Process" in *Soviet Social Problems* ed. Anthony Jones, Walter D. Connor and David E. Powell (Boulder: Westview, 1991), 270–295.

10. Larissa Lissyutkina, "Soviet Women at the Crossroads of Perestroika," in *Gender Politics and Postcommunism* eds. Nanette Funk and Magda Mueller (New York: Routledge, 1993), 284.

11. For a fuller discussion of this case, see Steven R. Galster, testimony on "The Sex Trade: Trafficking of Women and Children in Europe and the United States," Hearing before the Commission on Security and Cooperation in Europe (June 28, 1999), 14.

12. L. D. Erokhina, "Seksualnaia ekspolitatsiia zhenshchin i detei v rossii," research paper January 2001 for TraCCC grant (Transnational Crime and Corruption Center) on Sexual Exploitation of Women and Children, funded by USIA.

13. The nongovernmental organization, Miramed, has worked extensively in these areas with the most severe problems to combat trafficking.

14. Igor Kon and James Riordan, eds. *Sex and Russian Society* (Bloomington: Indiana University Press, 1993), 6.

15. Ibid.

16. United States of America vs. Alex Mishulovich, Case Number 98, CR645 in the United States District Court of Chicago, Illinois.

17. Anita Botti testimony on "The Sex trade: Trafficking of Women and Children in Europe and the United States," hearing before the Commission on Security and Cooperation in Europe (June 28, 1999), 4.

18. Amy O'Neill, "International Trafficking in Women from Central Europe and the NIS, Viewpoint, Bureau of Intelligence and Research, U.S. Department of State (December 16, 1997).

19. Gaukhar Isaeva, *Kazakhstan: Reket, moshennichestvo, suternerstvo* (Almaty: Al-Farabi, 1995).

20. Erokhina.

21. Botti, 5.

22. Galster, 14.

23. Ibid.

24. Cyrille Fijnaut, Frank Bovenkerk, Gerben Bruinsma and Henk van de Bunt, *Organized Crime in the Netherlands* (The Hague: Kluwer, 1998), 138.

25. Gerben J. N. Bruinsma and Guus Meershoek, "Organized Crime and Trafficking in Women from Eastern Europe in the Netherlands, *Transnational Organized Crime* Vol. 3, No. 4 (1997): 105–118.

26. Erokhina.

27. Daniel Jeffreys, "Beauty and the Banker," *The Moscow Times* (September 18, 1999).

28. Belgium is an exception in providing more protection for trafficked women.

29. "Overview: The Political Criminal Nexus," *Trends in Organized Crime* Vol. 4, No. 3 (1999): 3.

30. This represents an actual asylum case on which the author was consulted.

31. Pasuk Phongpaichit, Sungsidh Piriyaransan and Nualnoi Treerat, *Guns, Girls, Gambling and Ganja: Thailand's Illegal Economy and Public Policy* (Chinag Mai: Silkworm Books, 1998), 155–214.

32. Menachem Amir, "Organized Crime in Israel," in *Organized Crime: Uncertainties and Dilemmas* eds. S. Einstein and M. Amir (Chicago: Office of International Criminal Justice, 1999), 239–240.

33. Erokhina. Her research reveals a different situation in Khabarovsk, where they are actually investigating advertisements of traffickers.

34. The seminar to train law enforcement officers from Russia, Georgia and Moldova on how to combat trafficking crimes was conducted by TraCCC (Transnational Crime and Corruption Center) in Budapest, Hungary, at the International Law Enforcement Academy on Feb 14–22, 2001.

35. United States of America vs. Ludwig Fainberg, Case Number 97-054 in the United States District Court Southern District of Florida.

36. Donna M. Hughes, "The 'Natasha' Trade—the Transnational Shadow Market of Trafficking in Women," *Journal of International Affairs* (Spring 2000).

37. *Organized Crime Watch: Trafficking in Human Beings* 1, 2 (February 1999).

38. Louise Shelley and Anna Repetskaya, "Analysis:Corruption Research among Convicted Government and Law Enforcement Officials," *Organized Crime Watch* Vol. 1, No. 3 (March/April 1999).

39. Phongpaichit, et al.

40. Penelope Turnbull, "The Fusion of Immigration and Crime in the European Union: Problems of Cooperation and the Fight Against Trafficking in Women," *Transnational Organized Crime*, Vol. 3, No. 3 (1997), 189–213.

41. Interview with Dorothy Rosenberg, who had conducted research among members of Russian enterprises receiving advice from Western advisors and World Bank consultants.

IV
A WESTERN PERSPECTIVE

12

"A Failed Crusade?": The United States and Postcommunist Russia

Michael Cox

The conclusion of the Cold War and the implosion of the USSR constituted two of the most important moments in the late twentieth century, one of the more important consequences of which was to provide the United States with a breathing space within which it more adequately pursues its foreign policy goals. Boiled down to essentials these goals included the maintenance of its own hegemony within a stable global order (a task made all the more easy by the collapse of its old enemy), the control of the spread of nuclear weapons (a more difficult job to perform now that the USSR was no more), the global promotion of liberal democracy and human rights (though not where this did not coincide with the United States' larger economic and strategic objectives), and the extension of market capitalism to those countries attempting to make the transition out of planning and economic autarchy. Taken together, these formed the "core" of America's strategic mission in the 1990s.[1]

There was, however, a crucial connection between the achievement of these larger goals and developments in Russia.[2] Certainly, if reform in Russia failed, this would make it much more difficult for America to achieve its broader objectives. Indeed, if Russian democracy collapsed, or the transition from one economic system to another did not take place, then the United States, it was argued, would face a very insecure future with the strong possibility, according to one very senior official, of "a renewed nuclear threat, higher defence budgets, spreading instability, the loss of new markets and a devastating setback for the worldwide democratic movement."[3] Engaging with reform therefore was not just in Russia's interest, but in America's too.

It is within this larger context that we have to understand the U.S.-Russian relationship in the period after 1991, and the purpose of this chapter is to chart the history of that relationship and explore why the original American aim of facilitating the transition to democratic capitalism in Russia—pursued with great gusto but little economic support by the Clinton administration—has proved so elusive. Indeed, so elusive has it become, that by the beginning of the new century, the United States was prepared to live with almost any "solution" if it could stabilize the situation within Russia itself. To this extent, it is perfectly fair to speak, as commentators like Stephen Cohen have done, of a "failed American crusade" in Russia. Yet this implies that the United States could have made a great deal of difference in the first place, and that is disputable. We must also be careful not to exaggerate the threat, which a flawed transition in Russia represents to the West as a whole. The United States may not have been able to build a new Russia along liberal lines: on the other hand, it would be foolish to think that we are returning to anything resembling a "new" Cold War. Even the election of George Bush in 2000 does not represent a return to the bad old days of the superpower confrontation. Expelling "spies," deploying a missile defense, and raising the political temperature by talking of Russia as a competitor as much as a partner certainly represents a change of emphasis from what took place under Clinton. But it does not mean that the film of history is about to run backwards. The legacy of the past might still hang heavy over the U.S.-Russian relationship. Old assumptions born of seventy years of conflict die hard. But so much has changed since 1989 and 1991, that it would be quite wrong to think of the future in terms of the past. The world, and with it Russia's relationship with the West, has moved on.

In what follows we shall look at the relationship in stages. In part one we will examine some of the early problems after 1992, before looking at the U.S. response to the first of many crises in the relationship—the one that erupted in 1993 following the good showing of Zhirinovsky in the Duma elections. This did not undermine the new understanding; on the other hand, it did lead to what I term a new realism in Washington, one result of which was to make the case for NATO expansion almost irresistible. Next we will look at the unfolding of events before the next major crisis: the 1998 financial meltdown. Finally, we will analyze the election of Putin and its impact on U.S. foreign policy. Though his elevation created difficulties on the American side, once again it did not usher in a period of downright hostility. The relationship—it seemed—had established a new set of ground rules and it was going to take more than just the election of a nationalist in the Kremlin (or indeed a conservative in the White House) to upset these.

EARLY PROBLEMS: 1992–1994

Having defined Russia as America's number one security problem, Clinton made great play after 1992 of the need to build what his key adviser on Russian affairs, Strobe Talbott, liked to term a new "strategic partnership with Russian reform."

Indeed, for a period, it appeared that the only region in the world in which Clinton had any serious interest was Russia. Nevertheless, his apparent enthusiasm for Russia could not hide the fact that his strategy contained a number of obvious problems. These began to manifest themselves at the time of the "aid to Russia" campaign in the early summer of 1993, became more apparent as the political crisis unfolded in Russia in the autumn, continued during the late autumn of 1993 as the United States began to toy with the idea of extending security guarantees to the countries East-Central Europe, and reached a critical point when the December elections to the Russian Duma produced the wrong result. Thus by the beginning of 1994—and long before the "great Russian crash" of 1998—it looked as if Clinton's idea of an alliance with a reforming Russia had run its course, and that either an alternative strategy would have to be devised or a modification would have to be made to his original policy.

The first and most obvious problem with U.S. policy was that it made unwarranted assumptions about both Russia and what needed to be done to Russia to make it into a "normal" country. Assuming that there had been a genuine revolution in 1991, which had cleared the way for a relatively rapid forced march towards the market, policy makers were somewhat surprised to discover that the obstacles still standing in the way of reform were immense—much greater than they had originally anticipated.[4] Moreover, at no point did the United States seem ready to match its strong rhetorical endorsement of the market with concrete material support for the reform process itself. Having encouraged (some would even say, pushed) Russia down the path of painful economic restructuring, neither Congress nor the American people were prepared to extend very much material aid. The result was to leave the United States open to attack from critics in America for doing too little and enemies in Russia of failing to deliver on earlier promises.

The second problem with U.S. strategy was less economic than political. Although American officials spoke in warm terms of their support for post-Soviet reform in general, in reality the main thrust of American policy was always directed towards Russia. Naturally, Washington tried to reassure the other republics, arguing that backing for Russia did not imply indifference to, or neglect of, the other new independent states. Warren Christopher, the U.S. Secretary of State, indeed insisted that the United States was totally committed to the integrity of the different republics and would assist in their integration into the world community. Yet there was little disguising the fact that in its essentials U.S. policy was taken to mean, and certainly was perceived as being, a "Russia first" policy. This had a number of negative consequences. The most important perhaps was to fuel non-Russian suspicion of American motives. To most non-Russians, in fact, it now looked as if the United States either favored some partial reconstruction of the Union, or was prepared to turn a blind eye to Russian activities in the so-called near abroad. The other consequence, according to critics, was to encourage greater aggression by Russia itself. Working on the not illogical assumption that Washington had few serious objections to it throwing its weight around, Moscow started to assert itself in its so-called near abroad. In some cases the consequences were merely unfortunate: in Chechnya of course they turned out to be horrendous.

The final problem was to be found within Russia itself. Here the situation showed no sign of real improvement after 1992. For a president elected on the promise that he would push Russia more rapidly along the capitalist road, Clinton had little to show for his efforts during his first term in office. One need not blame Clinton personally but while he continued to talk up the reforms, Russia seemed to lurch from one near-fatal crisis to another. Yeltsin managed to negotiate his way through the first of these in April 1993, when he won his referendum. He then navigated the next crisis in October of the same year, but only after having bombed and then closed down the Russian parliament. The third crisis, however, proved far more difficult to resolve, not merely because the December elections in 1993 revealed strong opposition to economic change, but more significantly because those hostile to the market now had a genuine democratic mandate. This was a disaster of the first order that was bound to have serious consequences back in the United States.

Crisis and Response

Perhaps one indicator of the seriousness with which the Clinton administration viewed the situation in Russia was its half-hearted public attempts to play down the significance of the December elections and the "rise" of Vladimir Zhirinovsky. The official line at first was to make light of the anti-reform vote, more or less dismissing it as a "protest" against short-term problems that would evaporate once things improved. This exercise in damage limitation could not hide the administration's concern, however. According to one source, the White House was "startled and shaken" by the outcome. Al Gore, it is reliably reported, was "dazed and speechless" when the results came in. Indeed, so confused was he that he and others attempted to place at least some of the blame on western economic policies. In Talbott's famous or (infamous) phrase, there had been too much imposed "shock" and not enough "therapy" in Russia. Hence it was necessary, or so he implied, both to slow down the reforms and to take account of their negative social consequences.[5]

Once the dust had settled the White House set about picking its way through what looked like the debris of a failed policy. Some modifications would clearly have to be made to the original strategy. However, both Talbott and Clinton were determined to soldier on. The administration was not about to abandon Russia. Nor as one analyst suggested at the time, was it going to move Russia from being "the most highly favoured of nations beyond the old iron curtain to being only in the second rank." Clinton himself made this perfectly clear on his visit to Russia in early January 1994. During this, he went out of his way to reassure

Russians of America's continuing support and friendship. He also played to Russian amour propre by talking (somewhat over enthusiastically) of the nation's "greatness" and U.S. recognition of its special place in world affairs. A few days later Talbott followed up on these remarks in an important statement to the House Foreign Affairs Committee. He accepted that Russia was passing through its "time of troubles" and that "reformers in Russia were worried and demoralized." But this was no reason for America to jump ship. In fact, precisely because "there was" what he called a "titanic struggle" going on in Russia, in which the United States had a "huge stake," it was more important than ever to remain engaged. Moreover, according to Talbott, the situation was more "mixed" than the pessimists claimed. The democratic process was up and running. Over one-quarter of the labor force was now employed in the private sector. In the near abroad there had been progress, although there were some problems still left to resolve. On the security front, too, things were getting better, with Ukraine just having decided to transfer all its nuclear weapons to Russia, and the United States and Russia having agreed to "detarget" each other. It was not all doom and gloom, therefore.

Naturally, Talbott accepted that things could still go badly wrong. The "next two and a half years—between now and the elections scheduled for mid-1996— would be critical." But Russia had not yet passed beyond the point of no return. There was still everything to play for. What the United States should not do, he warned, was base its policy today on "worst-case assumptions about what tomorrow may bring." This would not only be foolish, but could lead the United Sates to "fall into the trap of the self-fulfilling prophecy." America had to remain patient and steady, therefore, and continue to work for the integration of Russia rather than begin planning for its containment. The advantages of doing so were self-evident, for "a Russia integrated rather than contained," he argued, would "mean fewer tax dollars spent on defence; a reduced threat from weapons of mass destruction; new markets for U.S. products; and a powerful, reliable partner for diplomacy as well as commerce in the twenty-first century." There was still a world to be won.[6]

Towards a New Realism?

If one result of the December "wake-up call" was to cause initial confusion followed by a resolute White House defense of its original strategy, the other was to open a floodgate out of which poured a tide of criticism. A good deal of this, clearly, had as much to do with Republican frustrations and right-wing dislike of the Clintons as it did with the administration's policy on Russia. Clinton's political opponents, moreover, saw his apparent discomfiture over the Russian question as a golden opportunity to erode further his diminishing credibility. Yet it would be wrong to conclude that all Clinton's critics were motivated only by political animus. There were genuine questions that needed an answer; about how to deal with a Russia in which communists and nationalists were now in a majority in the new parliament; a Russia that was also continuing to show an alarming tendency to reassert its prerogatives in the near abroad; and a Russia, too, in which the reformist Yeltsin only seemed able to hold on to power by stealing the rhetorical clothes of his anti-reformist enemies. To many, indeed, it looked in early 1994 as if Clinton's "love affair" with Yeltsin and his fear of "losing Russia" was now standing in the way of a more balanced American approach to post-Soviet problems.[7]

In good Cold War fashion the debate over Russia reached a critical point following the disclosure that a senior CIA official had been working for Moscow for several years, apparently with deadly consequences. As one of Clinton's more vocal opponents noted in late February, "Americans really did not need a major spy scandal to tell them that the honeymoon with Russia was over. But the arrest of the CIA's Aldrich Ames makes the point with some finality." With this discovery (coinciding as it did with a particularly tough statement by Yeltsin on Russian foreign policy) the attacks against Clinton intensified. The Republicans' chief spokesman on foreign affairs, Richard Lugar, declared that the United States had "to get over the idea" that it was involved in a "partnership" with Moscow. "This is a tough rivalry," he insisted. Much the same point was made at Talbott's confirmation hearings for the post of Deputy Secretary of State in February 1994. Here the Republicans launched a bitter attack on what one senator called a policy that endangered "our national interests." The Republicans also used the occasion to criticize Clinton's foreign policy more generally. "If Ambassador Talbott is confirmed by the Senate," argued Senator D'Amato, "another wrong signal will be sent: that the people who carry out our foreign policy offer nothing but inexperience and naiveté."[8]

The case against Clinton was certainly a powerful one, which logically led some of his more articulate critics—Zbigniew Brzezinski in particular—to some fairly radical conclusions. Brzezinski was no passive observer of the foreign policy scene, and since the collapse of the USSR had been indulging in what one observer called "a bit of freelance foreign policy," the primary goal of which was to cultivate links with the non-Russian states of the former Soviet Union, to which he thought "the American government should have been paying more attention." Believing that Talbott's "romantic fascination with Russia" (Russophilia even) was getting in the way of clear strategic thinking, Brzezinski called for a number of changes to U.S. policy. Most importantly, he argued that the countries of eastern and central Europe should be invited into NATO sooner rather than later. This was critical. Furthermore, in his view, the United States should set as its main objective "the consolidation of geopolitical pluralism within" the space once occupied by the old Soviet Union. Only in this way could countries like Ukraine be assured and America achieve a more balanced relationship with the new Europe as a whole. Indeed, according to Brzezinski, the creation of a belt of independent states around Russia, closely allied to the West, would not only serve America's interest but would help Russia as well; for only when its periphery was secured—and when Moscow was no longer tempted to play a spoiling role there—could it become both stable and democratic itself.[9]

The net result of all this was to bring about an adjustment in U.S. policy. This expressed itself in at least four ways. The first was at the level of public presentation. Hitherto, the Clinton team had talked quite boldly and optimistically about an alliance with Russia and Russian reform. Now this line was modified to include a recognition that on certain international issues at least, there were bound to be serious divergences between the two countries. As Defense Secretary William Perry pointed out in March 1994, "even with the best outcome imaginable in Russia, the new Russia" would have interests different to America's. Nor should the United States be particularly concerned about this, for as Perry pointed out (picking his countries carefully) "even with allies like France and Japan, we have rivalry and competition alongside our partnership," and so it will be with Russia.[10]

The second change in policy was in the U.S. attitude towards the other new republics. Sensitive to the charge that it had tilted too far towards Moscow and Yeltsin, Washington now began to make a much greater effort in building stronger relations with countries other than Russia. This not only pleased a number of countries in the former USSR, but Brzezinski too saw this as exactly the sort of initiative the Clinton administration should have taken much earlier. Whether the White House saw it this way is much less clear; but there was no mistaking the shift in policy. This expressed itself in many ways—both symbolic and practical. Thus during a scheduled visit by the new Ukrainian president to Washington in March 1994 (the first ever undertaken) Clinton reaffirmed "American support" for Ukrainian independence. Four months later Clinton met with the three leaders of the Baltic republics. Other meetings were held during the course of the year. At the same time, the United States issued a series of warnings to Moscow that good relations between Russia and the United States assumed—indeed presupposed—better relations with its neighbors.

These various moves were accompanied by perhaps the biggest change of all in U.S. policy: in its attitude towards NATO and NATO expansion. Accepting now that there could be no halfway house for the countries of Central and Eastern Europe, it decided during the course of 1994 that it was time to extend the privileges of full NATO membership to Poland, the Czech Republic and Hungary. Having initially been persuaded by Talbott back in 1992 that this was not the way to go (indeed a promise had been made to Moscow that NATO would not be expanded eastwards) after the events in Russia, the United States felt it had no alternative but to do so. Though in part a move designed to assuage critics both at home and abroad-and to find a new mission for NATO in a post-Soviet world—clearly underlying the move was a growing recognition that Russia's future could not be guaranteed. Once spoken of as only a theoretical possibility, by late 1994 the likelihood of the reform process in Russia going into reverse seemed far less unlikely. Thus there was good reason to hedge one's bets and secure the peace in Europe now by guarding against a resurgent Russia in the future.

The final shift in U.S. policy was less dramatic but still significant. Since being elected, President Clinton had not only promised a review of U.S. military objectives but important cuts in the U.S. military budget as well—and three months before the December elections in Russia he had made good on both promises with the publication of his defense review, suitably entitled the *Bottom Up Review*. Though hardly a radical document, it provoked a wave of criticism from conservatives in particular, who attacked it, in effect, for undermining American national security by failing to spend enough on the military. For a while, Clinton was able to fend off his opponents. However, with the Zhirinovsky "wake up call" it became increasingly difficult for him to do so. The result was to make him far more cautious on defense matters: partly out of political fear, but partly too because of a genuine concern about developments in Russia. With its future as yet undecided, it would have taken a much bolder American president than Clinton (who felt vulnerable on the issue) to have now argued the case for large cuts in American military spending.

PARTNERSHIP IN CRISIS AGAIN: 1994–1998

While the United States took what it regarded as sensible measures to guard against any future eventuality, it still did not accept that the situation in Russia was hopeless. As Talbott reminded the Senate in early 1994, though the United States would be acting cautiously, it had no intention of planning for the worse. Nor did it have any intention of cutting the Russians off from those all-too-important IMF loans. For a short while, things did begin to stabilize, leading some commentators to talk somewhat prematurely about Russia's "economic success story."[11] But the underlying trends were far from reassuring. Thus in December 1994 Yeltsin formally came out against NATO expansion. In the same month, Moscow launched its ill-fated "invasion" of Chechnaya. In early 1995, Russia then sold two light-water nuclear reactors to Iran. In December, the Russian communists did particularly well in elections to the Russian Duma. And in the race for the Russian presidency in June of the following year, Yeltsin only just managed to win.

Worse was yet to come and, as the economic situation continued to deteriorate in Russia, many began to express deep concerns about the country's future.[12] Nearly all of the main indicators pointed to further decline and possible political instability. One rather obvious sign of the times was Yeltsin's somewhat startling decision in March 1998 to sack his entire government, "good theatre but poor politics" opined one western source.[13] Another was the warning then delivered by the new Russian prime minister. According to Sergei Kiriyenko, Russia was living on the "never never." The young economist did not mince his words. Russia's foreign debt he noted stood at about $140bn, workers were not getting paid, and capital continued to leave the country at a far more rapid rate than it was coming in. As noted in chapter 1, living standards for all but the wealthy few continued to decline. Russia he warned was staring into the abyss. Extremely dangerous days lay ahead.[14]

How dangerous only became clear in August when Russia's financial system effectively collapsed, in the process wiping out ruble savings overnight. Furthermore, coming when it did (in the midst of a preexisting global financial crisis) the very real fear was that meltdown in Russia could easily spark a worldwide recession. As the normally staid *Wall Street Journal* pointed out, although the international weight of the Russian economy was small, accounting for only 1 percent of the world's gross domestic product, any move to default on its large foreign debt could easily precipitate similar actions elsewhere. Equally, if Russia took steps to prevent foreigners from getting their money out, then other "at risk" countries might be tempted to do the same. As the newspaper speculated, "already Malaysia has imposed rigid controls" and there was a genuine worry that if Russia did the same, then others would follow suit.[15]

The impact of these momentous events precipitated yet another "great debate" within the United States. One guru of doom was Martin Malia, the American historian who had earlier predicted the failure of perestroika. "The only certainty in Russia's present crisis," he argued, "is that it marks the end of an era—the Yeltsin years." In his view, it also marked the "end of a theory," the one advanced by Francis Fukuyama in the late 1980s, which suggested "that market democracy has triumphed as a universal ideal."[16] George Friedman was even more pessimistic. Indeed, whereas Malia had simply noted the passing of the liberal western model in Russia, Friedman predicted its replacement by a new form of Stalinism combining economic and geopolitical "anti-Westernism." And there was nothing the West could do about it. "The new Stalinism" could "not be stopped" he asserted. This left the United States with only one option: to abandon a strategy that assumed that reform was possible, and adopt a new policy that assumed it was not.[17]

Confronted with the crisis, U.S. officials charged with Russian policy clearly had an uphill task, one that was made all the more difficult by yet another change of government in Russia itself. Though rather less alarming in composition than some commentators assumed at the time—one stressed that Primakov, the new Russian prime minister, "was a former KGB agent, a friend of dictators in Iraq and Serbia, and an enemy of the West"[18]—the new team could hardly be described as reformist. Furthermore, while Primakov himself talked reassuringly about his commitment to the international community and his opposition to strident nationalism, his selection of economic advisers seemed to point backwards to the pre-Yeltsin years rather than forward to the market. As one seasoned observer noted, his choice "sent strong signals that his approach will be a throwback to another era when economists tried to introduce some

free market ideas within a Soviet system." The return of this cast of Soviet char-
acters according to Celestine Bohlen was "eerie, even alarming."[19]

American disquiet at the direction now being taken by Russia was expressed
most forcefully by Madelaine Albright, the U.S. Secretary of State. In her first
comprehensive review of United States-Russian relations since Primakov was
confirmed as prime minister in September, Mrs Albright was in no mood to
pour American oil onto Russia's troubled waters. Washington she declared was
"deeply concerned" about the direction in which Russia seemed to be moving.
Of particular concern was the apparent shift to the left in economic policy.
While praising Primakov as a foreign policy pragmatist, she was highly critical
of the new government's economic proposals, which included—amongst other
things—plans to print new money, index wages, impose price and capital controls and restore state management of "parts of the economy." This was not the
way to go. Indeed, she made it abundantly clear that Washington's "initial reaction to some of the directions" was not "particularly positive" at all; and if
Moscow continued along this particular road, it would raise a major question
mark about the future of the U.S.-Russian relationship. Though the United
States was keen to maintain the partnership and "help Russians help themselves," if the new leadership in Moscow took the country down the path of statism rather than free enterprise, America's ability to support Russia in any way
would "go from being very, very difficult to being absolutely impossible." [20]

The view that Russia had reached a crossroad was stated with equal force by
Strobe Talbott—the original architect of American policy. Talbott did his best to
defend his original creation. The partnership he argued had been a useful one,
and in a short space of time had done much to draw Russia out of its traditional
isolation. Russia moreover was now playing an increasingly responsible role in a
number of major international institutions such as the G8, the Council of Europe
and the United Nations. As he observed, Russia had "gone from being a spoiler
to a joiner." But there was no hiding the fact that the reform process in Russia
had reached an impasse to such an extent, he argued, that Western terms like *reform* and the *market* had gone from "being part of the vocabulary of triumph and
hope, to being, in the ears of many Russians, almost four-letter words." The situation was thus dire and could get a good deal worse. Nothing could be ruled out.
Hence even though democracy had struck some roots in Russia, it was in Talbott's opinion, "too early" to "proclaim Russian democratisation" to be irreversible;
and the "longer the economic meltdown continued, and the more serious it becomes, the harder it would be for Russia to sustain and consolidate the various
institutions and habits of what we call political normalcy." Furthermore, though
Russia had gone a long way to "joining the European mainstream," there was a
very real danger that it could take the wrong turn in the future. This would depend on many factors, but the most critical in his view was Russian economic
policy. If the country decided to persist with painful reform, then it had a chance
of rejoining the international community. If, on the other hand, it began to assert

its own economic identity and distance itself from the West, the most likely result would be "heightened tensions over security and diplomatic issues." Russia
had changed a good deal since the collapse of the USSR in 1991. But if it formally and finally abandoned western-style economic reform, then there is a very
real chance that the film of history could run backwards. It need not have to happen; but it could. [21]

FINALLY—THE PUTIN "PROBLEM"

The election of Putin seemed to confirm all of America's worst fears about the
unfolding events in Russia. A former member of the KGB who had come to
power on the back of a brutally conducted war in Chechnya hardly looked like
democracy's chosen emissary in postcommunist Russia. Even so, policy makers
in Washington were more than willing (or so it appeared from their public statements) to give Putin the benefit of the doubt. His smooth accession to power—
with Yeltsin's warm words of endorsement ringing in his ears—as well as his
early promises that there would be no great change in Russia's relations with
the West, did much to reassure U.S. officials. As Albright noted in December
1999, the United States had been especially pleased "by the way in which the
transition" had taken place. Washington had been equally reassured by promises made by Putin that there would be "no shift in terms" of Russian "foreign
policy." This was also confirmed in conversations with Foreign Minister Ivanov
with whom she had secured "agreement on a whole host of issues." Together,
these would ensure that Russia and the United States would be able to continue to work "together around the world." It was all very "encouraging," she
concluded.

The implication that Putin was a man with whom the United States could do
business was expressed with equal force by the influential U.S. Ambassador to
NATO, Alexander Vershbow. In the context of a wide-sweeping speech in the
first month of the new century, Vershbow provided a sober, but balanced assessment of the state of U.S.-Russian relations. There was, it was true, much to
be concerned about. The rule of law had not been established; Russia did not
yet have "an effective judicial system"; and there had been a worrying growth of
Russian chauvinism over the past year. But it was essential to maintain a sense
of balance. Putin obviously presented a challenge. On the other hand, statements made by him since December were decidedly reassuring. His commitment to the market (something he had talked about at some length in his important "Millennium Document"), his willingness to abide by the constitutional
process, and his stated desire to remain engaged with the West while encouraging further trade and investment had all been most welcome. There was no reason to be downhearted therefore: "a return to the competitive relationship of the
Cold War" was not on the cards.

The view expressed by Vershbow "that there were too many areas of common interest for Russia and NATO not to work together" was one also endorsed by the Director of the CIA in a statement to the Senate Foreign Relations Committee two months later. Though careful not to engage in idle speculation about Russia's future over the long term—though he did predict that "Acting President Putin" would win the 26 March election—Director Tenet pointed to what he saw as some positive signs. The most obvious perhaps was Putin's "voiced support for finalizing the START II agreement and moving toward further arm cuts in START III—though the Russians (he added) would "want U.S. reaffirmation of the 1972 ABM Treaty in return for Start endorsements." Putin and "many Russian officials" had also expressed "a desire to integrate more deeply Russia into the world economy." Finally, "with regard to its nuclear weapons, Moscow" appeared "to be maintaining adequate security and control." This did not mean there were no areas for U.S. concern. As he pointed out, there were several issues that would test U.S.-Russian relations in the coming months and years. That said, the prognosis was far from bleak. The proverbial glass still remained half-full.

U.S. efforts to put what many saw (and some criticized) as an unnecessarily positive gloss on the turn of events in Russia, did not mean that policy makers were insensitive to the problems that lay ahead. Indeed, for every upbeat statement made by officials there were equally significant downbeat evaluations made as well. This lent U.S. policy a somewhat schizophrenic tone in the new millennium. And at least five issues continued to cause concern amongst American policy makers.

The first was the situation in Chechnya. Here Washington was careful to balance between a felt need to protest the human consequences of Russia military actions, but without breaking with Moscow itself or challenging the integrity of Russia as a nation. In reality there was little or nothing America could do anyway—other than criticize Russia's scorched earth policy from afar, while all the time warning Moscow that the only consequence of its actions would be to lead to an ever-lengthening list of Russian casualties and a loss of goodwill abroad. Whether this would do much to deter a ruthless nationalist like Putin (who had cleverly exploited the war for his own political purposes) was far from certain. As Vershbow rather wearily admitted, "sad to say, it is hard to be optimistic that Russia will heed our calls for an end to an indiscriminate use of force." Politically it had no reason to do so. As another official observed, while the first Chechen war from 1994 to 1996 "ended in significant measure because it was so unpopular," the "current war" appeared to have "broad popular support." This is what made it so intractable and less likely to conclude in the political settlement favored by Washington.

If the brutal war in Chechnya hung like a Damocles sword over U.S.-Russian relations, so too did the figure of Putin himself. Efficient and young though he undoubtedly was, he was nonetheless a long-serving member of the KGB. He had also surrounded himself with advisers drawn from a similar background— key figures like Sergei Ivanov (head of the Security Council), Nikolai Patrushev (head of the Federal Security Service or FSB) and Viktor Cherkesov (the FSB's first deputy director). This "KGB-ization" of Russian politics at the highest level raised at least two critical questions for U.S. policy makers. The first concerned the future of Russian democracy and whether Putin could be trusted to protect basic human rights. There were severe doubts about this expressed not only by Americans, but even more significantly by civil rights campaigners in Russia itself who feared that Putin's elevation represented a new stage in Russian history or what Elena Bonner (Sakharov's widow) characterized as "modernized Stalinism." Others were equally wary of Putin's ready manipulation of enemy images as a way of consolidating his position at home. Thus while his initial pronouncements to western visitors sounded reassuring, when he spoke to other more Russian audiences he sent out quite different signals. It did not go unnoticed in Washington that in December 1999 he declared that "several years ago"—in the immediate aftermath of the collapse of the USSR—"we fell prey to an illusion that we have no enemies." Nor was it especially reassuring to hear the future president of Russia refer regularly to some of his political competitors at home not as legitimate opponents but as traitors to the country.

A third American worry was more precisely economic. Having confidently predicted in the early 1990s that a regimen of privatization and market reforms would in due course transform Russia, nearly ten years on U.S. officials were sounding decidedly less confident. Even the most upbeat of Americans could not ignore the fact that the form of "crony capitalism" that had emerged in Russia with its huge concentrations of economic power in a few hands, did not correspond to their preferred model of a market economy. Moreover, though an economic meltdown had been avoided after the great financial crash of 1998 (in part because of a rise in the price of oil and partly because of an improvement in the trade balance caused by devaluation and a sharp downturn in western imports) the situation for the majority of Russians remained grim. The U.S. response to this was not to deny the statistical evidence but to argue—somewhat unconvincingly—that it would take many more years than originally anticipated to reform the Russian economic system. As Undersecretary of State Pickering noted in a keynote speech a few days before Putin's election, the long view was needed when assessing Russia's economic future. Meanwhile, the outlook was far from rosy. Nor was there much expectation amongst U.S. policy makers that Putin would improve things very much; indeed, the consensus seemed to be that the same powerful oligarchs who had supported Yeltsin but limited the scope of economic reform, would also continue to shape Putin's options. To most Americans, in fact, it looked as if Putin was the creature of the powerful few, and that his primary political role was not to change things but rather protect their interests against any likely challenge. The economic outlook therefore looked less than optimistic; for if Putin was merely the plaything of what some viewed as a dangerous posse of plutocrats, there was little hope for any substantial economic reform.

If the favored elites of the Yeltsin years looked set to play a key background role in the Putin era, then so too were those who suspected NATO and opposed the expansion of NATO into East-Central Europe. Naturally enough American policy makers hoped they might be able to convince the Russians that NATO and Russia, to use Vershbow's words, could be "partners" rather than "protagonists." Indeed, Vershbow set out an eight-point plan of action, concrete measures that NATO and Russia could be working towards "over the long term." These included discussing respective military strategies, working together "to prevent further proliferation," cooperative efforts in "the area of theater missile defense against rogue states" and sorting out "ways to improve the capacity of their military forces to operate together in peace support operations." But Vershbow was hardly naïve and no doubt realized that Putin's own nationalist inclinations and stated objections to NATO expansion in the past meant that relations between the organization and Russia would remain difficult. Meanwhile the United States would continue to try and build bridges between the Alliance and Russia, partly because there was no alternative but more obviously because it was in America's interest to do so.

A final American worry concerned Putin's oft-repeated assertion that his ultimate objective was to rebuild Russian power after nearly a decade of neglect and decline. Talbott addressed this issue in some detail in a speech delivered at Oxford University in the new year. According to Talbott, there was one consistent theme in Putin's speeches and writings: "a desire to see Russia regain its strength, its sense of national pride and purpose." Talbott conceded that this was not an illegitimate objective; on the contrary, it was "not only understandable" but "indispensable" if Russia was going to prosper. There were two dangers however. One was that Putin might decide to rebuild Russia's strength at the expense of his immediate neighbors in the former USSR; the other was that he could easily come to define security in a zero sum fashion, which presupposed that one's own security could only be achieved in a unilateral rather than a mutually reinforcing way. This would not only fail to bring Russia the security it craved (and nor could it do so in "an age of global and regional interdependence") but could easily set off a chain reaction in the West. Putin thus had to choose between two concepts of security—"today's" or "yesterday's"—and how he chose could easily determine U.S.-Russian relations in the new millennium.[22]

Putin's emergence to the front rank of Russian politics at the turn of the century thus posed several difficult questions for American policy makers—ones they found difficult to answer and to which they readily admitted there was no easy answer. In many ways the only thing that could be done in the near term, it was reasoned, was simply to wait and see. As Albright noted, "there's little to be gained by trying to make final judgment at this point—because we don't really know the answer, because we're going to have to deal with what Putin does, not with what he thinks." And what he did was more likely to be determined by events within Russia rather than new initiatives coming out of Washington. The future remained uncertain.

The United States therefore seemed to be locked into a policy that promised little, but to which there appeared to be no realistic alternative. But it was not all gloom and doom, and policy makers could at least console themselves with the fact that even if Russian reform had failed, Russia itself was in such disarray that it simply did not have the capacity to challenge the West. As Vaclav Havel rather cynically pointed out, chaos in Russia might have been bad for Russians but for other countries it was perhaps a good thing. As he put it, "Better an ill Russia than a healthy Soviet Union." Furthermore, although there had been much talk throughout the 1990s about the rise of a new Russian nationalism, the dominant line in Moscow (as opposed to the noisiest) was that there was no longer any point in confrontation with the capitalist world. It was just not in the country's interest.[23] Finally, while most Russians agreed that capitalism was not feasible, few (including Russia's communists) advocated a return to a Soviet-style system. This might have been small comfort to U.S. policy makers as they gazed backwards at their original creation; but it suggested that some form of working relationship—if not partnership—would be possible in the future. This is not exactly what American policy makers had planned for back in 1992. It certainly represented a lower level goal than the one the IMF and the White House had in mind when they set out to remake Russia in the wake of the Soviet Union's collapse. But in an imperfect and increasingly unstable world it was perhaps the best they could now hope for.

NOTES

The chapter title is taken from Stephen Cohen, *Failed Crusade: America and the Tragedy of Post-Communist Russia* (New York: Norton Books, 2000).

1. See Michael Cox, *U.S. Foreign Policy after the Cold War: Superpower without a Mission?* (London: The Royal Institute of International Affairs, 1995).

2. See *A Strategic Alliance with Russian Reform*. U.S. Department of State Dispatch, 4:15 (12 April 1993).

3. *Securing U.S. Interests while Supporting Russian Reform*. U.S. Department of State Dispatch, 4:13 (29 March 1993).

4. See Stephen White, "Rethinking the Transition: 1991 and Beyond," in Michael Cox ed., *Rethinking the Soviet Collapse: Sovietology, the Death of Communism and the New Russia* (London: Pinter, 1998), 135–149.

5. "Reforming Russia's economy," *The Economist* (11 December 1993), 27–29.

6. Strobe Talbott, *America Must Remain Engaged with Russian Reform*, U.S. Department of State Dispatch, 5:5 (31 January 1994).

7. Charles Krauthammer, "Honeymoon Over, the Two Powers Must Go Their Own Way," *International Herald Tribune* (26–27 February 1994).

8. Helen Dewar, "Senate backs Talbott for State Department," *Washington Post* (23 February 1994).

9. Zbigniew Brzezinski, "The Premature Partnership," *Foreign Affairs*, 73:2 (March–April 1994): 67–82.

10. Michael R. Gordon, "Perry Says Caution Is Vital to Russian Partnership," *The New York Times* (15 March 1994).

11. See Anders Aslund, "Russia's Success Story," *Foreign Affairs*, 73:5 (September-October 1994): 58–71.

12. See "Russia's Reforms in Trouble," *The Economist* (22 November 1997).

13. John Lloyd, "Yeltsin Leaps into the Abyss," *The Times*, (24 March 1998).

14. James Meek, "Russia Stares into the Abyss," *The Guardian* (2 April 1998).

15. "Domino Effect: How a Little Market like Russia Set Off a Global Chain Reaction," *The Wall Street Journal Europe* (22 September 1998).

16. Martin Malia, "In Russia, the Liberal Western Model Has Failed," *International Herald Tribune* (5–6 September 1998).

17. George Friedman, "Russian Economic Failure Invites a New Stalinism," *International Herald Tribune* (11 September 1998).

18. William Safire, "Primakov Is No Short-termer," *International Herald Tribune* (18 September 1998).

19. Celestine Bohlen, "Gorbachev's Economists Back at the Helm," *International Herald Tribune* (16 September 1998).

20. Steven Erlanger, "Economy Shift in Russia Worries U.S.—Albright Says," *The New York Times* (3 October 1998).

21. Strobe Talbott, "Dealing with Russia in a Time of Troubles," *The Economist* (21 November 1998).

22. The previous section draws on published statements released on the U.S. Embassy Web site, London.

23. Alexei Arbatov, "Russian National Interest," in Robert D. Blackwill and Sergei Karaganov eds. *Damage Limitation or Crisis?* (London: Brasseys, 1998), 55–76.

Index

241

About the Contributors

Greg Andrusz is a reader in the sociology of the former Soviet Union at Middlesex University, where he is also head of the Kazakhstan-UK Centre. His publications include *The Co-operative Alternative in Europe: The Case of Housing* (1999) and *Cities after Socialism. Urban and Regional Change and Conflict in Post-Socialist Societies* (with M. Harloe and I. Szelenyi, 1996). His primary interest is housing policy in Russia.

Walter D. Connor is professor of political science, sociology, and international relations at Boston University and an associate of the Davis Center for Russian Studies at Harvard. His concerns include Russian and East-European politics, society, and foreign policy. His most recent book is *Tattered Banners: Labor, Conflict, and Corporatism in Postcommunist Russia* (1996).

Linda J. Cook is professor of political science and director of the International Relations Program at Brown University. She has been an associate at the Watson Institute and Harvard University's Davis Center for Russian Studies. She co-edited *Left Parties and Social Policy in Post-Communist Europe* (1999, with Mitchell Orenstein and Marilyn Rueschemeyer). Professor Cook received her Ph.D. in political science from Columbia University in 1985.

Michael Cox is professor of international politics at the University of Wales, Aberystwyth. His most recent books include *Rethinking the Soviet Collapse* (1998), *The Interregnum: Controversies in World Politics, 1989–1999* (1999) and *E. H. Carr: A Critical Appraisal* (2000).

Stefanie Harter studied in Konstanz and Dortmund, and at SSEES, University of London. She completed her doctoral dissertation at Birmingham University on "The civilianisation of the Russian economy—A Network Approach." She has been a Research Associate at the Institute for East European and International Studies (BIOST) in Cologne and is currently employed at GTZ, the German Agency for Technical Assistance, in charge of projects in the Former Soviet Union.

Irina Y. Kuzes has been studying political and economic dimensions of Russian reform since the beginning of the Yeltsin period. A visiting scholar at Virginia Commonwealth University, she is co-author of *Radical Reform in Yeltsin's Russia* (1995) and *Property to the People* (1994). She has published articles in a number of academic journals and other publications and is currently writing *The Politics of Interests in the New Russia* with Lynn Nelson.

David Lane has taught at the Universities of Essex, Birmingham, and Cambridge where he is currently senior research associate on a British Economic and Social Research Council project on the Russian banking sector. He is the author of many books on class, stratification, and socialism, including *The Rise and Fall of State Socialism* (1996), *The Transition from Communism to Capitalism* (with Cameron Ross, 1999), *The Political Economy of Russian Oil* (1999), and *Russian Banking: Evolution, Problems and Prospects* (2002).

Paul G. Lewis is a reader in Central and East European politics at the Open University, UK. His main recent research interests have been in the areas of democratization and party development, and his most recent publications include *Political Parties in Post-Communist Eastern Europe* (2000) and *Party Development and Democratic Change in Eastern Europe—The First Decade* (2001).

Lynn D. Nelson is a professor of sociology and political science at Virginia Commonwealth University. He has published a variety of articles about Russian political and economic change and is co-author of *Radical Reform in Yeltsin's Russia* (1995) and *Property to the People* (1944). He is currently writing *The Politics of Interests in the New Russia* with Irina Kuzes.

Cameron Ross is a lecturer in Russian politics in the department of politics, University of Dundee. His most recent books are *The Transition from Communism to Capitalism: Ruling Elites from Gorbachev to El'tsin* (with David Lane, 1999); *Russia after the Cold War* (with Mike Bowker, eds., 2000); *Regional Politics in Russia* (Cameron Ross, ed., 2002). At present he is completing a monograph on federalism and democratization in Russia.

Louise I. Shelley is a professor in the department of justice, law, and society at American University. She is also the founder and director of the Transnational Crime and Corruption Center at the university. She is the author of *Policing Soviet Society* (1996) and numerous articles and book chapters on international organized crime and corruption.

Ray Taras is professor of political science and Russian studies at Tulane University in New Orleans. He has served on the faculty of universities in Canada, Denmark, England, and Poland. His recent books include *Understanding Ethnic Conflict: The International Dimension* (with Rajat Ganguly, 2001) and *Going to Our Fathers' Land: Nationalisms, the State, and Beyond* (2002).

Stephen White is professor of politics and a senior associate member of the Institute of Central and East European Studies at the University of Glasgow, where he specializes in Russian electoral politics and public opinion. His recent writings include *Russia's New Politics* (2000) and *The Soviet Elite from Lenin to Gorbachev* (with Evan Mawdsley, 2000).